Collins

easy learning
English
Vocabulary

All the ~~~~
for natu~~

HarperCollins Publishers
Westerhill Road
Bishopbriggs
Glasgow
G64 2QT

Second edition 2015

10 9 8 7 6 5 4 3 2 1

© HarperCollins Publishers 2011, 2015

ISBN 978-0-00-810177-0

Collins ® is a registered trademark of
HarperCollins Publishers Limited

www.collinsdictionary.com/cobuild
www.collinselt.com

A catalogue record for this book is
available from the British Library

Typeset by Davidson Publishing
Solutions, Glasgow

Printed in Great Britain by Clays Ltd,
St Ives plc

Editorial staff

Senior editors:
Penny Hands
Kate Wild

Contributors:
Sandra Anderson
Katharine Coates
Kate Mohideen
Elspeth Summers

For the publisher:
Lucy Cooper
Kerry Ferguson
Elaine Higgleton
Lisa Sutherland
Celia Wigley

contents

contents

Collins Easy Learning English Vocabulary is designed for anyone who wants to broaden their knowledge of English words in everyday situations. Whether you need English at work, at school or university, or for a holiday, *Collins Easy Learning English Vocabulary* offers you the information you require in a clear and accessible format.

This book is divided into 50 subject areas. These cover topics such as 'air travel', 'business', 'food and drink' and 'science', arranged in alphabetical order. Arranging the words by subject area helps you to learn related words and phrases together. Because of this, you can always be sure that you are using the right word in the right context.

Within each topic, vocabulary is divided into nouns, verbs, adjectives, adverbs, phrases and idioms. Each word is defined in relation to the topic. For example, in 'air travel', the meaning that is given for the word *connection* is:

> 'a plane that leaves after another one arrives and allows you to continue your journey by changing from one to the other'.

In 'computers and the internet', on the other hand, *connection* is defined in terms of its computer-related sense:

> 'a link between a computer and a network'.

For each topic, there are plenty of authentic example sentences from the Collins Corpus. These show you how words and phrases are used in real English.

At the end of the book, there are sections on place names and people, numbers, measurements, times and dates. There is also an alphabetical index, and a list of irregular verbs.

We hope that this book will help you to expand your knowledge of English vocabulary in a wide range of situations. For more information on products to help you improve your English, please visit us at **www.collinselt.com**.

Topics are organized in alphabetical order.

→ air travel

Each topic is divided into word classes. These include nouns, verbs, adjectives, adverbs, phrases and idioms.

→ **NOUNS**

| **aeroplane** | ['eərəpleɪn] | a plane: a vehicle with wings and engines that can fly (*In American English*, use **airplane**) |
| **aircraft** (PL) **aircraft** | ['eəkrɑːft] | a plane or a helicopter |

Where a noun has an irregular plural form, this is shown below the main form.

| **airline** | ['eəlaɪn] | a company that carries people or goods in planes |

Common American words are shown.

| **airplane** (*American English*) | | *see* **aeroplane** |
| **airport** | ['eəpɔːt] | a place where planes come and go, with buildings and services for passengers |

The meaning of each word is given as it relates to the topic.

| **air-traffic controller** | [eə ˌtræfɪk kənˈtrəʊlə] | someone whose job is to organize where planes go |
| **aisle** | [aɪl] | the long narrow passage between the rows of seats on a plane |

Short phrases show you how the word is used in context.

| **arrivals** | [əˈraɪvəlz] | the part of an airport where passengers get off planes; *wait in arrivals* |
| **bag** | [bæg] | a container made of plastic or leather, used for carrying things |

The main form of the word is in bold.

→ | **baggage** | ['bægɪdʒ] | same as **luggage** |

These symbols show you how to say the word. See page vii for an explanation of these.

baggage reclaim	['bægɪdʒ rɪkleɪm]	the place where you collect your baggage after your flight; *go to baggage reclaim*
boarding card	['bɔːdɪŋ ˌkɑːd]	a card that you must show when you get on a plane
bureau de change (PL) **bureaux de change**	[ˌbjʊərəʊ də ˈʃɒnʒ] [ˌbjʊərəʊ də ˈʃɒnʒ]	a place where you can change your money to foreign money

Examples from the corpus show how words and phrases are used in real English.

→ **EXAMPLES**
Most low-cost airlines do not do not provide meals.
We checked in early and walked around the airport.

Phrasal verbs and other verb phrases are shown in the verb section.

→ | **check in** | | to tell the person at an airport desk that you have arrived |
check something in		to give your luggage to the person at an airport desk; *check in luggage*
delay	[dɪˈleɪ]	to make something later than expected; *The flight is delayed.*
depart	[dɪˈpɑːt]	to leave
fly	[flaɪ]	**1** to travel somewhere in an aircraft **2** when a pilot flies a plane, they make it move through the air

Where a word has more than one meaning that relates to the topic, each meaning is given.

In this dictionary the International Phonetic Alphabet (IPA) is used to show how the words are pronounced. The symbols used in the International Phonetic Alphabet are shown in the table below.

IPA Symbols

Vowel sounds

ɑː	calm, ah
æ	act, mass
aɪ	dive, cry
aɪə	fire, tyre
aʊ	out, down
aʊə	flour, sour
e	met, lend, pen
eɪ	say, weight
eə	fair, care
ɪ	fit, win
iː	seem, me
ɪə	near, beard
ɒ	lot, spot
eʊ	note, coat
ɔː	claw, more
ɔɪ	boy, joint
ʊ	could, stood
uː	you, use
ʊə	sure, pure
ɜː	turn, third
ʌ	fund, must
ə	the first vowel in about

Consonant Sounds

b	bed, rub
d	done, red
f	fit, if
g	good, dog
h	hat, horse
j	yellow, you
k	king, pick
l	lip, bill
m	mat, ram
n	not, tin
p	pay, lip
r	run, read
s	soon, bus
t	talk, bet
v	van, love
w	win, wool
x	loch
z	zoo, buzz
ʃ	ship, wish
ʒ	measure, leisure
ŋ	sing, working
tʃ	cheap, witch
θ	thin, myth
ð	then, bathe
dʒ	joy, bridge

Notes

Primary and secondary stress are shown by marks above and below the line, in front of the stressed syllable. For example, in the word *abbreviation*, /əˌbriːviˈeɪʃən/, the second syllable has secondary stress and the fourth syllable has primary stress.

We do not normally show pronunciations for compound words (words which are made up of more than one word). Pronunciations for the words that make up the compounds are usually found at their entries at other parts of the dictionary. However, compound words do have stress markers.

air travel

aeroplane ['eərəpleɪn] a plane: a vehicle with wings and engines that can fly (*In American English, use* **airplane**)

aircraft ['eəkrɑ:ft] a plane or a helicopter
(PL) **aircraft**

airline ['eəlaɪn] a company that carries people or goods in planes

airplane (*American English*) *see* **aeroplane**

airport ['eəpɔ:t] a place where planes come and go, with buildings and services for passengers

air-traffic [eə ˌtræfɪk someone whose job is to organize
  controller kən'trəʊlə] where planes go

aisle [aɪl] the long narrow passage between the rows of seats on a plane

arrivals [ə'raɪvəlz] the part of an airport where passengers get off planes; *wait in arrivals*

bag [bæg] a container made of plastic or leather, used for carrying things

baggage ['bægɪdʒ] same as **luggage**

baggage ['bægɪdʒ the place where you collect your baggage
  reclaim rɪkleɪm] after your flight; *go to baggage reclaim*

boarding card ['bɔ:dɪŋ ˌkɑ:d] a card that you must show when you get on a plane

bureau de [ˌbjʊərəʊ də a place where you can change your
  change 'ʃɒnʒ] money to foreign money
  (PL) **bureaux de** [ˌbjʊərəʊ də 'ʃɒnʒ]
  change

business class ['bɪznɪs ˌklɑ:s] seats that are cheaper than first class but more expensive than economy class; *in business class*

EXAMPLES

Most low-cost airlines do not provide meals.
We checked in early and walked around the airport.
Please do not leave bags in the aisle.
The police said the incident occurred last weekend in arrivals at Terminal 3.
We went to a bureau de change to change the Euros back into Sterling.
We had seats in business class on the flight from London to Los Angeles.

2 air travel

cabin	[ˈkæbɪn]	the part of a plane where people sit
cabin crew	[ˈkæbɪn ˌkruː]	the people whose job is to look after passengers on a plane; *The cabin crew were very nice.*
captain	[ˈkæptɪn]	the person who is in charge of a plane
car hire	[ˈkɑː ˌhaɪə]	paying money to borrow a car, for example when you are going on holiday (*In American English, use* **car rental**)
car rental (*American English*)		*see* **car hire**
check-in	[ˈtʃek ɪn]	the desk that you go to in an airport to say that you have arrived; *Go to check-in at once.*
connection	[kəˈnekʃən]	a plane that leaves after another one arrives and allows you to continue your journey by changing from one to the other
customs	[ˈkʌstəmz]	the place at an airport where you have to show certain goods that you have bought in another country, and, if necessary, pay tax on them
customs duty	[ˈkʌstəmz ˌdjuːti]	tax that you pay when bringing certain goods into a country from another country
departures	[dɪˈpɑːtʃəz]	the part of an airport where you wait before you get on a plane; *He was standing in departures.*
duration	[djʊˈreɪʃən]	the length of time that something lasts
economy class	[ɪˈkɒnəmi ˌklɑːs]	the cheapest seats on a plane; *in economy (class)*

EXAMPLES

Ask cabin crew or see leaflet for details.
The price includes flights, car hire and accommodation.
We got to the airport and went straight to check-in.
My flight was late and I missed my connection.
We walked through customs.
The government has reduced customs duty on imported machinery.
You must pay customs duty on these goods.
Please go to departures.
You must keep your mobile phone switched off for the duration of the flight.
Margarita sat in economy class on the flight to Bucharest.

emergency exit	[ɪˈmɜːdʒənsi ˌegzɪt]	a place where you leave a plane if there is an emergency, such as a crash or a fire
entrance	[ˈentrəns]	the door or gate where you go into a place
escalator	[ˈeskəˌleɪtə]	a set of moving stairs
e-ticket	[ˈiː-ˌtɪkɪt]	short for 'electronic ticket': a ticket that is stored on a computer rather than on paper
exit	[ˈeksɪt]	the door that you use to leave a public building
fare	[feə]	the money that you pay for a journey in a plane
first class	[fɜːst ˈklɑːs]	the best and most expensive seats on a plane; *in first class*
flight	[flaɪt]	a trip in an aircraft
flight attendant	[ˈflaɪt əˌtendənt]	a person whose job it is to look after passengers on a plane and to give them food and drink
flight number	[ˈflaɪt nʌmbə]	the unique number that is given to each flight
gate	[geɪt]	a place where you leave an airport and get on a plane
hand luggage	[ˈhænd ˌlʌgɪdʒ]	the bags that you take with you in the cabin, rather than the bags that are put in the hold; *lots of hand luggage*
helicopter	[ˈhelikɒptə]	an aircraft with long blades on top that go around very fast
hold	[həʊld]	the place in a plane where goods or luggage are stored

EXAMPLES

Take the escalator to the second floor.

Our flight was delayed by three hours because of fog.

There were no direct flights to San Francisco, so we had to change planes.

I asked the flight attendant for a glass of water.

He is on flight number 776 from Beijing.

How many pieces of hand luggage can I take on the plane?

This piece of luggage will have to go in the hold.

4 air travel

ID card	[ˌaɪ 'di: kɑ:d]	a card with your name, date of birth and photograph on it that shows who you are
information desk	[ˌɪnfə'meɪʃən ˌdesk]	a place where you can ask for information about your flight
jet lag	['dʒet læg]	the feeling of being very tired when you fly between two places where the time is different; *suffering from jet lag*
jumbo jet	['dʒʌmbəʊ ˌdʒet]	a large plane that can carry several hundred passengers
landing	['lændɪŋ]	the act of bringing a plane back down on to the ground; *a smooth landing*; *a bumpy landing*
layover (*American English*)		*see* **stopover**
luggage	['lʌgɪdʒ]	the bags that you take with you when you travel; *lots of luggage*
luggage label	['lʌgɪdʒ ˌleɪbəl]	a piece of plastic with your name and address that you attach to your luggage in case it gets lost
parachute	['pærəˌʃu:t]	a large piece of thin material that a person attaches to their body when they jump from an aircraft to help them float safely to the ground
passenger	['pæsɪndʒə]	a person who is travelling in a plane, but who is not flying it or working on it
passport	['pɑ:spɔ:t]	an official document that you have to show when you enter or leave a country
pilot	['paɪlət]	a person who controls an aircraft
plane	[pleɪn]	a vehicle with wings and engines that can fly
plane crash	['pleɪn kræʃ]	an accident in which a plane hits another plane or hits the ground
propeller	[prə'pelə]	a part of an aircraft that turns around very fast and makes the aircraft move

---

EXAMPLES
I had terrible jet lag for three days after my holiday.
How many pieces of luggage are you checking in?
Why does Ingrid need so much luggage for a short stay?
Could I see your passport and boarding card, please?

reservation	[ˌrezə'veɪʃən]	a seat on a flight that an airline keeps ready for you
runway	['rʌnweɪ]	a long road that a plane travels on before it starts flying
seat	[siːt]	something that you can sit on
seat belt	['siːt belt]	a long belt that you fasten around your body to keep you safe when you are on a plane
security	[sɪ'kjʊərɪti]	1 everything that is done to protect a place; *Security has been increased.* 2 the place in an airport where your bags are checked; *go through security*
stopover	['stɒpəʊvə]	a short stay in a place between parts of a journey (*In American English, use* **layover**)
suitcase	['suːtkeɪs]	a case for carrying your clothes when you are travelling
take-off	['teɪkɒf]	the beginning of a flight, when a plane leaves the ground; *a smooth take-off*
terminal	['tɜːmɪnəl]	a place where people begin or end a flight
ticket	['tɪkɪt]	a small piece of paper that shows that you have paid for a flight
timetable	['taɪmteɪbəl]	a list of the times when planes arrive and depart
tourist	['tʊərɪst]	a person who is visiting a place on holiday
travel agency	['trævəl ˌeɪdʒənsi]	a business that sells journeys and holidays
traveller	['trævələ]	1 a person who is on a trip 2 a person who travels a lot

EXAMPLES

You are in seat 35C.

Please fasten your seat belts during take-off and landing.

World leaders have announced plans to tighten up airline security.

We made a stopover in Bangkok to break up the journey between London and Brisbane.

What time is take-off?

We left the airport terminal and looked for the taxi rank.

Terminal 1 will handle Air Canada's domestic flights.

6 air travel

tray table	['treɪ ˌteɪbəl]	a small table that is attached to the back of the seat in front of you on a plane
trip	[trɪp]	a journey that you make to a particular place and back again
trolley	['trɒli]	a large container with wheels that you use at an airport for moving heavy luggage
window	['wɪndəʊ]	a space in the side of a plane that you can see through
wing	[wɪŋ]	one of the long flat parts at the side of a plane that support it while it is flying

VERBS

board	[bɔːd]	to get into a plane to travel somewhere
book	[bʊk]	to arrange and pay for a flight; *book a ticket*; *book a flight*
cancel	['kænsəl]	to say that something that has been planned will not happen; *cancel a flight*
check in		to tell the person at an airport desk that you have arrived
check something in		to give your luggage to the person at an airport desk; *check in luggage*
delay	[dɪ'leɪ]	to make something later than expected; *The flight is delayed.*
depart	[dɪ'pɑːt]	to leave
fly	[flaɪ]	**1** to travel somewhere in an aircraft **2** when a pilot flies a plane, they make it move through the air

EXAMPLES
I'm taking a short trip to France.
I pushed my luggage trolley towards the 'Nothing to Declare' green route.
Can I have a window seat, please?
I boarded the plane to Dubai.
British Airways cancelled several flights because of the bad weather.
Flight BA201 will depart from gate 21 in 30 minutes.
We are flying over London.

hijack	['haɪdʒæk]	to illegally take control of a plane
land	[lænd]	1 when a plane lands, it comes down to the ground after moving through the air 2 when a pilot lands a plane, it comes down to the ground after moving through the air
search	[sɜːtʃ]	to look carefully in a place for something; *search someone's luggage*
take off		when an aircraft takes off, it leaves the ground and starts to fly

ADJECTIVES

airsick	['eəsɪk]	feeling ill during a flight because of the movement of the plane
direct	[daɪ'rekt]	used to describe a flight that goes from one place to another without stopping
domestic	[də'mestɪk]	used to describe flights between airports in the same country
duty-free	[ˌdjuːti-'friː]	duty-free goods are sold at airports or on planes at a cheaper price than usual because they are not taxed; *duty-free perfume*
international	[ˌɪntə'næʃənəl]	used to describe flights between airports in different countries
on time	[ɒn 'taɪm]	not late or early; at the expected time; *The flight is on time.*

ADVERBS

| **on board** | [ɒn 'bɔːd] | on an aircraft |
| **on time** | [ɒn 'taɪm] | not late or early; at the expected time; *arrive on time* |

PHRASE

| **nothing to declare** | | used to describe the area of customs that you walk through if you do not have to pay customs duty on any goods |

EXAMPLES

The Boeing 737 was hijacked after taking off from London yesterday.
The plane landed on time, at eleven thirty.
The plane took off twenty minutes late.

the animal world

ANIMALS

animal	[ˈænɪməl]	**1** a creature such as a dog or a cat, but not a bird, fish, insect or human **2** any living creature, including a human
ant	[ænt]	a small crawling insect that lives in large groups
bat	[bæt]	a small animal, like a mouse with wings, that sleeps upside down during the day and comes out to fly at night
bear	[beə]	a large, strong wild animal with thick fur and sharp claws
bee	[biː]	a yellow and black striped flying insect that makes a sweet food (called honey) and can sting you
bird	[bɜːd]	an animal with feathers and wings
bull	[bʊl]	**1** a male animal of the cow family **2** a male animal of some other animal families, such as elephants and whales
butterfly	[ˈbʌtəflaɪ]	an insect with large coloured wings
calf (PL) **calves**	[kɑːf] [kɑːvz]	a young cow
camel	[ˈkæməl]	an animal with one or two large lumps on its back
cat	[kæt]	a small animal covered with fur, that people in some countries keep as a pet
caterpillar	[ˈkætəpɪlə]	a small animal with a long body, that develops into a butterfly
cockroach	[ˈkɒkrəʊtʃ]	a large brown insect that likes to live in places where food is kept
cod	[kɒd]	a large sea fish with white flesh
cow	[kaʊ]	a large female animal that is kept on farms for its milk
crab	[kræb]	a sea animal with a shell and ten legs. Crabs usually move sideways.

crocodile	['krɒkə͵daɪl]	a large animal with a long body, a long mouth, and sharp teeth. Crocodiles live in rivers in hot countries.
deer (PL) **deer**	[dɪə]	a large wild animal that eats grass and leaves. Male deer usually have antlers (= large horns that look like branches).
dog	[dɒg]	an animal that people in some countries keep as a pet, or use to guard buildings
donkey	['dɒŋki]	an animal like a small horse with long ears
duck	[dʌk]	a bird that lives near water
eagle	['iːgəl]	a large bird that eats small animals
eel	[iːl]	a long, thin fish that looks like a snake
elephant	['elɪfənt]	a very large grey animal with a long nose called a trunk
fish (PL) **fish**	[fɪʃ]	an animal that lives and swims in water, that people eat as food
fly	[flaɪ]	a small insect with two wings
fox	[fɒks]	a wild animal that looks like a dog, and has red fur and a thick tail
frog	[frɒg]	a small animal with smooth skin, big eyes and long back legs that it uses for jumping. Frogs live in or near water.
giraffe	[dʒɪˈrɑːf]	a large African animal with a very long neck, long legs and dark spots on its body
goat	[gəʊt]	an animal that has horns, and hairs on its chin that look like a beard
goose (PL) **geese**	[guːs] [giːs]	a large bird like a duck with a long neck
grasshopper	['grɑːsͺhɒpə]	an insect that jumps high into the air and makes a sound with its long back legs
hedgehog	['hedʒhɒg]	a small brown animal with sharp points covering its back
hen	[hen]	a female chicken

EXAMPLE
Where did you catch the fish?

hippopotamus [ˌhɪpə'pɒtəməs] a very large animal with short legs and thick skin, that lives in and near rivers

horse [hɔːs] a large animal that people can ride

insect ['ɪnsekt] a very small animal that has six legs. Most insects have wings.

jellyfish ['dʒeliˌfɪʃ] a sea animal that has a clear soft body and
(PL) **jellyfish** that can sting you

kangaroo [ˌkæŋgə'ruː] a large Australian animal. A female kangaroo carries her baby in a pocket (called a pouch) on her stomach.

kitten ['kɪtən] a very young cat

ladybird ['leɪdiˌbɜːd] a small round insect that is red or yellow with black spots

lamb [læm] a young sheep

lion ['laɪən] a large wild cat that lives in Africa. Lions have yellow fur, and male lions have manes (= long hair on their head and neck).

lizard ['lɪzəd] a small animal with a long tail and rough skin

lobster ['lɒbstə] a sea animal that has a hard shell and eight legs

mammal ['mæməl] an animal that feeds its babies with milk

mole [məʊl] a small animal with black fur, that lives under the ground

monkey ['mʌŋki] an animal that has a long tail and can climb trees

mosquito [mɒ'skiːtəʊ] a small flying insect that bites people and animals

moth [mɒθ] an insect that has large wings and is attracted by lights at night

mouse [maʊs] a small animal with a long tail
(PL) **mice** [maɪs]

octopus ['ɒktəpəs] a soft sea animal with eight long arms

ostrich ['ɒstrɪtʃ] a very large bird that cannot fly

owl [aʊl] a bird with large eyes that is active at night

oyster	[ˈɔɪstə]	a large flat shellfish that people often eat raw
panda	[ˈpændə]	a large animal from China with black and white fur
parrot	[ˈpærət]	a tropical bird with a curved beak and very bright feathers
penguin	[ˈpeŋgwɪn]	a black and white bird that lives in very cold places, that can swim but cannot fly
pet	[pet]	an animal that you keep in your home
pig	[pɪg]	a farm animal with a fat body and short legs, that is kept for its meat
pony	[ˈpəʊni]	a small or young horse
puppy	[ˈpʌpi]	a young dog
rabbit	[ˈræbɪt]	a small animal that has long ears and lives in a hole in the ground
rat	[ræt]	an animal that has a long tail and looks like a large mouse
rhinoceros	[raɪˈnɒsərəs]	a large animal from Asia or Africa with a horn on its nose
salmon (PL) **salmon**	[ˈsæmən]	a large fish with silver skin and pink flesh
seagull	[ˈsiːgʌl]	a common type of bird with white or grey feathers, that lives near the sea
seal	[siːl]	a large animal with a rounded body and short fur, that eats fish and lives near the sea
shark	[ʃɑːk]	a very large fish that often has very sharp teeth and may attack people
shellfish (PL) **shellfish**	[ˈʃelfɪʃ]	a small sea creature with a shell
snail	[sneɪl]	a small animal with a long soft body, no legs, and a round shell on its back
snake	[sneɪk]	a long, thin animal with no legs, that slides along the ground

EXAMPLE
We don't have any pets.

species (PL) **species**	['spi:ʃiz]	a related group of plants or animals; *a species of fish; an endangered species*
spider	['spaɪdə]	a small animal with eight legs
squid	[skwɪd]	a sea animal that has a long soft body and many soft arms (called tentacles)
squirrel	['skwɪrəl]	a small animal with a long thick tail, that lives mainly in trees
stag	[stæg]	an adult male deer
swan	[swɒn]	a large white bird with a very long neck, that lives on rivers and lakes
tadpole	['tædpəʊl]	a small water animal that looks like a black fish, and that develops into a frog or a toad
tiger	['taɪgə]	a large wild animal of the cat family. Tigers are orange with black stripes.
toad	[təʊd]	a small brown or green animal with long legs, that lives in water
tortoise	['tɔːtəs]	an animal with a shell on its back, that moves very slowly
turkey	['tɜːki]	a large bird that is kept on a farm for its meat
wasp	[wɒsp]	an insect with wings, and yellow and black stripes across its body. Wasps can sting people.
whale	[weɪl]	a very large mammal that lives in the sea
wolf (PL) **wolves**	[wʊlf] [wʊlvz]	a wild animal that looks like a large dog
worm	[wɜːm]	a small animal with a long, thin body, no bones and no legs
zebra	['zebrə, 'ziː-]	a wild horse with black and white stripes, that lives in Africa

PARTS OF ANIMALS

antenna (PL) **antennae**	[æn'tenə] [æn'teniː]	one of the two long, thin parts attached to the head of an insect, that it uses to feel things with
antler	['æntlə]	one of the two horns that are shaped like branches on the head of a male deer

beak	[biːk]	the hard, pointed part of a bird's mouth
hoof	[huːf]	one of the hard parts of the feet of horses,
(PL) **hooves**	[huːvz]	cows and some other animals
fur	[fɜː]	the thick hair that grows on the bodies of many animals
feather	[ˈfeðə]	one of the light soft things that cover a bird's body
claw	[klɔː]	the thin, hard, pointed part at the end of the foot of a bird or an animal
coat	[kəʊt]	an animal's fur or hair
hair	[heə]	the short threads that grow on the bodies of many animals
horn	[hɔːn]	one of the hard pointed things that grow from an animal's head
mane	[meɪn]	the long, thick hair that grows from the neck of some animals
paw	[pɔː]	the foot of an animal such as a cat, a dog or a bear
shell	[ʃel]	the hard part that covers the back of an animal such as a snail or a tortoise, and protects it
snout	[snaʊt]	the long nose of an animal such as a pig
tail	[teɪl]	the long thin part at the end of an animal's body
trunk	[trʌŋk]	the long nose of an elephant
tusk	[tʌsk]	a very long, curved, pointed tooth that grows beside the mouth of an elephant
wing	[wɪŋ]	one of the two parts of the body of a bird or an insect, that it uses for flying

EXAMPLES

He heard the sound of horses' hooves behind him.

Cat hair makes me sneeze.

The kitten was black, with white paws.

PLACES WHERE ANIMALS ARE FOUND

aquarium	[ə'kweərɪəm]	**1** a building where fish and sea animals are kept and people can go to look at them **2** a glass box filled with water, in which people keep fish as pets
cage	[keɪdʒ]	a structure made of metal bars where you keep birds or animals
field	[fiːld]	a piece of land where animals are kept
kennel	['kenəl]	a small house for a dog
nest	[nest]	the place where a bird, a small animal or an insect keeps its eggs or its babies; *build a nest*
web	[web]	the thin net that a spider makes in order to catch insects
zoo	[zuː]	a park where animals are kept and people can go to look at them

OTHER ANIMAL NOUNS

bite	[baɪt]	a painful mark on your body where an animal, a snake, or an insect has bitten you
collar	['kɒlə]	a band of leather or plastic that you can put around the neck of a dog or a cat
egg	[eg]	a round object that contains a baby bird, insect, snake or fish; *lay an egg*
sting	[stɪŋ]	a painful mark on your body where an insect has stung you
trap	[træp]	a piece of equipment for catching animals

EXAMPLES
A canary was singing in a cage.
How do you treat a wasp sting?
The rabbit was caught in a trap.

VERBS

NOISES ANIMALS MAKE

baa	[bɑː]	when a sheep baas, it makes its typical sound
bark	[bɑːk]	when a dog barks, it makes its typical short, loud sound
buzz	[bʌz]	when a bee or another insect buzzes, it makes its typical rough continuous sound
growl	[graʊl]	when a dog or another animal growls, it makes a low sound in its throat, usually because it is angry
hiss	[hɪs]	when an animal such as a snake or a cat hisses, it makes a sound like a long 's'
miaow	[mɪ'aʊ, mjaʊ]	when a cat miaows, it makes its typical sound
moo	[muː]	when a cow moos, it makes its typical long, low sound
neigh	[neɪ]	when a horse neighs, it makes its typical loud sound
purr	[pɜː]	when a cat purrs, it makes a low sound with its throat because it is happy
quack	[kwæk]	when a duck quacks, it makes its typical sound
roar	[rɔː]	when a lion roars, it makes its typical loud sound
snort	[snɔːt]	when an animal snorts, it breathes air noisily out through its nose

EXAMPLES

Our dog always barks at the postman.
Bees buzzed in the flowers.
The cat sat on the sofa, purring happily.

WAYS IN WHICH ANIMALS MOVE

crawl	[krɔːl]	when an insect crawls somewhere, it moves there quite slowly
fly	[flaɪ]	when a bird or an insect flies, it moves through the air
gallop	['gæləp]	when a horse gallops, it runs very fast so that all four legs are off the ground at the same time
hop	[hɒp]	when a bird or an animal hops, it moves by jumping on both of its feet or all four of its feet together
roam	[rəʊm]	when an animal roams, it moves freely around an area
slither	['slɪðə]	when a snake slithers, it moves along the ground, sliding from side to side
swim	[swɪm]	when a fish swims, it moves through water
trot	[trɒt]	when an animal such as a horse trots, it moves fairly fast, taking quick small steps
wag	[wæg]	when a dog wags its tail, it moves it from side to side

OTHER ANIMAL VERBS

bite	[baɪt]	if a snake or an insect bites you, it makes a mark or a hole in your skin with a sharp part of its body
feed	[fiːd]	1 when you feed an animal, you give it food to eat 2 when an animal feeds, it eats or drinks something
graze	[greɪz]	when an animal grazes, it eats the grass or other plants that are growing in a particular place
hibernate	['haɪbəneɪt]	when an animal hibernates, it spends the winter in a state like a deep sleep

EXAMPLES
The bird flew away as I came near.
The horse trotted around the field.

| **hunt** | [hʌnt] | to chase and kill wild animals for food or as a sport |
| **sting** | [stɪŋ] | if an insect stings you, a pointed part of it is pushed into your skin so that you feel a sharp pain |

ADJECTIVES

stray	[streɪ]	far away from home, or not having a home; *a stray dog*
tame	[teɪm]	not afraid of humans
wild	[waɪld]	living in nature, and not taken care of by people; *a wild animal*

EXAMPLE

The deer never became tame; they ran away if you went near them.

art and photography

NOUNS

art	[ɑːt]	**1** pictures or objects that are created for people to look at; *an art gallery* **2** the activity of creating pictures or objects for people to look at; *an art class*
art gallery	[ˈɑːt ˌɡæləri]	a place where people go to look at art
artist	[ˈɑːtɪst]	someone who draws, paints or creates works of art
background	[ˈbækɡraʊnd]	the part of a picture that is behind the main things or people in it
brush	[brʌʃ]	an object with a lot of bristles or hairs attached to it, that you use for painting
camera	[ˈkæmrə]	a piece of equipment for taking photographs or making films
canvas	[ˈkænvəs]	a piece of strong, heavy material that you paint on
clay	[kleɪ]	a type of earth that is used for making things such as pots and bricks; *a clay pot*
collage	[ˈkɒlɑːʒ]	a picture that you make by sticking pieces of paper or cloth on a surface
design	[dɪˈzaɪn]	**1** the process of planning and drawing things; *studying design* **2** a drawing that shows how something should be built or made; *drawing a design* **3** a pattern of lines or shapes that is used for decorating something; *a floral design*
designer	[dɪˈzaɪnə]	a person whose job is to design things; *a fashion designer*
digital camera	[ˌdɪdʒɪtəl ˈkæmrə]	a camera that produces digital pictures that can be stored on a computer
easel	[ˈiːzəl]	a stand that supports a picture while an artist is working on it

EXAMPLES

He studied art and design.

I looked at the man in the background of the photograph.

My brother has a talent for design.

The tablecloths come in three different designs.

exhibition	[ˌeksɪ'bɪʃən]	a public event where you can see art or interesting objects
foreground	['fɔːgraʊnd]	the part of a picture that seems nearest to you
frame	[freɪm]	the wood, metal or plastic border around a picture or photograph
graphics	['græfɪks]	drawings, pictures or symbols, especially when they are produced by a computer
illustration	[ˌɪlə'streɪʃən]	a picture, design or diagram in a book
landscape	['lændskeɪp]	a painting that shows a scene in the countryside
logo	['ləʊgəʊ]	a special design that an organization puts on all its products; *a corporate logo*
oil paint	['ɔɪl ˌpeɪnt]	a thick paint that artists use
oil painting	['ɔɪl ˌpeɪntɪŋ]	a picture that has been painted using oil paints
paint	[peɪnt]	a coloured liquid that you put onto a surface with a brush
painter	['peɪntə]	an artist who paints pictures
painting	['peɪntɪŋ]	**1** a picture that someone has painted; *a famous painting* **2** the activity of painting pictures; *I enjoy painting.*
pattern	['pætən]	an arrangement of lines or shapes that form a design
photograph	['fəʊtəˌgrɑːf]	a picture that you take with a camera; *take a photograph*
photographer	[fə'tɒgrəfə]	someone who takes photographs
photography	[fə'tɒgrəfi]	the skill or process of producing photographs

EXAMPLES

The game's graphics are very good, so you can see things clearly.
He is very good at painting flowers.
The carpet had a pattern of light and dark stripes.

picture	['pɪktʃə]	**1** a drawing or painting; *paint a picture* **2** a photograph; *take a picture*
portrait	['pɔːtrət]	a painting, drawing or photograph of a particular person
poster	['pəʊstə]	a large picture that you stick on a wall
pottery	['pɒtəri]	the activity of making pots, dishes, and other objects from clay; *pottery classes*
primary colour	['praɪməri ˌkʌlə]	one of the three colours (red, yellow and blue) that you can mix together to produce other colours
sculptor	['skʌlptə]	an artist who makes works of art out of stone, metal or wood
sculpture	['skʌlptʃə]	**1** a piece of art that is made into a shape from a material like stone or wood **2** the art of creating sculptures from materials like stone or wood
sketch	[sketʃ]	a drawing that you do quickly, without a lot of details
statue	['stætʃuː]	a large model of a person or an animal, made of stone or metal
still life	[stɪl 'laɪf]	**1** a painting or drawing of an arrangement of objects such as flowers or fruit **2** the type of painting or drawing that shows an arrangement of objects such as flowers or fruit
watercolour	['wɔːtəkʌlə]	**1** a coloured paint that is mixed with water and used for painting pictures **2** a picture that has been painted with watercolours

EXAMPLES
She drew a picture with a piece of coloured chalk.
Paul did a quick sketch in pencil.

VERBS

design	[dɪˈzaɪn]	to make a detailed plan or drawing that shows how something should be made
draw	[drɔː]	to use a pencil or a pen to make a picture
frame	[freɪm]	to put a picture or photograph in a frame; *a framed photograph*
paint	[peɪnt]	to produce a picture using paint
sketch	[sketʃ]	to make a quick drawing, without a lot of details

EXAMPLE
Monet painted hundreds of pictures of water lilies.

bikes

NOUNS

back light	[ˈbæk laɪt]	a red light on the back of a bicycle
bell	[bel]	a metal object on a bicycle that makes a ringing sound
bicycle	[ˈbaɪsɪkəl]	a vehicle with two wheels that you ride by sitting on it and using your legs to make the wheels turn
bike	[baɪk]	**1** a bicycle **2** a motorcycle
brake	[breɪk]	the part of a bicycle that makes it go more slowly or stop; *put the brakes on*
chain	[tʃeɪn]	a line of connected metal rings that turn the wheels of a bicycle
crossbar	[ˈkrɒsbɑː]	the horizontal bar between the handlebars and the saddle of a bicycle
cycle lane	[ˈsaɪkəl leɪn]	a section of a road that is marked for cyclists to use; *stay in the cycle lane*
cycle path	[ˈsaɪkəl pɑːθ]	a special path that cyclists can use separately from cars and other vehicles; *ride on the cycle path*
cycling	[ˈsaɪklɪŋ]	the activity of riding a bicycle
cyclist	[ˈsaɪklɪst]	someone who rides a bicycle
fall	[fɔːl]	an occasion when you move quickly to the ground by accident; *have a bad fall*
flat (*American English*)		*see* **puncture**
flat tyre	[flæt ˈtaɪə]	a tyre that has no air in it
frame	[freɪm]	the metal part of a bicycle between the wheels, handlebars and saddle
front light	[ˈfrʌnt laɪt]	a white light on the front of a bicycle
gears	[ɡɪəz]	the system of wheels with teeth that are driven by a chain on a bicycle, making it easier or more difficult to pedal

---

EXAMPLES

'How did you get there?' — 'I went by bike.'
'How did you get here?' — 'I came by bike.'
We rode along the cycle path through the forest.
On hills, you use low gears.

handlebars	['hændəlbɑːz]	a curved metal bar with handles at each end that you use to steer a bicycle
helmet	['helmɪt]	a hat made of a hard material, that you wear to protect your head
hub	[hʌb]	the centre of a wheel
inner tube	['ɪnə tjuːb]	a rubber tube containing air that is inside a tyre; *a spare inner tube*
motorcycle	['məʊtəsaɪkəl]	a large heavy bicycle with an engine
mountain bike	['maʊntɪn baɪk]	a type of bicycle with a strong frame and thick tyres
mudguard	['mʌdgɑːd]	a curved piece of metal or plastic above a bicycle wheel that protects the cyclist from dirt or water
padlock	['pædlɒk]	a metal lock that you use for fastening two things together
pedal	['pedəl]	one of the two parts that you push with your feet to make a bicycle move
pump	[pʌmp]	a machine that you use to fill a tyre with air; *a bicycle pump*
puncture	['pʌŋktʃə]	a small hole in a tyre that has been made by a sharp object; *have a puncture*; *mend a puncture* (In American English, use **flat**)
puncture repair kit	['pʌŋktʃə rɪ'peə kɪt]	the tools and materials you need to repair a puncture
reflector	[rɪ'flektə]	a small piece of special plastic on the front of a bicycle that becomes bright when light shines on it
ride	[raɪd]	a journey on a bicycle; *go for a ride*
saddle	['sædəl]	a seat on a bicycle or a motorcycle
speed	[spiːd]	**1** how fast something moves or is done; *increase/decrease your speed* **2** very fast movement or travel; *travel at speed*
spoke	[spəʊk]	a bar that connects the outer ring of a wheel to the centre

EXAMPLE

Cyclists should always wear helmets.

tyre	['taɪə]	a thick round piece of rubber that fits around the wheels of bicycles
valve	[vælv]	the part of a bicycle pump that controls the flow of air
wheel	[wiːl]	one of the two large round objects on a bicycle that allow it to move along the ground

VERBS

brake	[breɪk]	to make a vehicle go more slowly or stop
change gear		to make the chain of a bicycle move to another gear wheel; *change into first gear*
cycle	['saɪkəl]	to ride a bicycle
pedal	['pedəl]	to push the pedals of a bicycle around with your feet to make it move; *pedal faster/ more slowly*
pump up a tyre		to fill a tyre with air
ride	[raɪd]	to sit on a bicycle, control it and travel on it
signal	['sɪgnəl]	to make a movement that tells other people which way you intend to go; *to signal right/left*
stop	[stɒp]	to slow down and no longer move

ADJECTIVES

| shiny | ['ʃaɪni] | bright and reflecting light |
| rusty | ['rʌsti] | covered with rust (= a red-brown substance that can form on metal when it gets wet) |

EXAMPLES

My bike's got a flat tyre.
I need a new front/back wheel.
Belinda braked suddenly.
Every day he cycled to work.
When you ride a bike, you exercise all your leg muscles.

boats, water and the coast

NOUNS

anchor	[ˈæŋkə]	a heavy object that you drop into the water from a boat to stop it moving away
bank	[bæŋk]	a raised area of ground along the edge of a river
bay	[beɪ]	a part of a coast where the land goes in and forms a curve
beach	[biːtʃ]	an area of sand or stones next to a lake or the sea; *at the beach*
boat	[bəʊt]	a vehicle that people use to travel on water; *a fishing boat*; *a rowing boat*; *a sailing boat*; *a motor boat*
bridge	[brɪdʒ]	a structure that is built over a river so that people or vehicles can cross from one side to the other
cabin	[ˈkæbɪn]	a small room on a boat
canal	[kəˈnæl]	a long narrow river made by people for boats to travel along
canoe	[kəˈnuː]	a small, narrow boat that you move through the water using a paddle
captain	[ˈkæptɪn]	the person who is in charge of a ship
cargo	[ˈkɑːgəʊ]	the things that a ship is carrying
cliff	[klɪf]	a high area of land with a very steep side next to the sea
coast	[kəʊst]	the land that is next to the sea
cruise	[kruːz]	a holiday that you spend on a ship
current	[ˈkʌrənt]	a steady flow of water; *a strong current*

EXAMPLES

The bay is surrounded by steep cliffs.

We walked along the beach.

We went there by boat.

The ship was carrying a cargo of bananas.

We drove along the coast.

James and his wife went on a cruise around the world.

The couple were swept away by a strong current.

26 boats, water and the coast

deck	[dek]	one of the floors of a ship
dock	[dɒk]	an area of water beside land where ships go so that people can get on or off them
ferry	['feri]	a boat that regularly takes people or things a short distance across water
fisherman	['fɪʃəmən]	a person who catches fish as a job or for sport
harbour	['hɑːbə]	an area of water next to the land where boats can safely stay
horizon	[hə'raɪzən]	the line that appears between the sky and the sea; *on the horizon*
island™	['aɪlənd]	a piece of land that is completely surrounded by water
jet ski™	['dʒet skiː]	a small machine like a motorcycle that travels on water
kayak	['kaɪæk]	a covered canoe
lake	[leɪk]	a large area of water with land around it
lifebelt	['laɪfbelt]	a large ring that you can hold onto to stop you from going under water
lifeboat	['laɪfbəʊt]	a boat that is used for saving people who are in danger at sea
lifeguard	['laɪfgɑːd]	a person who works at a beach and helps people when they are in danger
lighthouse	['laɪthaʊs]	a tower that is built near or in the sea, with a flashing lamp that warns ships of danger
mouth	[maʊθ]	the place where a river goes into the sea
navy	['neɪvi]	the people who fight for a country at sea
oar	[ɔː]	a long pole with one flat end that you use for rowing a boat
ocean	['əʊʃən]	**1** one of the five very large areas of salt water on the Earth's surface; *the Indian Ocean* **2** same as **sea**; *The ocean was calm.*

EXAMPLES
We went on a luxury ship with five passenger decks.
The next ferry departs at 7 o'clock.
The fishing boats left the harbour.
A small boat appeared on the horizon.
Her son was in the Navy.

paddle	['pædəl]	a short pole with two flat ends that you use for rowing a small boat
pebble	['pebəl]	a small, smooth stone
pond	[pɒnd]	a small area of water
port	[pɔːt]	**1** an area of water next to land where ships arrive and leave. It is larger than a harbour. **2** a town by the sea where ships arrive and leave
quay	[kiː]	a long structure built next to water where boats can stop
river	['rɪvə]	a long line of water that flows into the sea
sail	[seɪl]	a large piece of cloth on a boat, that catches the wind and moves the boat along
sailing	['seɪlɪŋ]	the activity or sport of sailing boats; *go sailing*
sailor	['seɪlə]	**1** someone who works on a ship **2** someone who sails a boat for pleasure
sand	[sænd]	a powder made of very small pieces of stone that you find on most beaches
sea	[siː]	**1** the large area of salty water that covers the Earth's surface; *The sea was calm.* **2** a large area of salty water that is part of an ocean or is surrounded by land; *the North Sea*
seaside	['siːsaɪd]	an area that is close to the sea, especially where people go for their holidays; *at the seaside*
seaweed	['siːwiːd]	a plant that grows in the sea
shell	[ʃel]	the hard part of a small sea creature that you find on beaches
ship	[ʃɪp]	a very large boat that carries people or goods

EXAMPLES
We swam in the river.
I live by the sea.
Ayr is a seaside town on the west coast of Scotland.
We spent a day at the seaside.

shore	[ʃɔː]	the land along the edge of the sea or a lake
speedboat	['spiːdbəʊt]	a boat that can go very fast because it has a powerful engine
stream	[striːm]	a small narrow river
submarine	[ˌsʌbməˈriːn]	a type of ship that can travel below the surface of the sea
surfboard	['sɜːfbɔːd]	a long narrow board that people use for surfing
swimmer	['swɪmə]	**1** someone who swims, especially for sport or pleasure; *He's a fast swimmer.* **2** someone who is swimming; *There are swimmers in the lake.*
swimming	['swɪmɪŋ]	the activity of swimming, especially as a sport or for pleasure; *go swimming*
tide	[taɪd]	the change in the level of the sea towards the land and away from the land that happens twice a day; *at low/high tide*
voyage	['vɔɪɪdʒ]	a long trip on a boat
water	['wɔːtə]	a clear, thin liquid that has no colour or taste. It falls from clouds as rain.
wave	[weɪv]	a higher part of water on the surface of the sea, caused by the wind blowing on the water
yacht	[jɒt]	a large boat with sails or a motor, used for racing or for pleasure trips

VERBS

board	[bɔːd]	to get onto a boat in order to travel somewhere
dive	[daɪv]	**1** to jump into water with your arms and your head going in first

EXAMPLES
We walked along the shore.
I'm going to buy a surfboard and learn to surf.
They began the long voyage down the river.
Waves crashed against the rocks.
We went diving to look at fish.

2 to go under the surface of the sea or a lake, using special equipment for breathing

drown	[draʊn]	to die under water because you cannot breathe
float	[fləʊt]	to stay on the surface of a liquid, and not sink
launch	[lɔːntʃ]	to put a boat into water
navigate	[ˈnævɪˌgeɪt]	to find the direction that you need to travel in, using a map or the sun, for example
row	[rəʊ]	to make a boat move through the water by using oars
sail	[seɪl]	to move over water on a boat
sink	[sɪŋk]	to go below the surface of the water
steer	[stɪə]	to control a boat so that it goes in the direction that you want
surf	[sɜːf]	to ride on big waves using a special board
swim	[swɪm]	to move through water by making movements with your arms and legs

ADJECTIVES

calm	[kɑːm]	not moving much; *The sea was calm.*
coastal	[ˈkəʊstəl]	in the sea or on the land near the coast
marine	[məˈriːn]	relating to the sea or living in the sea; *marine animals*
rough	[rʌf]	with a lot of waves; *The sea was rough.*
sandy	[ˈsændi]	covered with sand
seasick	[ˈsiːsɪk]	feeling ill on a boat

EXAMPLES

Rubbish floated on the surface of the river.
The Titanic was launched in 1911.
We sailed across the bay.
The boat hit the rocks and began to sink.
Do you like swimming?
Coastal areas were flooded.
Nha Trang has a beautiful sandy beach.
Do you get seasick?

body
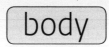

NOUNS

PARTS OF THE BODY

ankle	[ˈæŋkəl]	the part of your body where your foot joins your leg
arm	[ɑːm]	one of the two parts of your body between your shoulders and your hands
artery	[ˈɑːtəri]	one of the tubes in your body that carry blood from your heart to the rest of your body
back	[bæk]	the part of your body from your neck to your waist that is on the opposite side to your chest
blood	[blʌd]	the red liquid that flows inside your body
body	[ˈbɒdi]	all your physical parts
bone	[bəʊn]	one of the hard white parts inside your body
bottom	[ˈbɒtəm]	the part of your body that you sit on
brain	[breɪn]	the organ inside your head that controls your body and allows you to think and to feel things
breast	[brest]	one of the two soft, round parts on a woman's chest that can produce milk to feed a baby
calf (PL) **calves**	[kɑːf] [kɑːvz]	the thick part at the back of your leg, between your ankle and your knee
cheek	[tʃiːk]	one of the two sides of your face below your eyes
chest	[tʃest]	the top part of the front of your body
chin	[tʃɪn]	the part of your face below your mouth
ear	[ɪə]	one of the two parts of your body that you hear sounds with
elbow	[ˈelbəʊ]	the part in the middle of your arm where it bends
eye	[aɪ]	one of the two parts of your body that you see with

EXAMPLE

'What colour are your eyes?' – 'I have blue eyes.'

eyebrow	['aɪbraʊ]	one of the two lines of hair that grow above your eyes
eyelash	['aɪlæʃ]	one of the hairs that grow on the edges of your eyelids
eyelid	['aɪlɪd]	one of the pieces of skin that cover your eyes when they are closed
face	[feɪs]	the front part of your head
feature	['fiːtʃə]	any part of your face, such as your eyes, your nose or your mouth
finger	['fɪŋgə]	one of the long thin parts at the end of each hand
fist	[fɪst]	your hand with your fingers closed tightly together
flesh	[fleʃ]	the soft part of your body that is between your bones and your skin
foot (PL) **feet**	[fʊt] [fiːt]	the part of your body that is at the end of your leg, and that you stand on
forehead	['fɔːhed]	the front part of your head between your eyebrows and your hair
hair	[heə]	**1** the fine threads that grow on your head; *I have black hair.* **2** the short threads that grow on your body; *He has hair on his chest.*
hand	[hænd]	the part of your body at the end of your arm that you use for holding things
head	[hed]	the top part of your body that has your eyes, mouth and brain in it
heart	[hɑːt]	the part inside your chest that makes the blood move around your body
heel	[hiːl]	the back part of your foot, just below your ankle

EXAMPLES
Sarah made a gesture with her fist.
The doctor felt my forehead to see if it was hot.
'What colour is your hair?' – 'I have light-brown hair.'
Your hair looks nice – have you had it cut?

hip	[hɪp]	one of the two areas or bones at the sides of your body between the tops of your legs and your waist
jaw	[dʒɔː]	the top and bottom bones of your mouth
kidney	[ˈkɪdni]	one of the two organs in your body that remove waste liquid from your blood
knee	[niː]	the part in the middle of your leg where it bends
leg	[leg]	one of the long parts of your body that you use for walking and standing
lips	[lɪps]	the two soft outer parts at the edge of your mouth
liver	[ˈlɪvə]	the large organ in your body that cleans your blood
lung	[lʌŋ]	one of the two large organs inside your chest that you use for breathing
mouth	[maʊθ]	the part of your face that you use for eating or speaking
muscle	[ˈmʌsəl]	one of the parts inside your body that connect your bones, and that help you to move
nail	[neɪl]	the thin hard part that grows at the end of each of your fingers and toes
neck	[nek]	the part of your body between your head and the rest of your body
nose	[nəʊz]	the part of your face above your mouth, that you use for smelling and breathing
organ	[ˈɔːgən]	a part of your body, for example your brain or your heart, that has a particular purpose
rib	[rɪb]	one of the 12 pairs of curved bones that surround your chest
shoulder	[ˈʃəʊldə]	one of the two parts of your body between your neck and the tops of your arms
shin	[ʃɪn]	the front part of your leg between your knee and your ankle

EXAMPLE
She bites her nails.

skeleton	['skelɪtən]	all the bones in your body
skin	[skɪn]	the substance that covers the outside of your body
spine	[spaɪn]	the row of bones down your back
stomach	['stʌmək]	**1** the organ inside your body where food goes when you eat it; *a full stomach* **2** the front part of your body below your waist; *lie on your stomach*
thigh	[θaɪ]	the top part of your leg, above your knee
throat	[θrəʊt]	**1** the back of your mouth and inside your neck, where you swallow **2** the front part of your neck
thumb	[θʌm]	the short thick part on the side of your hand next to your four fingers
toe	[təʊ]	one of the five parts at the end of your foot
tongue	[tʌŋ]	the soft part inside your mouth that moves when you speak or eat
tooth (PL) **teeth**	[tuːθ] [tiːθ]	one of the hard white objects in your mouth, that you use for biting and eating
vein	[veɪn]	a thin tube in your body that carries blood to your heart
voice	[vɔɪs]	the sound that comes from your mouth when you speak or sing
waist	[weɪst]	the middle part of your body
wrist	[rɪst]	the part between your hand and your arm that bends when you move your hand

DESCRIBING PEOPLE

age	[eɪdʒ]	the number of years that you have lived
beard	[bɪəd]	the hair that grows on a man's chin and cheeks
complexion	[kəm'plekʃən]	the natural colour of the skin on your face; *a pale complexion*
expression	[ɪk'spreʃən]	the way that your face looks at a particular moment; *a shocked expression*
false teeth	[fɔːls 'tiːθ]	artificial teeth that someone wears if they do not have their natural teeth

fringe	[frɪndʒ]	hair that is cut so that it hangs over your forehead; *a short fringe*
freckles	['frekəlz]	small light-brown spots on someone's skin
gesture	['dʒestʃə]	a movement that you make with a part of your body, especially your hands, to express emotion or information; *make a gesture*
glasses	['glɑːsɪz]	two pieces of glass or plastic in a frame, that some people wear in front of their eyes to help them to see better; *wear glasses*
hairstyle	['heəstaɪl]	the way that your hair is cut or arranged; *a new hairstyle*
height	[haɪt]	your size from your feet to the top of your head; *a man of average height*
measurement	['meʒəmənt]	the size around a part of your body, that you need to know when you are buying clothes; *your hip/waist/chest measurement*
mole	[məʊl]	a natural dark spot on someone's skin
moustache	[mə'stɑːʃ]	the hair that grows between a man's nose and mouth
scar	[skɑː]	a mark that is left on someone's skin after a wound gets better
size	[saɪz]	how big or small something is
smile	[smaɪl]	an expression on your face when you curve up the corners of your mouth because you are happy or you think that something is funny; *give a smile*
spot	[spɒt]	a small red lump or mark on someone's skin
tears	[tɪəz]	drops of liquid that come from your eyes when you cry
weight	[weɪt]	how heavy a person or thing is

EXAMPLES

He has short red hair and freckles.
'What size are you?' – 'Size ten.'
I've got a big spot on my nose.
He had tears in his eyes.
She has put on weight.
He has lost weight.

| wrinkles | ['rɪŋkəlz] | lines that form on your face when you grow old |

VERBS

grow	[grəʊ]	to gradually become bigger
look	[lʊk]	to seem to have a particular quality; *He looks sad.*
look like		to have a particular appearance; *What does he look like?*
weigh	[weɪ]	to have a particular weight; *She weighs 50 kilos.*

THINGS PEOPLE DO WITH THEIR BODIES

blow your nose		to force air out of your nose in order to clear it
cry	[kraɪ]	to have tears coming from your eyes, usually because you are sad
fold your arms		to put one arm under the other and hold them over your chest
go red		if you go red, your face becomes red because you feel embarrassed
have your hair cut		if you have your hair cut, someone uses scissors to make your hair shorter
nod	[nɒd]	to move your head up and down to say 'yes'
shake your head		to move your head from side to side to say 'no'
shake hands with someone		to say hello or goodbye to someone by holding their right hand in your right hand and moving it up and down

EXAMPLES
His face was covered with wrinkles.
Sara has grown a lot.
Maria looks like her mother.
She was crying.
'Are you okay?' I asked. She nodded and smiled.
'Did you see Magda?' Anna shook her head.
Claude shook hands with David.

shrug	[ʃrʌg]	to move your shoulders up to show that you do not know or care about something
smile	[smaɪl]	to curve up the corners of your mouth because you are happy or you think that something is funny
wave at someone		to hold your hand up and wave it from side to side in order to say hello or goodbye to someone

SENSES

feel	[fiːl]	**1** to experience a particular physical feeling; *I feel cold.* **2** used for describing the way that something seems when you touch it or experience it; *This room feels cold.* **3** to touch something with your hand, so that you can find out what it is like; *feel someone's forehead* **4** to be aware of something because you touch it or it touches you; *feel the wind on your face*
hear	[hɪə]	to become aware of a sound through your ears
see	[siː]	to notice something using your eyes
smell	[smel]	**1** to have a quality that you notice by breathing in through your nose; *This flower smells sweet.* **2** to notice something when you breathe in through your nose; *I can smell smoke.*
taste	[teɪst]	**1** to have a particular flavour that you notice when you are eating or drinking; *This soup tastes delicious.* **2** to notice the flavour of something that you are eating or drinking; *I can taste salt in this soup.*

EXAMPLES
He was smiling.
It's too dark – I can't see anything.
I can hear music.

touch	[tʌtʃ]	to put your hand onto something

BODY POSITIONS

crouch	[kraʊtʃ]	to bend your legs so that you are close to the ground
kneel	[niːl]	to bend your legs and rest with one or both of your knees on the ground
lie	[laɪ]	to be in a flat position, and not standing or sitting; *lie on the ground*
lie down		to move your body so that it is flat on something, usually when you want to sleep or rest
sit	[sɪt]	to have the lower part of your body resting on a chair and the upper part straight
sit down		to move your body down until you are sitting on something
stand	[stænd]	to be on your feet
stand up		to move so that you are on your feet
stretch	[stretʃ]	to put your arms or legs out very straight

ADJECTIVES

bald	[bɔːld]	with no hair, or very little hair, on the top of your head
beautiful	[ˈbjuːtɪfʊl]	very attractive to look at
big	[bɪg]	large in size
blind	[blaɪnd]	unable to see

EXAMPLES

She reached down and touched her toes.
I crouched down to stroke the dog.
John was lying on the sofa.
Why don't you go upstairs and lie down?
Tom sat down beside me.
He yawned and stretched.
She was a beautiful woman with fine features.

blonde	[blɒnd]	**1** blonde hair is pale or yellow; *She has blonde hair.* **2** someone who is blonde has pale or yellow hair; *She is blonde.*
curly	['kɜːli]	shaped in curves; *curly hair*
dark	[dɑːk]	black or brown; *dark hair; dark eyes*
deaf	[def]	unable to hear anything or unable to hear very well
disabled	[dɪ'seɪbəld]	having an injury or a condition that makes it difficult for you to move around
dyed	[daɪd]	if you have dyed hair, you have changed the colour of your hair using a special substance
fair	[feə]	fair hair is pale or yellow; fair skin is very pale
fat	[fæt]	weighing too much
handsome	['hænsəm]	having an attractive face
old	[əʊld]	**1** having lived for many years; not young; *an old man* **2** used for talking or asking about someone's age; *six years old*
overweight	[ˌəʊvə'weɪt]	weighing more than is healthy or attractive
pretty	['prɪti]	attractive and pleasant
short	[ʃɔːt]	not tall
skinny	['skɪni]	extremely thin or too thin
slim	[slɪm]	thin in an attractive way
small	[smɔːl]	not large in size or amount
straight	[streɪt]	not bending or curving; *straight hair*

EXAMPLES
'How old are you?' – 'I'm 34.'
'What does she look like?' – 'She is short, and has curly blonde hair.'
A slim young girl was standing in the middle of the room.

tall	[tɔːl]	**1** of a greater height than other people; *a tall woman* **2** used when you are asking or talking about someone's height; *How tall are you?*
thin	[θɪn]	having no extra fat on your body
ugly	[ˈʌgli]	very unpleasant to look at
young	[jʌŋ]	not having lived for very long

EXAMPLES

He is taller than you.

She is 1.47 metres tall.

He was a tall, thin man with a grey beard.

business

NOUNS

accounts [ə'kaʊnts] records of all the money that a business receives and spends

ad (*mainly American English*) *see* **advert**

advert ['ædvɜːt] information that tells you about something such as a product, an event or a job (*In American English, use* **ad**)

advertising ['ædvətaɪzɪŋ] the business of creating information that tells people about a product in order to persuade them to buy it; *an advertising campaign*; *an advertising agency*

agent ['eɪdʒənt] someone whose job is to do business for another person or company

AGM [ˌeɪ dʒiː 'em] short for 'annual general meeting': a meeting that a company has once a year to discuss the previous year's activities and accounts

boom [buːm] an increase in the number of things that people are buying; *an economic boom*; *a boom in tourism*

brand [brænd] a product that has its own name and is made by a particular company

budget ['bʌdʒɪt] the amount of money that you have available to spend

business ['bɪznɪs] **1** work that is related to producing, buying and selling things; *do business with someone* **2** used to talk about how many products a company is selling; *Business is good.* **3** an organization that produces and sells goods or that provides a service; *a hairdressing business*

EXAMPLES

I work in advertising.

You are buying direct, rather than through an agent.

What is your favourite brand of coffee?

Our company does not have a large budget for training.

They worried that German companies would lose business.

My brother runs a thriving furniture business.

The government is not doing enough to help small and medium-sized businesses.

CEO	[ˌsiː iː ˈəʊ]	short for 'chief executive officer': the person who is responsible for the management of the whole company
chair	[tʃeə]	the person in charge of a company or an organization
client	[klaɪənt]	a person who pays someone for a service
commerce	[ˈkɒmɜːs]	the buying and selling of large amounts of things
company	[ˈkʌmpəni]	a business that sells goods or services
competition	[ˌkɒmpɪˈtɪʃən]	the activities of companies that are trying to sell more products than each other
consumer	[kənˈsjuːmə]	someone who buys something or uses a service
corporation	[ˌkɔːpəˈreɪʃən]	a large business or company
costs	[kɒsts]	the amount of money that you must spend in order to run your business
customer	[ˈkʌstəmə]	someone who buys something from a shop or a website; *customer services*; *customer relations*
deal	[diːl]	an agreement or an arrangement in business; *do a deal*
debt	[det]	**1** money that you owe to someone; *a £50,000 debt* **2** the state of owing money; *be in debt*
director	[daɪˈrektə]	one of the people who control a company or an organization, and meet regularly to make important decisions
executive	[ɪgˈzekjʊtɪv]	someone who has an important job at a company
firm	[fɜːm]	same as **company**

EXAMPLES

A lawyer and his client were sitting at the next table.
The company owes money to more than sixty banks.
They faced competition from new online companies.
We need to cut costs.
The supermarket wants to attract new customers.
They are still paying off their debts.
Many firms were facing bankruptcy.

growth	[grəʊθ]	increase in profits or sales
management ['mænɪdʒmənt]		**1** the control of a business **2** the people who control a business
manager	['mænɪdʒə]	someone who runs a business or part of a business
market	['mɑːkɪt]	the people who want to buy a particular product
market research	[ˌmɑːkɪt rɪ'sɜːtʃ]	the business activity of finding out about what people want, need and buy
marketing	['mɑːkɪtɪŋ]	the business of deciding how to sell a product, for example what price it is, where it is sold and how it is advertised
meeting	['miːtɪŋ]	an event in which a group of people come together to discuss things or make decisions
PR	[ˌpiː 'ɑː]	short for 'public relations': the part of a company's work that is concerned with getting people to like the company
product	['prɒdʌkt]	something that you make or grow in order to sell it
profit	['prɒfɪt]	the amount of money that you gain when you sell something for more than it cost to make it; *make a profit*
promotion	[prə'məʊʃən]	an attempt to make a product successful or popular, especially by advertising
publicity	[pʌ'blɪsɪti]	information that attracts the public's attention to a person or a product
retail	['riːteɪl]	the activity of selling goods directly to the public
sales	[seɪlz]	the quantity of a product that is sold
shareholder	['ʃeəhəʊldə]	someone who owns shares in a company

EXAMPLES

The zoo needed better management rather than more money.

The market for organic wines is growing.

There were meetings between senior management and staff.

This mobile phone is one of our most successful products.

The group made a profit of £1.05 million.

stocks and shares	[ˌstɒks ənd ˈʃeəz]	the parts of company that people buy in order to invest money in the company
supervisor	[ˈsuːpəvaɪzə]	someone who is in charge of activities or people
trade	[treɪd]	the activity of buying and selling goods
turnover	[ˈtɜːnəʊvə]	the value of the goods or services that are sold by a company during a particular period of time

VERBS

advertise	[ˈædvətaɪz]	to tell people about a product or a service in newspapers, on television, on signs, or on the internet
break even		to make enough money to pay for costs, but not enough to make a profit
buy	[baɪ]	to get something by paying money for it
employ	[ɪmˈplɔɪ]	to pay someone to work for a person or a company
expand	[ɪkˈspænd]	**1** to become bigger, with more people, goods or activities; *Our business expanded.* **2** to make something larger; *expand services*
go out of business		if a company goes out of business, it stops trading because it does not have enough money
improve	[ɪmˈpruːv]	to get better or to make something get better
invest	[ɪnˈvest]	to put money into a business, in order to try to make a profit from it

EXAMPLES

They bought shares in US-AIR.

Texas has a long history of trade with Mexico.

The company had a turnover of £3.8 million last year.

The airline hopes to break even next year and make a profit the following year.

The firm employs 800 staff.

I want to expand my business.

Many airlines could go out of business.

We need to improve performance.

launch	[lɔːntʃ]	to start selling a new product to the public
manage	['mænɪdʒ]	to control a business
market	['mɑːkɪt]	to advertise and sell a product
negotiate	[nɪ'gəʊʃieɪt]	to talk about a situation in order to reach an agreement
owe	[əʊ]	to have to pay money to someone; *owe someone money*
sell	[sel]	to let someone have something that you own in return for money

ADJECTIVES

bankrupt	['bæŋkrʌpt]	not having enough money to pay your debts; *go bankrupt*
commercial	[kə'mɜːʃəl]	relating to the buying and selling of things
medium-sized	['miːdiəm-saɪzd]	not large and not small; *a medium-sized firm*
online	['ɒnlaɪn]	using the internet to sell goods; *an online service*; *online retailing*; *online shopping*
private	['praɪvɪt]	not owned by the government
profitable	['prɒfɪtəbəl]	making a profit
senior	['siːnjə]	having an important job in an organization
small	[smɔːl]	not large in size or amount; *a small business*
thriving	[θraɪvɪŋ]	successful

IDIOMS

at the cutting edge	involved in the most exciting and new developments
blue-sky thinking	new creative ideas
think outside the box	to think in a new and creative way

EXAMPLES
The firm launched a new clothing range.
If the firm cannot sell its products, it will go bankrupt.
New York is a centre of commercial activity.
Drug manufacturing is the most profitable business in America.
This company is at the cutting edge of technology.

cars and road travel

NOUNS

accelerator	[æk'seləreɪtə]	the part in a vehicle that you press with your foot to make the vehicle go faster (*In American English, use* **gas pedal**)
accident	['æksɪdənt]	when a vehicle hits something and causes injury or damage
ambulance	['æmbjʊləns]	a vehicle for taking people to hospital; *call an ambulance*
bonnet	['bɒnɪt]	the front part of a car that covers the engine (*In American English, use* **hood**)
boot	[buːt]	the space at the back of a car that is used for carrying things in (*In American English, use* **trunk**)
brake	[breɪk]	the part in a vehicle that you press with your foot to make the vehicle go more slowly or stop
breakdown	['breɪkdaʊn]	an occasion when a vehicle stops working; *have a breakdown*
bumper	['bʌmpə]	a heavy bar at the front and back of a vehicle that protects the vehicle if it hits something
bus	[bʌs]	a large motor vehicle that carries passengers; *a school bus*; *a tour bus*; *a double-decker bus*; *catch a bus*
car	[kɑː]	a motor vehicle with space for about five people; *drive/park a car*; *a sports car*; *a racing car*; *a police car*
caravan	['kærəvæn]	a large vehicle that is pulled by a car. You can sleep and eat in a caravan on holiday.

EXAMPLES

There's been an accident.
Six people were injured in the accident.
He opened the boot and put my bags in.
He missed his last bus home.
They arrived by car.
The car won't start.

car park	['kɑː pɑːk]	an area or building where people can leave their cars (*In American English, use* **parking lot**)
clutch	[klʌtʃ]	the part of a vehicle that you press with your foot before you move the gear stick
coach	[kəʊtʃ]	a comfortable bus that travels between cities or takes people on long journeys; *a coach tour/trip*
crossroads	['krɒsrəʊdz]	a place where two roads cross each other
dashboard	['dæʃbɔːd]	the part of a car in front of the driver, where most of the controls are
direction	[daɪ'rekʃən]	the general line that you move in when you are going to a place
directions	[daɪ'rekʃənz]	instructions that tell you how to get somewhere; *give someone directions*
distance	['dɪstəns]	the amount of space between two places; *travel a short/long distance*
driver	['draɪvə]	someone who drives a bus, a car or a train, for example
driver's license (*American English*) *see* **driving licence**		
driving licence	['draɪvɪŋ ˌlaɪsəns]	a document showing that you are legally allowed to drive (*In American English, use* **driver's license**)
engine	['endʒɪn]	the part of a vehicle that produces the power to make it move
fire engine	['faɪə ˌendʒɪn]	a large vehicle that carries firemen and equipment for putting out fires (*In American English, use* **fire truck**)
fire truck (*American English*)		*see* **fire engine**
flat (*American English*)		*see* **puncture**
freeway (*American English*)		*see* **motorway**

EXAMPLES

Where's the nearest car park?
You're going in the wrong direction.
He gave us directions to the hospital.
Do you have a driving licence?
He got into the driving seat and started the engine.

garage	['gærɑːʒ]	**1** a building next to your house where you keep your car **2** a public building where you can park your car **3** a place where cars are repaired **4** same as **petrol station**
gas (American English)		see **petrol**
gas pedal (American English)		see **accelerator**
gear	[gɪə]	a part of an engine that changes power into movement
gear shift (American English)		see **gear stick**
gear stick	['gɪə stɪk]	the lever in a vehicle that you use to change gear (In American English, use **gear shift**)
handbrake	['hændbreɪk]	the brake in a car that you pull with your hand to stop it moving, for example, when you have parked
headlights	['hedlaɪts]	the large lights at the front of a vehicle
hood (American English)		see **bonnet**
horn	[hɔːn]	an object in a vehicle that makes a loud noise, and that you use as a warning of danger
indicator	['ɪndɪkeɪtə]	a flashing light on a vehicle that tells you when the vehicle is going to turn left or right (In American English, use **turn signal**)
journey	['dʒɜːni]	an occasion when you travel from one place to another
lane	[leɪn]	**1** a narrow road, especially in the countryside; *a country lane* **2** a part of a road that is marked by a painted line; *the fast lane*
license plate (American English)		see **number plate**
lorry	['lɒri]	a large vehicle that is used for transporting goods by road (In American English, use **truck**)

EXAMPLES

The car was in fourth gear.
It's a 3-hour journey.
Have a good journey!

make	[meɪk]	the name of the company that made a particular car; *a make of car*
motorbike	['məʊtəbaɪk]	same as **motorcycle**; *ride a motorbike*
motorcycle	['məʊtəsaɪkəl]	a vehicle with two wheels and an engine
motorway	['məʊtəweɪ]	a wide road that allows vehicles to travel very fast over a long distance (*In American English, use* **freeway**)
number plate	['nʌmbə pleɪt]	a sign on the front and back of a vehicle that shows its registration number (*In American English, use* **license plate**)
oil	[ɔɪl]	a smooth, thick liquid that is used for making machines work
one-way street	[,wʌn weɪ 'striːt]	a street where vehicles can only go in one direction
parking lot (*American English*)		*see* **car park**
parking space	['pɑːkɪŋ speɪs]	a place where you can park your car
passenger	['pæsɪndʒə]	someone who is travelling in a vehicle but is not driving it
pedestrian	[pɪ'destriən]	someone who is walking, especially in a town or city
petrol	['petrəl]	the fuel that you use in vehicles to make the engine work (*In American English, use* **gas**)
petrol station	['petrəl ,steɪʃən]	a place where you buy fuel for your vehicle
puncture	['pʌŋktʃə]	a small hole in a tyre that has been made by a sharp object (*In American English, use* **flat**)
rear-view mirror	['rɪə vjuː 'mɪrə]	the mirror on the front window of a vehicle that allows you to see behind the vehicle
registration number	[,redʒɪ'streɪʃən ,nʌmbə]	the official numbers and letters at the front and back of a vehicle

EXAMPLES
'What make of car do you drive?' – 'A Honda.'
Yesterday, traffic was light on the motorway.
We drove around for 20 minutes trying to find a parking space.
Mr Smith was a passenger in the car when it crashed.

road	[rəʊd]	a long piece of hard ground that cars travel on
road sign	['rəʊd saɪn]	a flat metal object at the side of a road that gives information to drivers
roof rack	['ruːf ræk]	a metal frame on top of a car where you can put things such as suitcases
roundabout	['raʊndəbaʊt]	a circle in the road where several roads meet, which vehicles must drive round until they reach the road they need
seat belt	['siːt belt]	a strap in a car that you put across your body to protect you in an accident
service station	['sɜːvɪs ˌsteɪʃən]	a place next to a motorway where you can buy petrol and food
side-view mirror *(American English) see* **wing mirror**		
spare part	[ˌspeə 'pɑːt]	a part that you can buy to replace an old or broken part of a vehicle
speed	[spiːd]	how fast something moves
speed camera	['spiːd ˌkæmrə]	a piece of equipment that takes pictures of vehicles if they are going too fast
speed limit	['spiːd ˌlɪmɪt]	the maximum speed that you are legally allowed to drive at
speedometer	[spiːˈdɒmɪtə]	a piece of equipment in a car that shows how fast you are driving
street	[striːt]	a road in a city or a town
taxi	['tæksi]	a car that you can hire, with its driver, to take you where you want to go; *take/catch a taxi*
traffic	['træfɪk]	all the vehicles that are moving along roads in a particular area; *heavy traffic*; *oncoming traffic*
traffic jam	['træfɪk dʒæm]	a long line of vehicles that cannot move because there is too much traffic, or because the road is blocked

EXAMPLES

Take the road to Nottingham.
Don't forget to put on your seat belt.
There was hardly any traffic on the road.
There is heavy traffic between Junctions 14 and 18.

50 cars and road travel

traffic lights	['træfɪk laɪts]	a set of red, yellow and green lights that show you when to stop and when to move forwards
traffic warden	['træfɪk ˌwɔːdən]	someone whose job is to make sure that vehicles are parked legally
trailer	['treɪlə]	a large container on wheels that is pulled by a lorry or other vehicle
transport	['trænspɔːt]	a system for taking people or things from one place to another in a vehicle; *road/air/rail transport*
truck (*American English*)		*see* **lorry**
trunk (*American English*)		*see* **boot**
turn signal (*American English*)		*see* **indicator**
tyre	['taɪə]	a thick round piece of rubber that fits around the wheels of cars
van	[væn]	a vehicle like a large car or a small lorry with space for carrying things in the back
vehicle	['viːɪkəl]	a machine that carries people or things from one place to another
wheel	[wiːl]	**1** one of the round objects under a vehicle that allow it to move along the ground; *the front/back wheel* **2** the round object on a vehicle that you turn to make the vehicle go in different directions; *a steering wheel*
windscreen	['wɪndskriːn]	the glass window at the front of a vehicle (*In American English, use* **windshield**)
windshield (*American English*)		*see* **windscreen**
wing mirror	['wɪŋ ˌmɪrə]	one of the two mirrors on each side of a car (*In American English, use* **side-view mirror**)

VERBS

accelerate	[æk'seləreɪt]	to go faster

EXAMPLE
There are too many vehicles on the road.

brake	[breɪk]	to use the brakes in order to make a vehicle stop or slow down
break down		to stop working; *The car broke down.*
crash	[kræʃ]	if a vehicle crashes, it hits something and is damaged
drive	[draɪv]	**1** to control the movement and direction of a vehicle; *Can you drive?* **2** to take someone somewhere in a vehicle; *I'll drive you home.*
give way		to let another vehicle go before you (*In American English, use* **yield**)
hitch-hike	['hɪtʃhaɪk]	to ask people to drive you somewhere, by standing by the side of a road and holding out your thumb
overtake	[ˌəʊvə'teɪk]	to pass another vehicle that is going in the same direction
park	[pɑːk]	to stop a vehicle and leave it somewhere
skid	[skɪd]	to slide sideways
speed	[spiːd]	to drive faster than the speed limit
steer	[stɪə]	to control a vehicle so that it goes in the direction you want
stop	[stɒp]	to not move any more
travel	['trævəl]	to go from one place to another, often to a place that is far away
tow	[təʊ]	to pull another vehicle along behind
yield (*American English*)		*see* **give way**

EXAMPLES

A dog ran across the road and I braked quickly.
I crashed into the back of a lorry.
We were driving at 100 kilometres an hour.
I'll drive you to work.
Jeff hitch-hiked to New York.
You should slow down when you are overtaking a cyclist.
The car skidded on the icy road.
People often travel hundreds of miles to get here.
He uses the lorry to tow his trailer.

52 cars and road travel

slow down	to reduce the speed you are driving at
speed up	to start driving more quickly
start up	when an engine starts up, it starts working

[PHRASES]

no entry	if a road sign says 'no entry', you must not go along that road
roadworks	if a road sign says 'roadworks', it means that people are fixing the road

EXAMPLES
You're going too fast – slow down.
Eric started the car and drove off.

celebrations and ceremonies

baptism	['bæptɪzəm]	a ceremony in which a person is baptized
bar mitzvah	[,bɑː 'mɪtsvə]	a ceremony for a Jewish boy on his thirteenth birthday
birth	[bɜːθ]	the time when a baby is born; *the birth of our daughter*
birthday	['bɜːθdeɪ]	a date when you celebrate the day that you were born
bride	[braɪd]	a woman on her wedding day
cemetery	['semətri]	a place where dead people are buried
ceremony	['serɪməni]	a formal event
christening	['krɪsənɪŋ]	a ceremony in which members of a church welcome a baby and give it a name
Christmas	['krɪsməs]	the period around the 25th December, when Christians celebrate the birth of Jesus Christ; *at Christmas*
Christmas Day	[,krɪsməs 'deɪ]	the 25th of December; *on Christmas Day*
Christmas Eve	[,krɪsməs 'iːv]	the 24th of December; *on Christmas Eve*
death	[deθ]	the end of a person's life
Easter	['iːstə]	a Christian festival in March or April when people celebrate Jesus Christ's return to life; *at Easter*
engagement	[ɪn'geɪdʒmənt]	an agreement to get married to somebody
Father's Day	['fɑːðəz deɪ]	a day when you give a card or present to your father to show that you love him; *on Father's Day*
festival	['festɪvəl]	a time when people celebrate a special event
festivities	[fes'tɪvɪtiz]	events that are organized in order to celebrate something

EXAMPLES

I'm going to my grandson's baptism tomorrow.
It's my birthday today.
I'm going to the cemetery to visit my grandma's grave.
The Christmas festivities lasted for more than a week.
I always visit my parents at Christmas.

fireworks	[ˈfaɪəwɜːks]	things that fly up into the air and explode, making bright colours in the sky; *a fireworks display*
funeral	[ˈfjuːnərəl]	a ceremony in which the body of a dead person is buried or cremated
gift	[gɪft]	same as **present**
graduation	[ˌgrædʒʊˈeɪʃən]	a ceremony for students when they have completed their studies at a university or college
grave	[greɪv]	a place in the ground where a dead person is buried
greetings card	[ˈgriːtɪŋz ˌkɑːd]	a folded card with a message inside that you give to someone on a special occasion
groom	[gruːm]	a man on his wedding day
Hanukkah	[ˈhɑːnʊkə]	a festival in November or December when Jewish people remember a special time when a temple was given back to them; *during Hanukkah*
honeymoon	[ˈhʌniˌmuːn]	a holiday that a man and woman take after their wedding
invitation	[ˌɪnvɪˈteɪʃən]	a written or spoken request to go to a party or a ceremony
Lent	[lent]	the forty days before Easter, when some Christians stop doing something that they enjoy; *during Lent*
marriage	[ˈmærɪdʒ]	**1** the relationship between a husband and wife; *a happy marriage* **2** same as **wedding**; *a marriage ceremony*
Mother's Day	[ˈmʌðəz deɪ]	a day when you give a card or present to your mother to show that you love her; *on Mother's Day*

EXAMPLES

We watched the fireworks from our balcony.
I need to choose a gift for my mum's birthday.
We went to Paris for our honeymoon.
We received an invitation to their wedding.
Maureen gave up chocolate for Lent.

New Year's Day	[ˌnjuː jɪəz ˈdeɪ]	the day when people celebrate the start of the year; *on New Year's Day*
New Year's Eve	[ˌnjuː jɪəz ˈiːv]	the last day of the year; *on New Year's Eve*
occasion	[əˈkeɪʒən]	an important event, ceremony, or celebration; *a special occasion*
party	[ˈpɑːti]	an event where you enjoy yourself with friends doing things like eating or dancing; *have a party*
Passover	[ˈpɑːsəʊvə]	a festival in March or April when Jewish people celebrate a special time when God helped them; *during Passover*
present	[ˈprɛzənt]	something that you give to someone on a special occasion
procession	[prəˈsɛʃən]	a line of people or vehicles that follow one another as part of a ceremony
public holiday	[ˌpʌblɪk ˈhɒlɪdeɪ]	a day when most of the shops, businesses and schools in a country are closed, often to celebrate a particular event
Ramadan	[ˈræmədæn]	the ninth month of the Muslim year, when Muslims celebrate the time that God spoke the words of their holy book; *during Ramadan*
retirement	[rɪˈtaɪəmənt]	the time when you stop work
Thanksgiving	[ˌθæŋksˈɡɪvɪŋ]	a holiday in November when families in America have a special meal together to celebrate all the good things in their lives; *on Thanksgiving*
Valentine's Day	[ˈvæləntaɪnz ˌdeɪ]	the 14th of February, when you give a card or flowers to the person you love; *on Valentine's Day*

EXAMPLES

We wished our neighbours a happy New Year.

I'm having a party on Friday night – would you like to come?

This necklace was an anniversary present from my husband.

The supermarket is closed on Sundays and public holidays.

We went out for dinner on Valentine's Day.

wake	[weɪk]	an event before or after a funeral when friends and family remember the person who died
wedding	['wedɪŋ]	a ceremony when two people get married
wedding anniversary	['wedɪŋ ænɪ,vɜːsəri]	a date when you celebrate the day you got married; *our 10th wedding anniversary*
wrapping paper	['ræpɪŋ peɪpə]	special paper that you use for wrapping presents

VERBS

baptize	[bæp'taɪz]	to touch someone with water, to show that they have become a member of the Christian church; *baptize a baby*
be born		when a baby is born, it comes out of its mother's body at the beginning of its life
bury	['beri]	to put the body of a dead person into a grave and cover it with earth
celebrate	['selɪ,breɪt]	to do something enjoyable for a special reason; *celebrate your birthday*
cremate	[krɪ'meɪt]	to burn the body of a dead person
die	[daɪ]	to stop living
fast	[fɑːst]	to not eat any food for a period of time
get married		1 when two people get married, they become husband and wife; *John and Linda got married.* 2 when you get married to someone, you become their husband or wife; *John got married to Linda.*
get engaged		1 when two people get engaged, they agree to marry each other; *Sue and Rishi got engaged.*

EXAMPLES
My sister was born in 1995.
We're celebrating the birth of our baby boy.
My dad died two years ago.
We fasted during Ramadan.

2 when you get engaged to someone, you agree to marry them; *I got engaged to my boyfriend.*

invite	[ɪnˈvaɪt]	to ask someone to come to an event; *invite someone to a party*
marry	[ˈmæri]	same as **get married**
organize	[ˈɔːɡəˌnaɪz]	to plan or arrange something; *organize a party*
turn	[tɜːn]	to reach a particular age; *turn 40*
wish	[wɪʃ]	to express the hope that someone will be lucky or happy; *wish someone a happy birthday*

[PHRASES]

Happy Christmas!	you say 'Happy Christmas!' to people when you meet them on Christmas Day
Happy birthday!	you say 'Happy birthday!' to someone when you meet them on their birthday

EXAMPLES
Let's invite some friends over for dinner.
My brother has just turned 17.

clothes

bathing suit *(American English)* *see* **swimsuit**

belt	[belt]	a strip of leather or cloth that you wear around your waist
bikini	[bɪˈkiːni]	a piece of clothing with two parts, that women wear for swimming
blouse	[blaʊz]	a shirt for a girl or a woman
boots	[buːts]	shoes that cover your whole foot and the lower part of your leg; *a pair of boots*
bra	[brɑː]	a piece of underwear that women wear to support their breasts
button	[ˈbʌtən]	a small hard object that you push through holes (= buttonholes) to fasten your clothes
cap	[kæp]	a soft, flat hat with a curved part at the front
cardigan	[ˈkɑːdɪgən]	a jumper that opens at the front like a jacket
clothes	[kləʊðz]	the things that people wear, such as shirts, coats, trousers and dresses
clothing	[ˈkləʊðɪŋ]	same as **clothes**
coat	[kəʊt]	a piece of clothing with long sleeves that you wear over other clothes when you go outside
collar	[ˈkɒlə]	the part of a shirt or coat that goes around your neck
dress	[dres]	**1** a piece of clothing that covers a woman's or girl's body and part of her legs; *a black dress* **2** a particular type of clothing; *people in traditional dress*
dressing gown	[ˈdresɪŋ gaʊn]	a long, loose piece of clothing that you wear over your night clothes when you are not in bed

---

EXAMPLES

He was dressed in a shirt, dark trousers and boots.
Isabel's striped dress suited her very well.

clothes 59

fashion	['fæʃən]	**1** the activity or business that involves styles of clothing and appearance; *a fashion designer; a fashion show* **2** a style of clothing that is popular at a particular time; *the latest fashion*
gloves	[glʌvz]	pieces of clothing that you wear on your hands, with a separate part for each finger; *a pair of gloves*
hat	[hæt]	a thing that you wear on your head
high heels	[haɪ 'hiːlz]	women's shoes that have high heels (= raised parts on the bottom of the shoe)
hood	[hʊd]	the part of a coat that you can pull up to cover your head
jacket	['dʒækɪt]	a short coat with long sleeves
jeans	[dʒiːnz]	trousers made from strong cotton cloth
jumper	['dʒʌmpə]	a warm piece of clothing that covers the top part of your body (*In American English, use* **sweater**)
kaftan	['kæftæn]	a long loose piece of clothing with long sleeves, that men in Arab countries wear
kimono	[kɪ'məʊnəʊ]	a long piece of clothing shaped like a coat, that some Japanese people wear
knickers	['nɪkəz]	a piece of underwear for women and girls, that covers the area between the waist and the legs (*In American English, use* **panties**)
leggings	['legɪŋz]	a piece of tight clothing that covers the lower body to the ankles, usually worn by women and girls; *a pair of leggings*
nightdress	['naɪtdres]	a loose dress that a woman or girl wears in bed
onesie	['wʌnzi]	a piece of clothing that covers the whole body, usually worn in bed or at home
panties (*American English*)		*see* **knickers**
pants	[pænts]	**1** a piece of underwear that covers the area between your waist and your legs **2** (*American English*) *see* **trousers**

pantyhose (*American English*)		*see* **tights**
pattern	['pætən]	an arrangement of lines or shapes that form a design
pocket	['pɒkɪt]	a part of a piece of clothing that you can put things in
pyjamas	[pə'dʒɑːməz]	loose trousers and a top that people wear in bed
sandals	['sændəlz]	light shoes that you wear in warm weather
sari	['sɑːri]	a long piece of material that you wrap around your body, often worn by Indian women
scarf (PL) **scarves**	[skɑːf] [skɑːvz]	a piece of cloth that you wear around your neck or head
shirt	[ʃɜːt]	a piece of clothing with a collar and buttons, that you wear on the top part of your body
shoes	[ʃuːz]	things made of leather or another strong material, that you wear on your feet over socks
shoelaces	['ʃuːleɪsɪz]	thin pieces of material that go through holes in shoes in order to make the shoes tighter
shorts	[ʃɔːts]	trousers with very short legs; *a pair of shorts*
size	[saɪz]	one of a series of particular measurements for clothes and shoes
skirt	[skɜːt]	a piece of clothing for women and girls that hangs down from the waist and covers part of the legs
sleeve	[sliːv]	one of the two parts of a piece of clothing that cover your arms
slippers	['slɪpəz]	loose, soft shoes that you wear indoors

EXAMPLES

I take size 38 in shoes.
I need a new pair of shoes.
What size do you take?
What shoe size do you take?

sneakers *(American English)*	*see* **trainers**	
socks	[sɒks]	pieces of clothing that cover your feet and ankles and that you wear inside shoes
suit	[su:t]	a jacket and trousers or a jacket and skirt that are both made from the same cloth
sweater *(American English)*	*see* **jumper**	
swimming trunks	['swɪmɪŋ trʌŋks]	shorts that men and boys wear when they go swimming
swimsuit	['swɪmsu:t]	a piece of clothing that women and girls wear when they go swimming (*In American English, use* **bathing suit**)
tie	[taɪ]	a long narrow piece of cloth that you wear around your neck with a shirt
tights	[taɪts]	a piece of tight clothing that covers the lower body, worn by women, girls and dancers (*In American English, use* **pantyhose**); *a pair of tights*
top	[tɒp]	[INFORMAL] a piece of clothing, for example a blouse or a shirt, that you wear on the upper part of your body
trainers	['treɪnəz]	shoes that people wear for running and other sports, or with informal clothes (*In American English, use* **sneakers**)
trousers	['traʊzəz]	a piece of clothing that covers the body from the waist downwards, and that covers each leg separately (*In American English, use* **pants**); *a pair of trousers*
T-shirt	['ti:ʃɜ:t]	a cotton shirt with short sleeves and no collar or buttons
turban	['tɜ:bən]	a long piece of cloth that Sikh, Hindu and Muslim men wrap around their heads

EXAMPLE

He was wearing a dark business suit.

underpants	[ˈʌndəpænts]	a short piece of underwear for men and boys, that covers the area between the waist and the top of the legs
underwear	[ˈʌndəweə]	clothes that you wear next to your skin, under your other clothes
uniform	[ˈjuːnɪfɔːm]	the special clothes that some people wear to work, and that some children wear at school
vest	[vest]	**1** a piece of clothing that you wear under your shirt or t-shirt in order to keep warm **2** (American English) see **waistcoat**
waistcoat	[ˈweɪstkəʊt]	a piece of clothing without sleeves that people usually wear over a shirt (In American English, use **vest**)
zip	[zɪp]	a long metal or plastic object with two rows of teeth that join together, and a small part that you pull in order to open and close clothes or bags (In American English, use **zipper**)
zipper (American English)		see **zip**

VERBS

dress up		**1** to put on more formal clothes **2** to put on different clothes in order to look like someone else, for fun
fit	[fɪt]	to be the right size for you
get changed		to take off some or all of your clothes, and put on different clothes
get dressed		to put on your clothes

EXAMPLES

You don't need to dress up for dinner.
My son dressed up as a cowboy for the fancy dress party.
The dress fitted me perfectly.
When I get home from school I get changed.
In the morning I get dressed.
Sarah got dressed quickly and went to work.

get undressed		to take off your clothes
put something on		to put a piece of clothing onto your body
suit	[suːt]	to make you look attractive
take something off		to take a piece of clothing off your body
wear	[weə]	to have something such as clothes, shoes or jewellery on your body
zip	[zɪp]	to fasten something such as a piece of clothing using its zip

ADJECTIVES

casual	['kæʒʊəl]	worn at home or on holiday, and not at work or on formal occasions
checked	[tʃekt]	with a pattern of small squares, usually of two colours
fashionable	['fæʃənəbəl]	1 popular at a particular time; *fashionable clothes* 2 wearing fashionable clothes; *a fashionable woman*
formal	['fɔːməl]	formal clothes are worn on serious or official occasions
long	[lɒŋ]	measuring a great distance from one end to the other; *a long coat*
old-fashioned	[ˌəʊld'fæʃənd]	no longer fashionable or modern
short	[ʃɔːt]	measuring only a small amount from one end to the other; *a short skirt*

EXAMPLES

In the evening I get undressed.
He put his shirt on.
Jason took off his jacket and loosened his tie.
He wore formal evening dress to the dinner.
That suits you.
He zipped up his jeans.
You need to wear warm clothes when you go out today.

smart	[smɑːt]	**1** clean and tidy, and wearing attractive clothes; *You look smart.*
		2 tidy and attractive, and worn at work or on slightly formal occasions; *a smart suit*
spotted	['spɒtɪd]	having a pattern of spots (= small round coloured areas); *a spotted handkerchief*
striped	[straɪpt]	having a pattern of stripes (= long lines of different colours); *a pair of striped pyjamas*
tight	[taɪt]	small, and fitting closely to your body; *a tight skirt*
trendy	['trendi]	fashionable and modern

EXAMPLE
That's very smart.

college and university

NOUNS

art school	['ɑːt skuːl]	a college where people study subjects such as painting and photography
arts	[ɑːts]	subjects such as history, literature and language, which are not scientific
assignment	[ə'saɪnmənt]	a task that you are given to do as part of your studies
bachelor's degree	['bætʃələz dɪ,griː]	a first university degree (= course of study), that usually lasts three or four years
bursary	['bɜːsəri]	an amount of money that is given to someone so that they can study in a college or university
campus	['kæmpəs]	an area of land that contains the main buildings of a university or college
college	['kɒlɪdʒ]	a place where students study after they leave secondary school
course	[kɔːs]	a series of lessons on a particular subject; *complete a course*
coursework	['kɔːswɜːk]	work that students do during a course, rather than in exams
degree	[dɪ'griː]	**1** a course of study that you do at a university or college; *do a degree* **2** the qualification that you get when you have passed this course; *have a degree*
department	[dɪ'pɑːtmənt]	one of the sections in a university or college; *the English Literature department*
diploma	[dɪ'pləʊmə]	**1** a course of study that you do at a university or college, often in order to do a particular job; *do a diploma in journalism* **2** the qualification that you get when you have passed this course; *have a diploma*

EXAMPLES
We have to do written assignments as well as fieldwork.
Cars are not allowed on campus.
Joanna is doing business studies at a local college.
I did a course in computing.
He was awarded a diploma in social work.

distance learning	['dɪstəns ˌlɜːnɪŋ]	a system of education in which people study at home
essay	['eseɪ]	a short piece of writing on a subject
exam	[ɪg'zæm]	a formal test that you take to show your knowledge of a subject; *sit an exam*
examination [ɪg,zæmɪ'neɪʃən]		[FORMAL] same as **exam**
faculty	['fækəlti]	a group of related departments in a university; *the Faculty of Arts*
fieldwork	['fiːldwɜːk]	the activity of gathering information about something in the real world, rather than studying it in a classroom
finals	['faɪnəlz]	the last and most important exams in a university or college course; *sit your finals*
first	[fɜːst]	in British universities, the highest honours degree you can get
graduate	['grædʒʊət]	a student who has completed a course at a college or university
graduation	[,grædʒʊ'eɪʃən]	a special ceremony for students when they have completed their studies at a university or college
grant	[grɑːnt]	an amount of money that a government gives to a person or to an organization for a special purpose
halls of residence	[,hɔːlz əv 'rezɪdəns]	buildings with rooms or flats, usually built by universities or colleges, in which students live during the term
honours degree	['ɒnəz dɪ,griː]	a type of university degree which is of a higher standard than an ordinary degree
invigilator	[ɪn'vɪdʒɪleɪtə]	someone who checks that an exam starts and finishes at the correct time, and that there is no cheating

EXAMPLES
We had to write an essay on Shakespeare.
Professor Akimoto is Dean of the Science faculty.
She has a first in Biology.

college and university

law school	['lɔː skuːl]	a college where people study to become lawyers
lecture	['lektʃə]	a talk that someone gives in order to teach people about a particular subject
lecturer	['lektʃərə]	a teacher at a university or college
major	['meɪdʒə]	in the United States, the main subject that someone is studying
master's degree	['mɑːstəz dɪˌɡriː]	a second university degree, that usually lasts one or two years
medical school	['medɪkəl ˌskuːl]	a college where people study to become doctors and nurses
natural sciences	[ˌnætʃərəl 'saɪənsɪz]	subjects such as physics, biology and chemistry, that are concerned with the physical world
PGCE	[ˌpiː dʒiː siː 'iː]	short for 'Postgraduate Certificate of Education': a second degree, usually lasting one year, that people take in order to become school teachers
PhD	[ˌpiː eɪtʃ 'diː]	**1** short for 'Doctor of Philosophy': the highest degree in a particular subject; *do a PhD* **2** the qualification that you get when you have passed this degree; *have a PhD*
plagiarism	['pleɪdʒərɪzəm]	the practice of copying someone else's work and pretending that you did the work
prospectus	[prə'spektəs]	a document that gives details about a college or university and the courses it provides
reading list	['riːdɪŋ lɪst]	a document that a lecturer gives to students, with suggestions for books that they should read for a particular course
research	[rɪ'sɜːtʃ]	work that involves studying something and trying to discover facts about it

EXAMPLES
He is a lecturer in the Geography department of Moscow University.
He has a master's degree in Business Administration.
Marc has a PhD in Linguistics.

scholarship	['skɒləʃɪp]	an amount of money that is given to someone who has achieved good results, so that they can continue studying
school	[skuːl]	a department of a university or college; *the School of Humanities*
semester	[sə'mestə]	half of a college or university year
seminar	['semɪnɑː]	a class at a college or university in which the teacher and a small group of students discuss a topic
social sciences	['səʊʃəl ˌsaɪənsiz]	subjects such as sociology and politics, that are concerned with society
student	['stjuːdənt]	a person who is studying at a university or a college
student accommodation ['stjuːdənt əkɒmə'deɪʃən]		buildings or rooms where students live
student loan	['stjuːdənt 'ləʊn]	an amount of money that students can borrow from the government; *apply for a student loan*
student union	['stjuːdənt 'juːnjən]	**1** an organization in a university or college that helps students **2** a building where this organization has an office, and where there is usually a shop and a coffee bar
syllabus	['sɪləbəs]	a list of subjects that are covered in a university or college course
technical college	['teknɪkəl ˌkɒlɪdʒ]	a college where you can study practical subjects, often in order to do a particular job
term	[tɜːm]	one of the periods of time that a college or university year is divided into
thesis (PL) **theses**	['θiːsɪs] ['θiːsiːz]	a long piece of writing based on your own ideas and research, that you do as part of a degree

---

EXAMPLES

Phuong was awarded a scholarship to study business management.
Please read this chapter before next week's seminar.
He was awarded his PhD for a thesis on industrial robots.

tuition fees	[tjʊˈɪʃən ˌfiːz]	the money that you pay to be taught at a university or college
tutor	[ˈtjuːtə]	a teacher at a university or college, who usually teaches small groups
tutorial	[tjuːˈtɔːriəl]	**1** same as **seminar**; *attend a tutorial* **2** in some universities, a regular meeting in which a tutor and one student discuss the student's work
undergraduate [ˌʌndəˈɡrædʒʊət]		a university or college student who has not yet passed their final exams
university	[ˌjuːnɪˈvɜːsɪti]	a place where you can study for a degree, and where people do academic research
viva	[ˈvaɪvə]	a university examination in which a student answers questions by speaking rather than writing
vocational course	[vəʊˈkeɪʃənəl ˌkɔːs]	a course that someone does in order to do a particular job

VERBS

enrol	[ɪnˈrəʊl]	to officially join a class
graduate	[ˈɡrædʒʊeɪt]	to complete your studies at college or university
invigilate	[ɪnˈvɪdʒɪleɪt]	to check that an exam starts and finishes at the correct time, and that no-one cheats
register	[ˈredʒɪstə]	to put your name on an official list, in order to be able to do a particular course
study	[ˈstʌdi]	to spend time learning about a particular subject
work	[wɜːk]	to do an activity that uses a lot of your time or effort

---

EXAMPLES

The government are planning to increase tuition fees.
She went to university where she got a BA and then an MA.
She graduated in English and Drama from Manchester University.
What do you want to do after you graduate?
She spends most of her time studying.
He studied History and Geography at university.

(**ADJECTIVES**)

academic	[ˌækəˈdemɪk]	relating to the work done in universities and colleges; *an academic journal*
full-time	[ˈfʊltaɪm]	relating to a course that takes up the whole of each normal working week; *a full-time course*; *a full-time student*
part-time	[ˈpɑːttaɪm]	relating to a course that takes up only part of each day or week; *a part-time course*; *a part-time student*

EXAMPLE
Their academic standards are high.

colours

NOUNS AND ADJECTIVES

beige	[beɪʒ]	(having) a pale brown colour
black	[blæk]	1 (having) the colour of the sky at night 2 black coffee or tea has no milk in it
blue	[blu:]	(having) the colour of the sky on a sunny day
brown	[braʊn]	(having) the colour of earth or wood
cream	[kri:m]	(having) a yellowish-white colour
gold	[gəʊld]	(having) a bright yellow colour that is often shiny
green	[gri:n]	(having) the colour of grass or leaves
grey	[greɪ]	(having) the colour of ashes, or clouds on a rainy day
navy blue	['neɪvi 'blu:]	(having) a very dark blue colour; *a navy blue suit*
orange	['ɒrɪndʒ]	(having) a colour between red and yellow
pink	[pɪŋk]	(having) a colour between red and white
purple	['pɜːpəl]	(having) a colour between red and blue
red	[red]	(having) the colour of blood or of a tomato
silver	['sɪlvə]	(having) a shiny and pale grey colour
turquoise	['tɜːkwɔɪz]	(having) a light greenish-blue colour
white	[waɪt]	1 (having) the colour of snow or milk 2 white wine is a pale-yellow colour 3 white coffee or tea has milk in it
yellow	['jeləʊ]	(having) the colour of lemons or butter

EXAMPLES

Blue suits you.
'What colour are your eyes?' – 'Blue.'
I bought some blue shoes.
'What colour is your hair?' – 'Brown.'
The room is decorated in soft browns and creams.
She has green eyes.
'Do you have this t-shirt in green?
'What's your favourite colour?' – 'Red.'
You look good in white.

ADJECTIVES

bright	[braɪt]	strong and noticeable in colour; *a bright red dress*
dark	[dɑːk]	close to black, or containing some black; *dark brown hair*
light	[laɪt]	pale in colour; *light brown hair*
pale	[peɪl]	not strong or bright in colour; *pale blue eyes*
rich	[rɪtʃ]	dark in colour and pleasant to look at
soft	[sɒft]	not bright, and pleasant to look at

VERBS

blush	[blʌʃ]	to become red in the face because you are ashamed or embarrassed
change colour		to become a different colour
go red		to become red in the face because you are embarrassed or angry
paint	[peɪnt]	to cover a wall or an object with paint; *paint something blue*

PHRASE

a black eye	a dark area of skin around your eye where someone has hit you

EXAMPLES
She's wearing a light blue t-shirt.
The leaves on the trees are changing colour.
Mum went red in the face with anger.
He had a black eye, and several cuts on his face.

computers and the internet

attachment	[ə'tætʃmənt]	a file that you send with an email message
avatar	['ævətɑː]	a picture that you use to represent yourself on a website where you are having a conversation with other people
blog	[blɒg]	a website that describes the daily life and thoughts of the person who writes it
blogpost	['blɒgpoʊst]	a short piece of writing on a blog
broadband	['brɔːdbænd]	a very fast method of sending information over the internet
browser	['braʊzə]	a piece of software that allows you to search for information on the internet
bug	[bʌg]	a mistake in a computer program
CD-ROM	[ˌsiː diː 'rɒm]	a CD that stores information that you can read using a computer
chat	[tʃæt]	a way of communicating with friends by exchanging written messages using the internet; *internet chat*
cloud computing	['klaʊd kəmˌpjuːtɪŋ]	the practice of storing and sending information using the internet rather than keeping and managing it on a personal computer
computer	[kəm'pjuːtə]	an electronic machine that stores and deals with large amounts of information; *a computer game*; *a computer system*
connection	[kə'nekʃən]	a link between a computer and a network; *an internet connection*
cursor	['kɜːsə]	a small line on a computer screen that shows where you are working
data	['deɪtə]	information that can be used by a computer program

EXAMPLES
My broadband keeps dropping out.
You need to update your browser.
There is a bug in the software.
A CD-ROM can hold huge amounts of data.

database	['deɪtəbeɪs]	a collection of information on a computer that is stored in such a way that you can use it and add to it easily
desktop	['desktɒp]	the images that you see on a computer screen when the computer is ready to use
disk	[dɪsk]	a flat metal object that stores information and can be put into a computer
disk drive	['dɪsk draɪv]	the part of a computer that holds a disk
document	['dɒkjəmənt]	a piece of text that is stored on a computer
email	['iːmeɪl]	**1** short for 'electronic mail': a system of sending written messages from one computer to another; *send a file by email* **2** a written message that you send by computer; *send an email*
email address	['iːmeɪl ə,dres]	a combination of letters and symbols that identifies where emails are sent
emoji	[ɪ'məʊdʒi]	a symbol that you use in an email or text message to show how you feel
e-reader	['iː riːdə]	a digital device that you use for reading books
file	[faɪl]	a collection of information that you keep on your computer
folder	['fəʊldə]	a group of files that are stored together on a computer
font	[fɒnt]	a set of letters of the same style and size
friend	[frend]	someone who you are connected with on a social media website such as Facebook
Google™	['guːgəl]	a website that you can use to look for information on the internet
hacker	['hækə]	a person who illegally gets access to another computer

EXAMPLES

You can rearrange the icons on your desktop.

You can cut and paste whole paragraphs from one document to another.

Could you send David an email to arrange a meeting?

How many friends have you got on Facebook?

We looked him up on Google.

hard disk	[hɑːd ˈdɪsk]	the part inside a computer where data and programs are stored
hard drive	[hɑːd ˈdraɪv]	the part inside a computer that contains the hard disk
hardware	[ˈhɑːdweə]	things in computer systems such as the computer, the keyboard and the screen, rather than the programs
hashtag	[ˈhæʃtæg]	a word with the symbol [#] before it, used in messages on social media websites to help other people to search for messages on that topic
home page	[ˈhəʊm peɪdʒ]	the main page of a website
I.T.	[aɪ ˈtiː]	short for 'information technology': the study and practice of using computers
icon	[ˈaɪkɒn]	a picture on a computer screen that you can choose, in order to open a particular program
inbox	[ˈɪnbɒks]	the place where your computer stores emails that people have sent to you
ink cartridge	[ˈɪŋk ˌkɑːtrɪdʒ]	a container of ink that you put in a printer
the internet	[ðɪ ˈɪntənet]	the network that connects computers all over the world
italics	[ɪˈtælɪks]	letters and numbers that slope to the right; *This sentence is in italics*.
key	[kiː]	one of the buttons that you press in order to operate a computer
keyboard	[ˈkiːbɔːd]	the set of keys that you press in order to operate a computer
laptop	[ˈlæptɒp]	a small computer that you carry with you
LOL	[lɒl]	short for 'laughing out loud': used in emails and text messages to show that you find something funny

EXAMPLES

You can add a hashtag to your message so that it reaches more people, for example, #londonchristmaslights.

The company needs people with I.T. skills.

I had 50 emails in my inbox.

I found all the information I needed on the internet.

memory	['meməri]	the part of a computer where it stores information
memory stick	['meməri ˌstɪk]	a small object for storing digital information that you can carry with you
menu	['menjuː]	a list of choices on a computer screen, showing things that you can do using a particular program; *a drop-down menu*
modem	['məʊdem]	a piece of equipment that uses a telephone line to connect computers
monitor	['mɒnɪtə]	a computer screen
mouse	[maʊs]	an object that you use to do things on a computer without using the keyboard
mouse mat	['maʊs mæt]	a flat piece of plastic that you rest a mouse on
network	['netwɜːk]	a system of connected computers
OMG	[ˌəʊ em 'dʒiː]	short for 'oh my God': used in emails and text messages to show that you are surprised or excited about something
operating system	['ɒpəreɪtɪŋ ˌsɪstəm]	a system in a computer that controls all the other programs
password	['pɑːswɜːd]	a secret word or phrase that allows you to use a computer system
PC	[piː 'siː]	short for 'personal computer': a computer that people use at school, at home or in an office
post	[pəʊst]	a short piece of writing that is published on the internet, for example, on a social media website
printer	['prɪntə]	a machine for printing copies of computer documents on paper
printout	['prɪntaʊt]	a piece of paper with information from a computer printed on it
program	['prəʊgræm]	a set of instructions that a computer uses to do a particular task

---

EXAMPLES
OMG, that cake looks amazing!
The printer plugs into the computer's USB port.

retweet	['riːtwiːt]	a message on the social media website Twitter that repeats a message that another person sent
screen	[skriːn]	a flat surface on a computer where you see pictures or words
selfie	['selfi]	a photo that you take of yourself, especially to show on a social media website; *take a selfie*
social media	[ˌsəʊʃəl 'miːdiə]	websites and programs that people use for sharing information, pictures, etc. with other people
social networking	[ˌsəʊʃəl 'netwɜːkɪŋ]	the activity of contacting friends and making new friends on particular websites
software	['sɒftweə]	computer programs
spam	[spæm]	advertising messages that are sent automatically by email to large numbers of people
spreadsheet	['spredʃiːt]	a program that deals with numbers, and is mainly used for financial planning
status	['steɪtəs]	a short piece of writing on a social media website that tells other people what you are thinking about; *put up a status*
tablet	['tæblət]	a small computer that you operate by touching the screen; *a tablet computer*
tweet	[twiːt]	a message on the social media website Twitter
USB	[juː es 'biː]	short for 'Universal Serial Bus': a way of connecting equipment to a computer; *a USB port*

EXAMPLES

My wedding announcement got 250 retweets!

I clicked on the link and a message appeared on the screen.

Did you see Sam's tweet from the concert last night?

How much time do you spend on social networking sites like Twitter and Facebook?

Keep your system updated with the latest software downloads.

username	['juːzəneɪm]	the name that you type onto your screen each time you open a particular program or website
virus	['vaɪərəs]	a program that enters a computer system and changes or destroys the information that is there
the web	[ðə web]	a computer system that helps you find information. You can use it anywhere in the world.
webcam	['webkæm]	a camera on a computer that produces images that can be seen on a website
website	['websaɪt]	a set of information on the internet about a particular subject
website address	['websaɪt ə,dres]	the location of a website on the internet, for example, http://www.harpercollins.com
window	['wɪndəʊ]	one of the work areas that a screen can be divided into

VERBS

browse	[braʊz]	to search for information on the internet; *browse the internet*
back something up		to make a copy of a computer file that you can use if the original file is lost; *back up a file*
boot up a computer		to make a computer start working
click	[klɪk]	to press one of the buttons on a mouse in order to make something happen on the screen; *click on a link*
copy	['kɒpi]	to make a new version of a file or disk that is exactly the same as the old one; *copy a file*
crash	[kræʃ]	used for saying that a computer or a program suddenly stops working; *The computer crashed.*

EXAMPLES
You should protect your computer against viruses.
Go over to your computer and boot it up.
My computer crashed for the second time that day.

computers and the internet

cut and paste		to move words or pictures on a computer from one place to another place
delete	[dɪ'li:t]	**1** to remove a file or document from a computer; *delete a file* **2** to remove text from a document; *delete a paragraph*
download	[daʊn'ləʊd]	to copy a file, a program or other information from a bigger computer, a network or the internet to your own computer
email	['i:meɪl]	to send a message from one computer to another; *email someone*
format	['fɔ:mæt]	to change the arrangement of the text of a document
friend	[frend]	to add someone to your list of friends on a social media website such as Facebook
google	['gu:gəl]	to use the search engine Google™ to look for information on the internet; *google someone's name*
key something in		to put information into a computer using the keyboard; *key in data*
log in		to type your username and password so that you can start using a computer or website
log off		to stop using a computer or website by clicking on an instruction
post	[pəʊst]	to publish a short piece of writing on the internet, for example, on a social media website
print	[prɪnt]	to use a machine to produce a copy of a computer file on paper; *print ten copies of a document*

EXAMPLES

The report was too long so I deleted a few paragraphs.

You can download software from this website.

My mum wants to friend me on Facebook. Is that a good idea?

If you don't know the answer, just google it.

She turned on her computer and logged in.

Katie posted some pictures from her holiday on Facebook.

program	['prəʊgræm]	to give a computer a set of instructions so that it can do a particular task; *program a computer*
retweet	[riː'twiːt]	to send a message on the website Twitter that repeats a message that another person sent
save	[seɪv]	to give a computer an instruction to store some information; *save your work*
scroll	[skrəʊl]	to move the text on a computer screen up or down to find the information that you need; *scroll down the page*
tweet	[twiːt]	to send a message on the social media website Twitter
zip	[zɪp]	to make a file smaller so that you can send it to someone using the internet

ADJECTIVES

bold	[bəʊld]	letters and numbers that are bold are thicker and darker than ordinary ones; *bold capitals*
cloud-based	['klaʊdbeɪst]	cloud-based services store and send information to computers using the internet
desktop	['desktɒp]	of a convenient size for using on a desk or a table; *a desktop computer*
electronic	[ɪlek'trɒnɪk]	using electricity and small electrical parts
offline	[ɒf'laɪn]	not connected to the internet; *The computer is offline.*
online	[ɒn'laɪn]	1 available on the internet; *an online store* 2 connected to the internet; *people who are online*

EXAMPLES

That's really funny. I'm going to retweet it.
Sara tweeted a photo of herself in Florida.
Everyone's tweeting about the election results.
This is how to zip files so that you can send them via email.
Your computer is currently offline.
I buy most of my clothes online.

portable	['pɔːtəbəl]	designed to be carried or moved around
wireless	['waɪələs]	using radio waves (= a form of power that travels through the air) instead of wires; *a wireless connection*

ADVERBS

offline	[ɒf'laɪn]	not using the internet; *work offline*
online	[ɒn'laɪn]	using the internet; *search online*

PHRASE

in the cloud	computer services that are in the cloud store and send information to computers using the internet

IDIOM

surf the net	to spend time looking at different websites on the internet

EXAMPLE
Your data is stored safely in the cloud.

cooking

NOUNS

barbecue [ˈbɑːbɪkjuː] a piece of equipment that you use for cooking outdoors

blender [ˈblendə] a piece of electrical equipment for mixing liquids and soft foods together or for turning fruit or vegetables into liquid

bottle opener [ˈbɒtəl ˌəʊpənə] a metal tool for removing tops from bottles

broiler (American English) see **grill**

cake tin [ˈkeɪk tɪn] **1** a metal container that you use for baking a cake
2 a metal container that you put a cake in to keep it fresh

chopping board [ˈtʃɒpɪŋ bɔːd] a flat piece of wood or plastic that you chop meat or vegetables on

coffee maker [ˈkɒfi ˌmeɪkə] a machine for making coffee

cook [kʊk] someone who prepares and cooks food

cooker [ˈkʊkə] a piece of kitchen equipment that you use for cooking food

corkscrew [ˈkɔːkskruː] a tool for pulling corks out of bottles

dish [dɪʃ] a wide shallow container with no cover, that you use for cooking and serving food

food processor [ˈfuːd ˌprəʊsesə] a piece of electrical equipment for mixing or chopping food, or for turning food into liquid

fork [fɔːk] a tool with a handle and three or four long metal points at the end, that you use for eating and cooking

frying pan [ˈfraɪɪŋ pæn] a flat metal pan with a long handle, that you use for frying food

grater [ˈgreɪtə] a tool with a rough surface, that you use for cutting food into very small pieces

---

EXAMPLES
My mum is a good cook.
We bought a new cooker.

grill	[grɪl]	**1** the part of a cooker where you cook food under strong heat **2** a flat frame of metal bars that you can use to cook food over a fire (*In American English, use* **broiler**)
hob	[hɒb]	the top part of a cooker where you put pans
kettle	[ˈketəl]	a metal container with a lid and a handle, that you use for boiling water
knife	[naɪf]	a tool with a handle and a sharp flat piece of metal, that you use for eating and cooking; *a carving knife*; *a bread knife*
ladle	[ˈleɪdəl]	a large, round, deep spoon with a long handle, that you use for serving soup
microwave	[ˈmaɪkrəʊweɪv]	an oven that cooks food very quickly using electric waves
mixing bowl	[ˈmɪksɪŋ ˌbəʊl]	a large bowl that you use for mixing ingredients
oven	[ˈʌvən]	a piece of equipment for cooking that is like a large metal box with a door
pan	[pæn]	a round metal container with a long handle, that you use for cooking food
peeler	[ˈpiːlə]	a tool for removing the skin from fruit and vegetables; *a potato peeler*
pot	[pɒt]	a deep round container that you use for cooking soup and other food
recipe	[ˈresɪpi]	a set of instructions telling you how to cook something
rolling pin	[ˈrəʊlɪŋ pɪn]	a long wooden tool that you roll over pastry in order to make it flat
saucepan	[ˈsɔːspən]	a deep metal cooking pot, usually with a long handle and a lid
scale (*American English*)		*see* **scales**

EXAMPLES

Put the pan on the hob, add flour, and cook for one minute.
Put the dish in the oven for 40 minutes.
No salt is required in this recipe.

scales	[skeɪlz]	a piece of equipment that you use for weighing food (*In American English, use* **scale**)
sieve	[sɪv]	a tool with a fine metal net, that you use for separating food from liquids
spatula	['spætʃʊlə]	a tool like a knife with a wide flat blade, that you use for lifting hot food
spoon	[spuːn]	a tool with a handle and a part like a shallow bowl, that you use for eating and cooking; *a wooden spoon*
toaster	['təʊstə]	a piece of electrical equipment that you use to heat bread
timer	['taɪmə]	a piece of equipment that you use for measuring how long you need to cook something for
tin opener	['tɪn ˌəʊpənə]	a tool for opening tins of food
tongs	[tɒŋz]	a tool consisting of two connected pieces of metal, that you use for picking up food
whisk	[wɪsk]	a tool for stirring eggs or cream very fast; *an electric whisk*; *a hand whisk*

VERBS

bake	[beɪk]	to cook food in an oven without extra oil or liquid
beat	[biːt]	to mix food quickly with a spoon or a fork; *beat an egg*
boil	[bɔɪl]	**1** to heat water until bubbles appear and the water starts to change into steam; *boil water* **2** to cook food in boiling water; *boil potatoes*
bring something to the boil		to heat liquid until it boils
broil (*American English*)		*see* **grill**
carve	[kɑːv]	to cut slices from meat; *carve the meat*

EXAMPLES
Beat the eggs with a wooden spoon.
Gradually bring the sauce to the boil.
Carve the beef into thin slices.

chop	[tʃɒp]	to cut something into pieces with a knife; *chop the vegetables*
cook	[kʊk]	to prepare and heat food
fry	[fraɪ]	to cook food in hot fat or oil
grill	[grɪl]	to cook food on metal bars above a fire or barbecue or under a grill (*In American English, use* **broil**)
mash	[mæʃ]	to press food to make it soft
melt	[melt]	to heat a solid food so that it becomes a liquid
peel	[piːl]	to remove the skin of fruit or vegetables
prepare	[prɪ'peə]	to get food ready
roast	[rəʊst]	to cook meat or other food in an oven or over a fire
serve	[sɜːv]	to give people food and drinks
slice	[slaɪs]	to cut food into thin pieces; *slice the mushrooms*
stir	[stɜː]	to mix a liquid in a container using a spoon
weigh	[weɪ]	to measure how heavy something is
whisk	[wɪsk]	to stir eggs or cream very fast

ADJECTIVES

baked	[beɪkt]	cooked in the oven without extra oil or liquid; *a baked potato*
boiled	[bɔɪld]	cooked in boiling water; *a boiled egg*
chopped	[tʃɒpt]	cut into pieces with a knife; *a tin of chopped tomatoes*
fried	[fraɪd]	cooked in hot fat or oil; *fried rice*
grated	[greɪtɪd]	cut into very small pieces using a grater; *grated cheese*

EXAMPLES

Chop the butter into small pieces.
Mash the bananas with a fork.
Top with whipped cream and serve.
Serve the soup with crusty bread.
Helen sliced the cake.

mashed	[mæʃt]	pressed until soft; *mashed potatoes*
medium	['mi:diəm]	used for describing meat that is cooked so that the inside is still slightly pink
poached	[pəʊtʃt]	cooked gently in boiling liquid; *a poached egg*
rare	[reə]	used for describing meat that is cooked very lightly so that the inside is still red
roast	[rəʊst]	cooked in the oven or over a fire; *roast beef*
scrambled	['skræmbəld]	used to describe eggs that have been mixed together and heated in a pan
steamed	[sti:md]	cooked in steam rather than water; *steamed vegetables*
well done	[ˌwel 'dʌn]	if meat is well done, it has been cooked thoroughly

EXAMPLE
I'd like my steak well done.

countryside

NOUNS

agriculture	[ˈægrɪkʌltʃə]	the business or activity of taking care of crops and farm animals
barn	[bɑːn]	a building on a farm where animals and crops are kept
bulldozer	[ˈbʊldəʊzə]	a large vehicle that is used for moving large amounts of earth
cave	[keɪv]	a large hole in the side of a hill or under the ground; *an underground cave*
cliff	[klɪf]	a high area of land with a very steep side next to the sea; *walk along the cliffs*
combine harvester	[ˌkɔmbaɪn ˈhɑːvɪstə]	a large machine that is used on farms to cut, sort and clean grain
country	[ˈkʌntri]	same as **countryside**
countryside	[ˈkʌntrɪˌsaɪd]	land that is away from cities and towns; *We live in the countryside.*
crop	[krɒp]	a plant that people grow for food; *plant a crop*
ditch	[dɪtʃ]	a deep, long, narrow hole that carries water away from a road or a field
estate	[ɪˈsteɪt]	a large house in a large area of land in the country
farm	[fɑːm]	an area of land and buildings where people grow crops and keep animals
farmer	[ˈfɑːmə]	a person who owns or works on a farm
farmyard	[ˈfɑːmjɑːd]	an area near a farmhouse that is enclosed by walls or buildings; *farmyard animals*
fence	[fens]	a wooden or metal wall around a piece of land
field	[fiːld]	a piece of land where crops are grown, or where animals are kept

EXAMPLES

Lisa and Andrew live in the country.
Both of the boys work on the farm.
There is not enough good farm land here.
We drove past fields of sunflowers.

fishing	[ˈfɪʃɪŋ]	the sport or business of catching fish
forest	[ˈfɒrɪst]	a large area where trees grow close together
gate	[geɪt]	a structure like a door that you use to enter a field; *close the gate*
ground	[graʊnd]	the soil on the Earth's surface in which you can grow plants
harvest	[ˈhɑːvɪst]	**1** the activity of collecting a crop, or the time when this is done **2** the amount of a crop that is collected; *a good/poor harvest*
hay	[heɪ]	grass that has been cut and dried so that it can be used for feeding animals
hedge	[hedʒ]	a row of small trees growing close together around a field
hike	[haɪk]	a long walk, especially in the countryside
hill	[hɪl]	an area of land that is higher than the land around it; *a steep hill*; *climb a hill*
hunt	[hʌnt]	an organized event when a group of people follow and kill wild animals as a sport; *go on a hunt*
hunter	[ˈhʌntə]	a person who hunts wild animals for food or as a sport
lake	[leɪk]	a large area of water with land around it
land	[lænd]	an area of ground that is used for farming
market	[ˈmɑːkɪt]	a place where people buy and sell products
marsh	[mɑːʃ]	a soft, wet area of land
meadow	[ˈmedəʊ]	a field that has grass and flowers growing in it
moor	[mʊə]	an area of high open ground covered mainly with rough grass and heather
mountain	[ˈmaʊntɪn]	a very high area of land with steep sides; *climb a mountain*

EXAMPLES

I walked through the gate and into the field.
The women prepare the ground for planting.
Mt. McKinley is the highest mountain in North America.

mud	[mʌd]	a sticky mixture of earth and water
path	[pɑːθ]	a long, narrow piece of ground that people walk along
picnic	['pɪknɪk]	an occasion when you eat a meal outdoors, usually in a park or a forest, or at the beach
plough	[plaʊ]	a large farming tool that is pulled across the soil to turn it over, usually before seeds are planted
pond	[pɒnd]	a small area of water
produce	['prɒdjuːs]	food that you grow on a farm to sell
quarry	['kwɒri]	a place where stone or minerals are dug out of the ground
river	['rɪvə]	a long line of water that flows into a sea; *a river bank*
rock	[rɒk]	**1** the hard substance that is in the ground and in mountains **2** a large piece of rock
ruins	['ruːɪnz]	the parts of a building that remain after something destroys the rest
scarecrow	['skeəkrəʊ]	an object, in the shape of a person, that stands in a field where crops are growing in order to frighten birds away
scenery	['siːnəri]	the land, water or plants that you can see around you in a country area
soil	[sɔɪl]	the substance on the surface of the Earth in which plants grow
spring	[sprɪŋ]	a place where water comes up through the ground; *an underground spring*
stable	['steɪbəl]	a building in which horses are kept
stick	[stɪk]	a thin branch from a tree

EXAMPLES

We went for a picnic.

The restaurant uses as much local produce as possible.

We tried to dig, but the ground was solid rock.

Maria sat on a rock and looked out across the sea.

The soil here is good for growing vegetables.

stone	[stəʊn]	**1** a hard solid substance that is found in the ground and is often used for building **2** a small piece of rock that is found on the ground
stream	[striːm]	a small narrow river
track	[træk]	**1** a rough road or path; *a muddy track* **2** the marks that an animal leaves on the ground; *animal tracks*
tractor	['træktə]	a vehicle that a farmer uses to pull farm machinery; *drive a tractor*
valley	['væli]	a low area of land between hills; *a steep mountain valley*
view	[vjuː]	everything that you can see from a place
village	['vɪlɪdʒ]	a very small town in the countryside
walk	[wɔːk]	a trip that you make by walking, usually for pleasure; *go for a walk*
waterfall	['wɔːtə,fɔːl]	a place where water flows over the edge of a steep part of hills or mountains, and falls into a pool below
well	[wel]	a deep hole in the ground from which people take water or oil
wellingtons	['welɪŋtənz]	long rubber boots that you wear to keep your feet dry
windmill	['wɪndmɪl]	a building with long, flat parts on the outside that turn as the wind blows to make machinery move inside
wood	[wʊd]	**1** the hard material that trees are made of **2** a large area of trees growing near each other; *in the woods*

EXAMPLES
She could feel cool, smooth stone beneath her feet.
Loose stones on the ground made walking difficult.
Zak found fresh bear tracks in the snow.
The view from the top of the hill was magnificent.

VERBS

climb [klaɪm] to move towards the top of something; *climb a hill*; *climb to the top*

go camping to stay in a tent or a caravan for a short time

harvest ['hɑːvɪst] to collect a farm crop; *harvest crops*

hike [haɪk] to go for a long walk

hunt [hʌnt] to chase and kill wild animals for food or as a sport

plough [plaʊ] to turn earth over, usually before seeds are planted

ADJECTIVES

peaceful ['piːsfʊl] quiet and calm

rural ['rʊərəl] not near cities or large towns

PHRASE

in the open air outside rather than in a building

EXAMPLES

The group hiked along a track in the forest.
The service is ideal for people who live in rural areas.
We eat our meals in the open air.

employment

NOUNS

annual leave [ˈænjʊəl ˈliːv] an amount of time in every year when you are paid, but you do not have to go to work; *take annual leave*; *be on annual leave*

application form [ˌæplɪˈkeɪʃən fɔːm] a document with questions that you must answer when you apply for a job; *fill in an application form*

apprentice [əˈprentɪs] a young person who works for someone in order to learn their skill

benefits [ˈbenɪfɪts] money that is given by the government to people who do not have a job; *live on benefits*

bonus [ˈbəʊnəs] an extra amount of money that you earn, usually because you have worked very hard; *a bonus payment*

boss [bɒs] the person who is in charge of you at the place where you work

career [kəˈrɪə] a job that you do for a long time, or the years of your life that you spend working

colleague [ˈkɒliːg] a person someone works with

company [ˈkʌmpəni] a business that sells goods or services

contract [ˈkɒntrækt] an official agreement between two companies or two people

covering letter [ˌkʌvərɪŋ ˈletə] a letter that you send with an application form in order to provide extra information

co-worker [kəʊˈwɜːkə] a person you work with

CV [siː ˈviː] short for 'curriculum vitae': a document giving details of your education and work experience. You send a CV to someone when you are trying to get a new job.

disability [ˌdɪsəˈbɪlɪti] a permanent injury or condition that makes it difficult for you to work or live normally

---

EXAMPLES

Their son Dominic is an apprentice woodworker.

Please send your CV and a covering letter to the following address.

discrimination [dɪsˌkrɪmɪˈneɪʃən]		the practice of treating one person or group unfairly, for example, by paying them less money than other people; *age discrimination*; *racial/sexual discrimination*
employee	[ɪmˈplɔɪiː]	a person who is paid to work for another person or a company
employer	[ɪmˈplɔɪə]	the person or the company that you work for
employment	[ɪmˈplɔɪmənt]	work that you are paid for
equality	[ɪˈkwɒlɪti]	the fair treatment of all the people in a group
flexitime	[ˈfleksitaɪm]	a system that allows employees to start or finish work at different times, provided that they work an agreed number of hours in total
freelancer	[ˈfriːlɑːnsə]	someone who is not employed by an organization, and does work for more than one company
human resources	[ˌhjuːmən rɪˈzɔːsiːz]	the department in a company that finds, trains and looks after the staff
income	[ˈɪnkʌm]	the money that a person earns or receives
interview	[ˈɪntəvjuː]	a formal meeting in which someone asks you questions to find out if you are the right person for a job; *ask someone for an interview*
job	[dʒɒb]	**1** the work that someone does to earn money; *get a good job* **2** a particular task; *do a good job*
job centre	[ˈdʒɒb ˌsentə]	a place where people can get advice on finding a job, and look at job advertisements
maternity leave	[məˈtɜːnɪti ˌliːv]	a period of time when a woman leaves her job to have a baby

EXAMPLES

His former chauffeur is claiming unfair dismissal on the grounds of racial discrimination.

When I went for my first interview for this job I arrived early.

minimum wage	[ˌmɪnɪməm ˈweɪdʒ]	the lowest wage that an employer is allowed to pay an employee; *on the minimum wage*
notice	[ˈnəʊtɪs]	the act of telling your employer that you are going to leave your job; *give in/hand in your notice*
occupation	[ˌɒkjʊˈpeɪʃən]	someone's job; *What is your occupation?*
overtime	[ˈəʊvətaɪm]	extra time that you spend doing your job
paternity leave	[pəˈtɜːnɪti ˌliːv]	a period of time when a man does not go to work because his child has just been born
pay	[peɪ]	to give someone money for the work that they do
profession	[prəˈfeʃən]	a type of job for which you need special education or training
promotion	[prəˈməʊʃən]	a move to a more important job or rank in the organization that you work for; *get promotion*
rate of pay	[reɪt əv ˈpeɪ]	the money that workers can earn for a particular amount of work; *a higher/lower rate of pay*
recruitment	[rɪˈkruːtmənt]	the process of selecting people to work for an organization
redundancy	[rɪˈdʌndənsi]	a situation in which you lose your job because it is no longer necessary or because the organization can no longer afford to pay you; *redundancy pay*
reference	[ˈrefərəns]	a statement from someone who knows you, describing your character and your abilities
retirement	[rɪˈtaɪəmənt]	the period in someone's life after they retire
rise	[raɪz]	an increase in the money that you earn; *get a rise*

EXAMPLES

These workers are not even on the minimum wage.

You have to give one month's notice.

Thousands of bank employees are facing redundancy as their employers cut costs.

Could you write me a reference?

salary	['sæləri]	the money that you earn from your employer
seasonal work	['si:zənəl ˌwɜ:k]	work that is only available at particular times of the year
sick leave	['sɪk li:v]	the time that a person spends away from work because of illness or injury
staff	[stɑ:f]	the people who work for an organization
strike	[straɪk]	a period of time when workers refuse to work, usually in order to try to get more money; *go on strike*
temp	[temp]	a temporary office worker
temping agency	['tempɪŋ ˌeɪdʒənsi]	a company that finds jobs for people who want to work in different offices for short periods of time
trade union	[treɪd 'ju:njən]	an organization formed by workers in order to improve conditions for workers
training	['treɪnɪŋ]	the process of learning the skills that you need for a particular job; *a training course*
the unemployed	[ði ˌʌnɪm'plɔɪd]	people who do not have a job
unemployment [ˌʌnɪm'plɔɪmənt]		a situation in which people cannot work because there are not enough jobs
wages	['weɪdʒɪz]	money that is paid to someone for the work that they do; *get your wages*
work	[wɜ:k]	**1** a job that you do to earn money; *find work* **2** the place where you do your job; *go to work*
working week	[ˌwɜ:kɪŋ 'wi:k]	the total amount of time that you spend at work during the week; *a 35-hour working week*

VERBS

apply for a job		to write a letter or write on a form in order to ask for a job

EXAMPLES

Staff at the hospital went on strike yesterday.
We want to create jobs for the unemployed
I start work at 8.30 a.m. and finish at 5 p.m.
I'm lucky. I can walk to work.

discriminate	[dɪs'krɪmɪneɪt]	to treat a person or a group of people unfairly
dismiss	[dɪs'mɪs]	to tell someone that they have to leave their job
earn	[ɜːn]	to receive money for work that you do; *earn money*
employ	[ɪm'plɔɪ]	to pay someone to work for a person or a company
fire	[faɪə]	[INFORMAL] to tell someone that they have to leave their job; *She was fired from that job.*
give someone the sack		to tell someone that they must leave their job because they have done something wrong or because their work is not good enough
hire	[haɪə]	to pay someone to do a job for you
interview	['ɪntəvjuː]	to ask someone questions to find out if they are the right person for a particular job
pay	[peɪ]	to give someone money for the work that they do; *well/badly paid*
promote	[prə'məʊt]	to give someone a more important job in the same organization
recruit	[rɪ'kruːt]	to choose people to work in an organization
resign	[rɪ'zaɪn]	to tell your employer that you are leaving a job
retire	[rɪ'taɪə]	to leave your job and stop working, usually because of your age
strike	[straɪk]	to refuse to work, usually to try to get more money
temp	[temp]	to work as a temp
work	[wɜːk]	to have a job and earn money for it

EXAMPLES

Richard has just been promoted to general manager.

Workers have the right to strike.

Mrs Lee has been temping since losing her job.

Many people in the country are still working for less than the minimum wage.

ADJECTIVES

absent	['æbsənt]	not at work
blue-collar	[blu:'kɒlə]	working in industry, doing physical work, rather than in offices
freelance	['fri:lɑ:ns]	working alone for different companies, rather than being employed by one company that pays you regularly
full-time	[fʊl'taɪm]	working for the whole of each normal working week
part-time	[pɑ:t'taɪm]	working for only part of each day or week
permanent	['pɜ:mənənt]	employed for an unlimited length of time
redundant	[rɪ'dʌndənt]	without a job because there is not enough work or money to keep you
temporary	['tempərəri]	lasting or working for only a certain period of time; *a temporary job*; *temporary workers*
unemployed	[ʌnɪm'plɔɪd]	able to work but without a job
white-collar	[waɪt'kɒlə]	working in offices rather than doing physical work in industry

PHRASE

What do you do (for a living)?	you ask 'What do you do (for a living)?' when you want to know what someone's job is

IDIOMS

a golden handshake	a large sum of money that a company may give to an employee when he or she leaves
get a foot in the door	to manage to enter an organization that you hope to succeed in
the rat race	a job or way of life in which people compete aggressively with each other to be successful; *get out of the rat race*

EXAMPLE

Have you been unemployed for over six months?

environment

NOUNS

bottle bank ['bɒtəl bæŋk] a large container where you can put empty bottles so that the glass can be recycled

carbon dioxide [ˌkɑːbən daɪˈɒksaɪd] a gas that is produced when animals and people breathe out, and by certain chemical processes

carbon monoxide [ˌkɑːbən məˈnɒksaɪd] a harmful gas that is produced by the engines of vehicles

chemical ['kemɪkəl] a substance that is made by changing or combining other substances

climate change ['klaɪmət tʃeɪndʒ] changes in the Earth's climate (= normal weather) over a long period of time

conservation [ˌkɒnsəˈveɪʃən] the activity of taking care of the environment; *a conservation group*

crisis (PL) **crises** ['kraɪsɪs] ['kraɪsiːz] a situation that is very serious or dangerous

damage ['dæmɪdʒ] physical harm that happens to something

diesel ['diːzəl] a type of oil that is used in the engines of some vehicles instead of petrol

disaster [dɪˈzɑːstə] a very bad accident or event that may hurt many people

Earth [ɜːθ] the planet that we live on

electric car [ɪˌlektrɪk ˈkɑː] a car that is powered by electricity

endangered species [ɪnˈdeɪndʒəd ˈspiːʃiz] a type of animal or plant that may soon disappear from the world

energy ['enədʒi] the power that makes machines work or that provides heat

the environment [ði ɪnˈvaɪərənmənt] the natural world, consisting of land, the seas, the air, plants and animals

exhaust fumes [ɪgˈzɔːst fjuːmz] gases that cars give out as waste

---

EXAMPLES

I'm going to take these bottles to the bottle bank.

Pandas are an endangered species.

You can save energy by switching off your computer when you are not using it.

These gases are harmful to the environment.

fuel	[fjuːəl]	a substance such as coal or oil that is burned to provide heat or power
fumes	[fjuːmz]	the unpleasant and harmful gases that are produced by things such as chemicals and fuel
global warming	[ˌɡləʊbəl ˈwɔːmɪŋ]	the slow rise in the Earth's temperature
greenhouse effect	[ˈɡriːnhaʊs ɪˌfekt]	the rise in the Earth's temperature caused by a build-up of gases around the Earth
habitat	[ˈhæbɪtæt]	the place where an animal or a plant lives or grows
hydro-electric power [haɪdrəʊɪˌlektrɪk ˈpaʊə]		electricity that is produced by water power
industrial waste	[ɪnˌdʌstriəl ˈweɪst]	rubbish produced by factories
landfill	[ˈlændfɪl]	**1** a method of disposing of a lot of rubbish by burying it in a large deep hole; *the cost of landfill* **2** a large deep hole that rubbish is buried in; *a landfill site*
low-energy bulb	[ləʊ ˌenədʒi ˈbʌlb]	a light bulb that uses less electricity than normal light bulbs
nature	[ˈneɪtʃə]	all the animals and plants in the world, as well as the land and the sea
nuclear power	[ˌnjuːkliə ˈpaʊə]	energy that is produced when the central part of an atom is split
nuclear waste	[ˌnjuːkliə ˈweɪst]	harmful material from nuclear plants
oxygen	[ˈɒksɪdʒən]	a colourless gas that people, plants and animals need to breathe in order to live
ozone layer	[ˈəʊzəʊn ˌleɪə]	a part of the atmosphere that protects us from harmful rays from the sun; *a hole in the ozone layer*

EXAMPLES

Scientists are trying to find a solution to global warming.
The pollution of rivers destroys the habitats of many fish.
Millions of plastic bags go to landfill every day.

planet	['plænɪt]	a large, round object in space that moves around a star. The Earth is a planet.
pollution	[pə'luːʃən]	**1** the process of making water, air or land dirty and dangerous; *the pollution of our oceans* **2** harmful substances that make water, air or land dirty and dangerous; *high levels of pollution*
population	[ˌpɒpjʊ'leɪʃən]	all the people who live in a country or an area
rainforest	['reɪnfɒrɪst]	a thick forest of tall trees that grows in tropical areas where there is a lot of rain
recycling	[ˌriː'saɪklɪŋ]	processing things such as paper and glass so that they can be used again
renewable energy	[rɪˌnjuːəbəl 'enədʒi]	power from wind, water and sunlight, which are always available
sewage	['suːɪdʒ]	waste material, especially from people's bodies, which flows away through underground pipes
solar panel	[ˌsəʊlə 'pænəl]	a piece of equipment on a roof that collects energy from sunlight in order to heat water and produce electricity
solar power	[ˌsəʊlə 'paʊə]	energy from the sun that is used to heat water and produce electricity
solution	[sə'luːʃən]	a way of dealing with a problem
unleaded petrol	[ʌnˌledɪd 'petrəl]	petrol that contains less lead than normal petrol and causes less damage to the environment
wildlife	['waɪldlaɪf]	the animals and other living things that live in nature
wind power	['wɪnd paʊə]	energy from the wind that can be used to make electricity
world	[wɜːld]	the planet that we live on

EXAMPLES

The government have plans to reduce air pollution.
The population of Bangladesh is rising every year.
We watched a programme about the destruction of the Amazon rainforest.
We installed solar panels on our roof last year.
This car runs on unleaded petrol.

VERBS

ban	[bæn]	to say officially that something must not be done, shown or used; *ban the use of chemicals*
damage	['dæmɪdʒ]	to have a bad effect on something so that it is less strong or successful
destroy	[dɪ'strɔɪ]	to cause so much damage to something that it cannot be used any longer, or does not exist any longer
dispose of something		to get rid of something; *dispose of waste*
dump	[dʌmp]	to leave something somewhere quickly and carelessly
harm	[hɑːm]	same as **damage**
pollute	[pə'luːt]	to make water, air or land dirty
preserve	[prɪ'zɜːv]	to take action to save something or protect it; *preserve nature*
protect	[prə'tekt]	to keep someone or something safe from harm or damage; *protect wildlife*
recycle	[riː'saɪkəl]	to process things such as paper or bottles so that they can be used again
save	[seɪv]	**1** to protect something from harm; *save the rainforests* **2** to use less of something; *save paper*
use something up		to finish something so that none of it is left; *use up resources*

ADJECTIVES

biodegradable [ˌbaɪəʊdɪ'greɪdəbəl]		able to decay naturally without harming the environment; *biodegradable packaging*
eco-friendly	[ˌiːkəʊ'frendli]	same as **environmentally friendly**; *an eco-friendly product*

EXAMPLES

This book was printed on recycled paper.
We should recycle our rubbish.
They are developing a new kind of biodegradable plastic.
These houses were built using eco-friendly materials.

environmentally friendly [ɪnˌvaɪərənˌmentəli 'frendli]		not harmful to the environment, or less harmful to the environment
extinct	[ɪk'stɪŋkt]	not existing any more; *this species is extinct*
green	[griːn]	relating to the protection of the environment; *green policies*
harmful	['hɑːmfʊl]	having a bad effect on someone or something
organic	[ɔː'gænɪk]	grown without using chemicals
sustainable	[sə'steɪnəbəl]	using natural products in a way that does not damage the environment; *sustainable farming*; *sustainable development*

EXAMPLES

How can we make our company more environmentally friendly?
Many animals will soon be extinct.
We are trying to be greener by walking to work rather than driving.
This shop sells organic food.
All our furniture is made of wood from sustainable sources.

feelings and personal qualities

NOUNS

anger	['æŋgə]	the strong emotion that you feel when you think that someone has behaved badly or has treated you unfairly
excitement	[ɪk'saɪtmənt]	the feeling you have when you are excited
fear	[fɪə]	the unpleasant feeling you have when you think that you are in danger
feeling	['fi:lɪŋ]	a state in which you feel something such as anger or happiness
feelings	['fi:lɪŋz]	your emotions; *hurt someone's feelings*
guilt	[gɪlt]	an unhappy feeling that you have when you think that you have done something wrong
happiness	['hæpinəs]	a feeling of being pleased and satisfied
honesty	['ɒnɪsti]	the quality of being honest
intelligence	[ɪn'telɪdʒəns]	the ability to understand and learn things quickly and well
kindness	['kaɪndnəs]	the quality of being friendly and helpful
mood	[mu:d]	the way you are feeling at a particular time
nature	['neɪtʃə]	a person's character, which they show by the way they behave; *a friendly nature*
personality	[ˌpɜːsə'nælɪti]	the qualities that make you different from other people

EXAMPLES

Everyone is in a state of great excitement.
My whole body was shaking with fear.
Sara has a fear of mice.
I have a feeling that everything will be all right.
They have strong feelings about politics.
She felt a lot of guilt about her children's unhappiness.
I am always in a good mood.
He is in a bad mood.
She is a very good-natured child.

pride	[praɪd]	**1** a feeling of satisfaction that you have because you have done something well; *a sense of pride* **2** a sense of dignity and self-respect
quality	['kwɒlɪti]	a particular characteristic that a person has
regret	[rɪ'gret]	a feeling of sadness caused by something that you have done or not done; *express regret*
relief	[rɪ'liːf]	the feeling of happiness that you get when something unpleasant has not happened or is no longer happening
spite	[spaɪt]	a feeling that makes you do something to hurt or upset someone; *He did it out of spite.*
stupidity	[stjuː'pɪdɪti]	lack of intelligence or consideration
surprise	[sə'praɪz]	the feeling you have when something that you do not expect happens

ADJECTIVES

ambitious	[æm'bɪʃəs]	having a strong feeling that you want to be successful, rich or powerful
angry	['æŋgri]	feeling a strong emotion when someone has done something bad or has treated you unfairly
annoyed	[ə'nɔɪd]	angry about something
anxious	['æŋkʃəs]	nervous or worried
ashamed	[ə'ʃeɪmd]	feeling embarrassed or guilty

EXAMPLES

He takes great pride in his work.
His pride wouldn't allow him to ask for help.
She has lots of good qualities.
He had no regrets about leaving.
I breathed a sigh of relief.
To my surprise, I found I liked working hard.
I was ashamed of myself for getting so angry.

feelings and personal qualities

bored	[bɔːd]	not interested in something, or having nothing to do; *get bored*
calm	[kɑːm]	not worried, angry or excited; *Try to keep calm.*
cheerful	['tʃɪəfʊl]	happy
competent	['kɒmpɪtənt]	able to do something well
confident	['kɒnfɪdənt]	feeling sure about your own abilities and ideas
curious	['kjʊəriəs]	wanting to know more about something
depressed	[dɪ'prest]	feeling very sad
dishonest	[dɪs'ɒnɪst]	not honest
dissatisfied	[dɪs'sætɪsfaɪd]	not happy about something; *dissatisfied customers*
embarrassed	[ɪm'bærəst]	feeling shy, ashamed or guilty about something
enthusiastic [ɪnˌθjuːzi'æstɪk]		showing how much you like or enjoy something
envious	['enviəs]	wanting something that someone else has
excited	[ɪk'saɪtɪd]	very happy or enthusiastic
friendly	['frendli]	behaving in a pleasant, kind way; *Samir was friendly to me.*
frightened	['fraɪtənd]	anxious or afraid
frustrated	[frʌ'streɪtɪd]	upset or angry because there is nothing you can do about a problem
funny	['fʌni]	amusing and likely to make you smile or laugh
furious	['fjʊəriəs]	extremely angry
glad	[glæd]	happy and pleased about something

EXAMPLES

She was very depressed after her husband died.
He looked a bit embarrassed when he noticed his mistake.
Tom was not very enthusiastic about the idea.
I have to admit I was a little envious
I was excited about playing football again.
She was frightened of making a mistake.
They seemed glad to see me.

grateful	['greɪtfʊl]	wanting to thank someone for something that they have given you or done for you
guilty	['gɪlti]	feeling unhappy because you think that you have done something wrong; *feel guilty*
happy	['hæpi]	feeling pleased and satisfied; *a happy child*
helpful	['helpfʊl]	helping you by doing something useful for you
honest	['ɒnɪst]	always telling the truth and not stealing or cheating
hurt	[hɜːt]	upset because of something that someone has said or done
impatient	[ɪm'peɪʃənt]	**1** annoyed because you have to wait too long for something **2** becoming annoyed very quickly
independent	[ˌɪndɪ'pendənt]	able to take care of yourself without needing help or money from anyone else
insecure	[ˌɪnsɪ'kjʊə]	not confident
intelligent	[ɪn'telɪdʒənt]	able to understand and learn things quickly and well
jealous	['dʒeləs]	**1** feeling angry because you think that another person is trying to take away someone or something that you love **2** feeling angry or unhappy because you do not have something that someone else has
kind	[kaɪnd]	friendly and helpful
lonely	['ləʊnli]	unhappy because you are alone

EXAMPLES

She was grateful to him for being so helpful.
She was deeply hurt by Ali's remarks.
People are impatient for the war to be over.
Try not to be impatient with your kids.
Children become more independent as they grow.
Most people are a little insecure about their looks.
He got jealous and there was a fight.
She was jealous of her sister's success.

loving	['lʌvɪŋ]	feeling or showing love for other people; *a loving husband*
mean	[miːn]	unkind or cruel
miserable	['mɪzərəbəl]	very unhappy
naughty	['nɔːti]	badly behaved, and not doing what someone tells you to do; *a naughty boy*
nervous	['nɜːvəs]	frightened or worried
nice	[naɪs]	friendly and pleasant
optimistic	[ˌɒptɪ'mɪstɪk]	hopeful about the success of something
pessimistic	[ˌpesɪ'mɪstɪk]	thinking that bad things are going to happen
pleased	[pliːzd]	happy about something or satisfied with something; *I am very pleased with your work.*
polite	[pə'laɪt]	behaving with respect towards other people
proud	[praʊd]	**1** pleased and satisfied about something good that you or other people close to you have done **2** thinking that you are better than other people
relaxed	[rɪ'lækst]	calm and not worried
relieved	[rɪ'liːvd]	feeling happy because something unpleasant has not happened or is no longer happening
rude	[ruːd]	not polite
sad	[sæd]	unhappy
satisfied	['sætɪsfaɪd]	happy because you have what you wanted
scared	[skeəd]	frightened; *I'm not scared of him.*
selfish	['selfɪʃ]	caring only about yourself, and not about other people

---

EXAMPLES

Don't be mean to your brother!
They were extremely nice to me.
His dad was very proud of him.
We are relieved to be back home.

feelings and personal qualities

sensitive	['sensɪtɪv]	**1** showing that you understand other people's feelings **2** easily worried and offended about something when people talk about it
serious	['sɪərɪəs]	thinking a lot, and not smiling or laughing much
shocked	[ʃɒkt]	very upset because of something unpleasant that has happened
shy	[ʃaɪ]	nervous about talking to people that you do not know well
stupid	['stjuːpɪd]	not intelligent, and not able to behave in a sensible way
surprised	[sə'praɪzd]	having the feeling you get when something happens that you did not expect
suspicious	[sə'spɪʃəs]	not trusting someone or something
thoughtful	['θɔːtfʊl]	thinking about other people's feelings
thoughtless	['θɔːtləs]	not thinking about other people's feelings
uncomfortable	[ʌn'kʌmftəbəl]	slightly worried or embarrassed
unhappy	[ʌn'hæpi]	**1** sad **2** not satisfied with something
upset	[ʌp'set]	unhappy because something bad has happened; *Marta looked upset.*
well-behaved	[ˌwelbɪ'heɪvd]	behaving in a way that other people think is polite and correct; *well-behaved little boys*
worried	['wʌrid]	thinking about problems that you have or about unpleasant things that might happen

EXAMPLES

The classroom teacher must be sensitive to a child's needs.
Young people can be sensitive about their appearance.
She was deeply shocked when she heard the news.
We were surprised by the play's success.
It was thoughtless of me to forget your birthday.
The request for money made them feel uncomfortable.
We were unhappy with the way we played on Friday.
When she did not come home, they became worried.

VERBS

become	[bɪˈkʌm]	to start to feel a particular way; *become anxious*
behave	[bɪˈheɪv]	to do and say things in a particular way; *behave strangely*
calm down		to become less upset or excited
enjoy	[ɪnˈdʒɔɪ]	to like doing something
enjoy yourself		to get pleasure from an experience
feel	[fiːl]	to experience a particular emotion; *How do you feel?*
grow	[grəʊ]	to begin to have a particular feeling; *Lisbet soon grew bored.*
hurt	[hɜːt]	to say or do something that makes someone unhappy
suffer	[ˈsʌfə]	to feel pain, sadness or worry
upset	[ʌpˈset]	to make you feel worried or unhappy

IDIOMS

down in the dumps	unhappy or depressed
get on someone's nerves	to annoy someone
hit the roof	to suddenly become very angry
over the moon	extremely happy and excited

EXAMPLES

I enjoyed playing basketball.
I'm really sorry if I hurt your feelings.
His behaviour really upset me.

food and drink

food	[fuːd]	the things that people and animals eat

MEAT AND FISH

bacon	['beɪkən]	slices of salted or smoked meat that comes from a pig; *eggs and bacon for breakfast*
beef	[biːf]	meat from a cow
chicken	['tʃɪkɪn]	**1** a bird that is kept on a farm for its eggs and meat **2** the meat of this bird; *chicken sandwiches*
fish	[fɪʃ]	an animal that lives and swims in water, that people eat as food
gravy	['greɪvi]	a sauce made from the juices that come from meat when it cooks
ground beef (American English)	*see* **mince**	
ham	[hæm]	meat from a pig that has been prepared with salt and spices; *ham sandwiches*
hamburger	['hæmbɜːgə]	a type of food made from small pieces of meat that have been shaped into a flat circle. Hamburgers are fried or grilled and are often eaten in a round bread roll
lamb	[læm]	the flesh of a young sheep eaten as food
meat	[miːt]	the part of an animal that people cook and eat
mince	[mɪns]	meat that has been cut into very small pieces using a machine (*In American English, use* **ground beef**)
pork	[pɔːk]	meat from a pig
sausage	['sɒsɪdʒ]	a mixture of very small pieces of meat, spices and other foods, inside a long thin skin
seafood	['siːfuːd]	fish and other small animals from the sea that you can eat; *a seafood restaurant*

EXAMPLES
We had roast beef for lunch.
I don't eat meat or fish.
For supper, she served lamb and vegetables.
Fry the mince in a frying pan.
They ate sausages for breakfast.

steak	[steɪk]	**1** a large flat piece of beef without much fat on it; *steak and chips* **2** a large piece of fish that does not contain many bones; *a salmon steak*

EGGS, CHEESE AND MILK PRODUCTS

butter	['bʌtə]	a soft yellow food made from cream that you spread on bread or use in cooking
cheese	[tʃiːz]	a solid food that is usually white or yellow and and is made from milk
cream	[kriːm]	a thick liquid that is made from milk; *whipped cream*
custard	['kʌstəd]	a sweet yellow sauce made of milk, eggs and sugar
egg	[eg]	a hen's egg, that people eat as food in many countries; *a boiled egg*; *a hard-boiled egg*; *a poached egg*; *scrambled eggs*
ice cream	['aɪs kriːm]	**1** a frozen sweet food made from cream, sugar, and sometimes fruit or chocolate; *chocolate ice cream* **2** a portion of ice cream; *two ice creams*
margarine	[mɑːdʒə'riːn]	a yellow substance that is made from vegetable oil, and is similar to butter; *a tub of margarine*
mayonnaise	[meɪə'neɪz]	a cold, thick sauce made from eggs and oil
omelette	['ɒmlət]	a type of food made by mixing eggs and cooking them in a frying pan; *a cheese omelette*
yoghurt	['jɒgət]	a thick liquid food that is made from milk

BREAD, CAKES AND BISCUITS

biscuit	['bɪskɪt]	a type of hard, dry cake that is usually sweet and round in shape; *a chocolate biscuit* (In American English, use **cookie**)

EXAMPLES

Jordi spread some butter on a roll.
We had apple pie and custard for dessert.
Break the eggs into a bowl.

bread	[bred]	a food made mostly from flour and water and baked in an oven; *a slice of bread*
cake	[keɪk]	a sweet food that you make from flour, eggs, sugar and butter; *a birthday cake*
cookie (mainly American English)		*see* **biscuit**
loaf	[ləʊf]	bread that has been shaped and baked in one large piece; *a loaf of bread*
pancake	['pænkeɪk]	a thin, round food made from milk, flour and eggs, cooked in a frying pan
roll	[rəʊl]	bread in a small round or long shape
sandwich	['sænwɪdʒ]	two slices of bread with another food such as cheese or meat between them; *a cheese sandwich*; *a toasted sandwich*
toast	[təʊst]	slices of bread that you have heated until they are hard and brown; *slices of toast*

OTHER FOOD

candy (American English)		*see* **sweets**
cereal	['sɪəriəl]	**1** a food made from grain, that people eat with milk for breakfast; *a bowl of cereal* **2** a plant that produces grain for food; *cereal grains such as corn and wheat*
chips	[tʃɪps]	**1** long thin pieces of potato, cooked in oil and eaten hot; *fish and chips* (In American English, use **fries**) **2** (American English) *see* **crisps**
chocolate	['tʃɒklət]	**1** a brown food eaten as a sweet; *a bar of chocolate* **2** a small sweet covered with chocolate; *a box of chocolates*
crisps	[krɪsps]	very thin slices of potato that have been cooked in oil and are eaten as a snack; *a bag of crisps* (In American English, use **chips**)

EXAMPLES

Patricia put two pieces of bread on a plate and buttered them.

He spread some butter on a roll.

I blew out the candles and Mum sliced the cake.

Raul ate a piece of chocolate cake.

food and drink

curry	[ˈkʌri]	a dish, originally from Asia, that is cooked with hot spices; *vegetable curry*
dish	[dɪʃ]	food that is prepared in a particular way; *a chicken dish*
fast food	[fɑːst ˈfuːd]	hot food, such as hamburgers, that is served quickly after you order it; *a fast food restaurant*
flour	[ˈflaʊə]	a fine powder that is used for making bread, cakes and pastry; *wholemeal flour*
fries *(American English)*		*see* **chips**
honey	[ˈhʌni]	a sweet, sticky food that is made by bees (= black-and-yellow insects); *a jar of honey*
jam	[dʒæm]	a sweet food containing soft fruit and sugar, that is usually spread on bread; *strawberry jam* (*In American English, use* **jelly**)
jelly	[ˈdʒeli]	**1** a soft sweet food made from fruit juice and sugar that moves from side to side when you touch it; *jelly and ice cream* **2** *(American English) see* **jam**
lasagne	[ləˈsænjə]	a dish that consists of layers of pasta, sauce, and a filling such as meat or cheese, baked in an oven
noodles	[ˈnuːdəlz]	long, thin strips of pasta, used especially in Chinese and Italian cooking; *a bowl of noodles*
oil	[ɔɪl]	a smooth, thick liquid made from plants, that is often used for cooking; *vegetable oil*
pasta	[ˈpæstə]	a type of food made from a mixture of flour, eggs and water that is made into different shapes and then boiled

EXAMPLES
Shall we go for a curry tonight?
My favourite dish is lasagne.
The pasta is cooked in a garlic and tomato sauce.

pastry	[ˈpeɪstri]	a food made from flour, fat and water that is often used for making pies
pâté	[ˈpæteɪ]	a mixture of meat, fish or vegetables that is mixed into a paste and eaten cold; *liver pâté*
pepper	[ˈpepə]	a brown or black spice with a hot taste that you put on food; *salt and pepper*
pie	[paɪ]	a dish consisting of meat, vegetables or fruit with a cover made of pastry
pizza	[ˈpiːtsə]	a flat, round piece of bread that is covered with tomatoes, cheese and sometimes other foods, and then baked in an oven
rice	[raɪs]	white or brown grains from a plant that grows in warm, wet areas; *plain boiled rice*
salad	[ˈsæləd]	a mixture of foods, especially vegetables, that you usually serve cold; *a green salad*; *a mixed salad*
salt	[sɔːlt]	a white substance that you use to improve the flavour of food
sauce	[sɔːs]	a thick liquid that you eat with other food; *pasta sauce*
snack	[snæk]	a simple meal that is quick to prepare and eat; *have a snack*
soup	[suːp]	a liquid food made by boiling meat, fish or vegetables in water; *home-made soup*
spaghetti	[spəˈgeti]	a type of pasta that looks like long pieces of string
stew	[stjuː]	a meal that you make by cooking meat and vegetables slowly in liquid
sugar	[ˈʃʊgə]	a sweet substance used for making food and drinks taste sweet; *a spoonful of sugar*

EXAMPLES
Bruno ordered a thin-crust pizza.
The children have a snack when they come home from school.
She gave him a bowl of beef stew.
Do you take sugar in your coffee?

sweets	[swiːts]	small pieces of sweet food such as chocolates (*In American English, use* **candy**)
vinegar	['vɪnɪgə]	a sour, sharp-tasting liquid that is used in cooking

DRINKS

alcoholic drink [ˌælkə,hɒlɪk 'drɪŋk]		a drink that contains alcohol
beer	[bɪə]	an alcoholic drink made from grain
cider	['saɪdə]	an alcoholic drink made from apples
coffee	['kɒfi]	a drink made from boiling water and the beans of the coffee plant, made into a powder; *strong coffee*; *Two coffees, please.*
hot chocolate	[hɒt 'tʃɒklɪt]	a drink made by mixing chocolate powder with milk
ice cube	['aɪs kjuːb]	a small block of ice that you put into a drink to make it cold
juice	[dʒuːs]	the liquid that comes from a fruit or a vegetable; *orange/apple/lemon/fruit juice*
lemonade	[lemə'neɪd]	a drink that is made from lemons, sugar and water
milk	[mɪlk]	the white liquid that cows and some other animals produce, which people drink
mineral water	['mɪnərəl ˌwɔːtə]	water that comes out of the ground naturally and is considered healthy to drink
soft drink	[sɒft 'drɪŋk]	a cold non-alcoholic drink such as lemonade
tap water	['tæp wɔːtə]	the water that comes out of a tap in a building such as a house or a hotel
tea	[tiː]	a drink that you make by pouring boiling water on the dry leaves of a plant called the tea bush; *a pot of tea*
whisky	['wɪski]	a strong alcoholic drink made from grain
wine	[waɪn]	an alcoholic drink made from grapes (= small green or purple fruit); *red/white wine*; *a glass of wine*

EXAMPLES

Eat more fruit and vegetables and fewer sweets.
We ordered a couple of beers and asked for the menu.

ITEMS USED FOR EATING, DRINKING AND SERVING MEALS

bottle	['bɒtəl]	a glass or plastic container in which drinks and other liquids are kept
bowl	[bəʊl]	a round container that is used for mixing and serving food
chopsticks	['tʃɒpstɪks]	a pair of thin sticks that people in East Asia use for eating food
cup	[kʌp]	a small round container that you drink from; *a cup of coffee*
dish	[dɪʃ]	a shallow container for cooking or serving food; *a serving dish*; *a dish of hot vegetables*
fork	[fɔːk]	a tool with long metal points, used for eating food; *knives and forks*
glass	[glɑːs]	a container made from glass, which you can drink from
jug	[dʒʌg]	a container with a handle, used for holding and pouring liquids; *a milk jug*
knife (PL) **knives**	[naɪf] [naɪvz]	a sharp flat piece of metal with a handle, used for cutting things; *a sharp/blunt knife*
mug	[mʌg]	a deep cup with straight sides; *a mug of coffee*
napkin	['næpkɪn]	a square of cloth or paper that you use when you are eating to protect your clothes, or to wipe your mouth or hands
plate	[pleɪt]	a flat dish that is used for holding food; *a plate of sandwiches*
saucer	['sɔːsə]	a small curved plate that you put under a cup
spoon	[spuːn]	a long object with a round end that is used for eating, serving or mixing food; *a serving spoon*
straw	[strɔː]	a thin tube that you use to suck a drink into your mouth
teapot	['tiːpɒt]	a container that is used for making and serving tea

EXAMPLES

Put the soup in a bowl.
Maisie was drinking juice with a straw.

teaspoon	['tiːspuːn]	a small spoon that you use for putting sugar into tea or coffee

CAFÉS AND RESTAURANTS

à la carte	[,ɑː lɑː 'kɑːt]	an à la carte menu in a restaurant is a list of dishes that each have a different price
bar	[bɑː]	a place where you can buy and drink alcoholic drinks
bill	[bɪl]	a document that shows how much money you must pay for something (*In American English, use* **check**)
café	[kæfeɪ]	a place where you can buy drinks and small meals
check (*American English*)		*see* **bill**
chef	[ʃef]	a person who prepares and cooks food in a restaurant
menu	['menjuː]	a list of the food and drink that you can have in a restaurant
order	['ɔːdə]	the food or drink that you ask for in a bar, café or restaurant
pub	[pʌb]	a building where people can buy and drink alcoholic drinks; *go to the pub*
restaurant	['restərɒnt]	a place where you can buy and eat a meal
service	['sɜːvɪs]	the help that people in a restaurant or a shop give you; *give/get good/poor service*
tip	[tɪp]	money that you give to a waiter or waitress to thank them for a job they have done for you
waiter	['weɪtə]	a man whose job is to serve food in a restaurant
waitress	['weɪtrəs]	a woman whose job is to serve food in a restaurant
wine list	['waɪn lɪst]	a menu of wines that are available in a restaurant

EXAMPLES

Can we have the bill please?

Is service included in the price?

I gave the waiter a tip.

The waitress brought our food and said, 'Enjoy your meal!'

EXPERIENCING FOOD

flavour	['fleɪvə]	the taste of a food or drink
hunger	['hʌŋgə]	the feeling that you get when you need something to eat
smell	[smel]	the quality of something that you notice when you breathe in through your nose; *a lovely smell*
taste	[teɪst]	**1** the particular quality that something has when you put it in your mouth, for example whether it is sweet or salty; *the taste of chocolate*; *a horrible taste* **2** a small amount of food or drink that you try in order to see what the flavour is like; *Have a taste of this.*
thirst	[θɜːst]	the feeling that you get when you want to drink something

MEALS AND PARTS OF MEALS

breakfast	['brekfəst]	the first meal of the day; *have breakfast*
course	[kɔːs]	one part of a meal; *a three-course meal*
dessert	[dɪ'zɜːt]	something sweet that you eat at the end of a meal
dinner	['dɪnə]	the main meal of the day, usually served in the evening; *have dinner*; *invite someone for dinner*
lunch	[lʌntʃ]	the meal that you have in the middle of the day; *have lunch*
main course	['meɪn kɔːs]	the most important course of a meal
meal	[miːl]	**1** an occasion when people sit down and eat **2** the food that you eat during a meal
starter	['stɑːtə]	a small amount of food that you eat as the first part of a meal

---

EXAMPLES

I added some pepper for extra flavour.
There was a horrible smell in the fridge.
I just love the smell of freshly baked bread.
The meal consisted of chicken, rice and vegetables.

| **sweet** | [swiːt] | same as **dessert** |
| **tea** | [tiː] | a meal that some people eat in the late afternoon or the early evening |

drink	[drɪŋk]	1 to take liquid into your mouth and swallow it; *drink some water* 2 to drink alcohol; *I don't drink.*
eat	[iːt]	to put something into your mouth and swallow it
order	[ˈɔːdə]	to ask for food or drink in a bar, café or restaurant
serve	[sɜːv]	to give people food and drinks in a restaurant or bar; *A waiter served us.*
smell	[smel]	1 to have a quality that you notice by breathing in through your nose; *That cake smells delicious.* 2 to notice something when you breathe in through your nose; *I can smell garlic.*
swallow	[ˈswɒləʊ]	to make something go from your mouth down into your stomach
taste	[teɪst]	1 to have a particular flavour; *It tastes of lemons.* 2 to eat or drink a small amount of food or drink in order to see what the flavour is like; *Taste the soup.* 3 to be aware of the flavour of something that you are eating or drinking; *Can you taste the garlic?*

EXAMPLES

Noah served me coffee and chocolate cake.
That smells good!
Polly took a bite of the apple and swallowed it.
The water tasted of metal.
Don't add salt until you've tasted the food.
The pizza tastes delicious.

ADJECTIVES

canned *(American English)*		see **tinned**
delicious	[dɪˈlɪʃəs]	very good to eat
disgusting	[dɪsˈgʌstɪŋ]	extremely unpleasant
fizzy	[ˈfɪzi]	fizzy drinks contain small bubbles
fresh	[freʃ]	picked or prepared recently; *fresh vegetables*
frozen	[ˈfrəʊzən]	used for describing food that has been stored at a very low temperature; *frozen vegetables*
hungry	[ˈhʌngri]	wanting to eat
juicy	[ˈdʒuːsi]	containing a lot of juice in a pleasant way
off	[ɒf]	food that is off tastes and smells bad because it is no longer fresh enough to be eaten; *gone off*
organic	[ɔːˈgænɪk]	grown without using chemicals
raw	[rɔː]	not cooked; *raw fish*
salty	[ˈsɔːlti]	containing salt or tasting of salt
savoury	[ˈseɪvəri]	having a salty flavour rather than a sweet one
sour	[ˈsaʊə]	**1** with a sharp taste like the taste of a lemon **2** tasting bad; not fresh; *sour milk*
stale	[steɪl]	no longer fresh; *stale bread*
sweet	[swiːt]	containing a lot of sugar
thirsty	[ˈθɜːsti]	wanting to drink something
tinned	[tɪnd]	tinned food lasts a long time because it is in a strong metal container (called a tin); *tinned tomatoes* (In American English, use **canned**)

PHRASES

Can I take your order?	used by a waiter to ask what you would like to eat
Cheers!	you say 'Cheers!' to each other as you lift up your glasses to drink
Enjoy your meal!	you say 'Enjoy your meal!' to someone just before they begin to eat
Is everything all right?	used by a waiter to ask if you are enjoying your food

friends and family

NOUNS

acquaintance [ə'kweɪntəns] someone you have met, but that you don't know well

adult ['ædʌlt] a fully grown person or animal

aunt [ɑːnt] the sister of your mother or father, or the wife of your uncle

aunty ['ɑːnti] [INFORMAL] aunt

baby ['beɪbi] a very young child

baby boy [beɪbi 'bɔɪ] a very young boy

baby girl [beɪbi 'gɜːl] a very young girl

bachelor ['bætʃələ] a man who has never married

best friend [best 'frend] your best friend is the friend that you like most

bestie ['besti] [INFORMAL] best friend

boy [bɔɪ] a male child

boyfriend ['bɔɪfrend] a man or a boy that someone is having a romantic relationship with

brother ['brʌðə] a boy or a man who has the same parents as you

brother-in-law ['brʌðərɪn,lɔː] the brother of your husband or wife, or the man who is married to your sister.

child [tʃaɪld] **1** a young boy or girl
2 someone's son or daughter

Christian name ['krɪstʃən neɪm] same as **first name**

couple ['kʌpəl] two people who are married or having a romantic relationship

cousin ['kʌzən] the child of your uncle or your aunt

dad ['dæd] [INFORMAL] **1** father; *This is my dad.*
2 a word you use when you are talking to your father; *Hi, Dad!*

EXAMPLES
He was just a casual acquaintance.
Hannah is going to have a baby.
Congratulations on the birth of your baby boy!
Here are some lovely gift ideas for your bestie.
Do you have any brothers or sisters?

daughter	[ˈdɔːtə]	a person's female child
daughter-in-law	[ˈdɔːtərɪnˌlɔː]	the wife of your son
family	[ˈfæmɪli]	a group of people who are related to each other, usually parents and their children
father	[ˈfɑːðə]	your male parent
father-in-law	[ˈfɑːðərɪnˌlɔː]	the father of your husband or wife
fiancé	[fiˈɒnseɪ]	the man that a woman is going to marry
fiancée	[fiˈɒnseɪ]	the woman that a man is going to marry
first name	[ˈfɜːst neɪm]	the name that you were given when you were born
friend	[frend]	someone who you like and know well
girl	[gɜːl]	a female child
girlfriend	[ˈgɜːlfrend]	a girl or woman who someone is having a romantic relationship with
grandchild	[ˈgræntʃaɪld]	the child of your son or daughter
granddaughter	[ˈgrændɔːtə]	the daughter of your son or daughter
grandfather	[ˈgrænfɑːðə]	the father of your father or mother
grandma	[ˈgrænmɑː]	[INFORMAL] 1 grandmother; *My grandma lives with us.* 2 a word you use when you are talking to your grandmother; *Look, Grandma!*
grandmother	[ˈgrænmʌðə]	the mother of your father or mother
grandpa	[ˈgrænpɑː]	[INFORMAL] 1 grandfather; *My grandpa is nearly 70.* 2 a word you use when you are talking to your grandfather; *Hello, Grandpa!*
grandparents [ˈgrænpeərənts]		the parents of your mother or father
grandson	[ˈgrænsʌn]	the son of your son or daughter
grown-up	[ˈgrəʊnʌp]	a child's word for an adult
husband	[ˈhʌzbənd]	the man that a woman is married to

EXAMPLES
May I introduce my fiancée, Cheryl Ferguson?
How many grandchildren have you got?
I visit my grandma every weekend.

maiden name	['meɪdən neɪm]	a woman's surname before she married
mother	['mʌðə]	your female parent
mother-in-law	['mʌðərɪnˌlɔː]	the mother of your husband or wife
mum	['mʌm]	[INFORMAL] **1** mother; *This is my mum.* **2** a word you use when you are talking to your mother; *Can I go out, Mum?*
name	[neɪm]	the word or words that you use to talk to a particular person, or to talk about them
neighbour	['neɪbə]	someone who lives near you
nephew	['nefjuː]	the son of your sister or brother
nickname	['nɪkneɪm]	an informal name that people use for a particular person
niece	[niːs]	the daughter of your sister or brother
old age	[əʊld'eɪdʒ]	the period of years towards the end of your life
only child	['əʊnli tʃaɪld]	a child who does not have any brothers or sisters
orphan	['ɔːfən]	a child whose parents are dead
parents	['peərənts]	your mother and father
relative	['relətɪv]	a member of your family
single man	[ˌsɪŋɡəl 'mæn]	a man who is not married
single parent	[ˌsɪŋɡəl 'peərənt]	someone who looks after their children alone, because the other parent does not live with them
single woman	[ˌsɪŋɡəl 'wʊmən]	a woman who is not married
sister	['sɪstə]	a girl or woman who has the same parents as you

EXAMPLES

'What is your name?' — 'Daniela.'
His name is Paolo.
I am an only child.
I get on well with my parents.
I don't have any brothers or sisters.
My older sister is at university.

sister-in-law	[ˈsɪstərɪnˌlɔː]	the sister of your husband or wife, or the woman who is married to your brother
son	[sʌn]	your male child
son-in-law	[ˈsʌnɪnˌlɔː]	the husband of your daughter
stepbrother	[ˈstepbrʌðə]	the son of your stepfather or stepmother
stepdaughter	[ˈstepdɔːtə]	a daughter who was born to your husband or wife during a previous relationship
stepfather	[ˈstepfɑːðə]	the man who has married someone's mother but who is not their father
stepmother	[ˈstepmʌðə]	the woman who has married someone's father but who is not their mother
stepsister	[ˈstepsɪstə]	the daughter of your stepfather or stepmother
stepson	[ˈstepsʌn]	a son who was born to your husband or wife during a previous relationship
surname	[ˈsɜːneɪm]	the name that you share with other members of your family
teenager	[ˈtiːneɪdʒə]	someone who is between thirteen and nineteen years old
triplets	[ˈtrɪpləts]	three children who were born at the same time to the same mother
twins	[twɪnz]	two children who were born at the same time to the same mother
uncle	[ˈʌŋkəl]	the brother of your mother or father, or the husband of your aunt
widow	[ˈwɪdəʊ]	a woman whose husband has died
widower	[ˈwɪdəʊə]	a man whose wife has died
wife	[waɪf]	the woman a man is married to

EXAMPLES
I have three stepsisters.
'What is your surname?' — 'Smith.'
My father is a widower.

VERBS

adopt	[ə'dɒpt]	to take someone else's child into your own family and make them legally your son or daughter; *adopt a child*
be born		when a baby is born, it comes out of its mother's body at the beginning of its life
break up		**1** if two people break up, their relationship ends; *Marianne and Pierre broke up last year.*
		2 if a marriage or relationship breaks up, it ends; *Their marriage broke up.*
		3 if you break up with your boyfriend, girlfriend, husband or wife, your relationship with that person ends; *I've broken up with Jamie.*
die	[daɪ]	to stop living
divorce	[dɪ'vɔːs]	if one person divorces another, their marriage is legally ended
fall out		**1** if two people fall out, they have an argument; *We fell out.*
		2 if you fall out with someone, you have an argument and stop being friendly with them; *Chris fell out with Mike.*
foster	['fɒstə]	to take a child into your family for a period of time, without becoming its legal parent; *foster a child*
get divorced		if a man and woman get divorced, their marriage is legally ended
get married		**1** when two people get married they become husband and wife in a special ceremony; *John and Linda got married.*
		2 when you get married to someone, you become their husband or wife in a special ceremony; *John got married to Linda.*

EXAMPLES

I was born in 1990.
She died in 1995.
I fell out with my girlfriend last week, but we've made up now.

live	[lɪv]	to stay alive until you are a particular age; *live to the age of 94*
marry	['mæri]	to legally become someone's husband or wife in a special ceremony
give birth		when a woman gives birth, she produces a baby from her body
go out with someone		to have a romantic or sexual relationship with someone
grow up		to gradually change from a child into an adult
make friends		**1** when two people make friends, they begin a friendship **2** when you make friends with someone, you begin a friendship with them
make up		to become friends again after an argument
split up		same as **break up**

ADJECTIVES		
dead	[ded]	not alive
divorced	[dɪ'vɔːst]	no longer legally married to your former husband or wife
engaged	[ɪn'geɪdʒd]	if two people are engaged, they have agreed to marry each other
grown-up	[grəʊn'ʌp]	mature, and no longer dependent on your parents or another adult
married	['mærid]	having a husband or wife
pregnant	['pregnənt]	having a baby or babies developing in your body
separated	['sepəreɪtɪd]	living apart from your husband or wife, but not divorced
single	['sɪŋgəl]	not married

EXAMPLES

She married David Nichols in 2012.
'Are you going out with John?' — 'No; we're just good friends.'
I grew up in France.
I've just split up with my boyfriend.
My parents are divorced.

IDIOMS

get on like a house on fire	if two people get on like a house on fire, they quickly become close friends
go back a long way	if two people go back a long way, they have known each other for a long time
just good friends	used to say that two people are not having a romantic relationship
your nearest and dearest	your close relatives and friends
something runs in the family	used to say that a characteristic or medical condition is often found in members of a particular family
a tower of strength	a person that you can rely on to help and protect you
you would not give someone the time of day	used to say that you do not like someone at all

EXAMPLES
Singing runs in the family.
Judith was a tower of strength when my mum died.

fruit, nuts and vegetables

NOUNS

FRUIT

apple [ˈæpəl] a firm round fruit with green, red or yellow skin; *apple pie*; *cooking apples*

apricot [ˈeɪprɪkɒt] a small, soft, round fruit with yellow flesh and a large seed inside; *apricot jam*

avocado [ˌævəˈkɑːdəʊ] a fruit that does not taste sweet, with dark green skin and a large seed in the middle

banana [bəˈnɑːnə] a long curved fruit with yellow skin; *a bunch of bananas*

berry [ˈberi] a small, round fruit that grows on a bush or a tree

cherry [ˈtʃeri] a small, round fruit with red skin

coconut [ˈkəʊkənʌt] **1** a very large nut with a hairy shell and white flesh
2 the white flesh of a coconut

date [deɪt] a small, dark-brown, sticky fruit with a stone inside

fig [fɪg] a soft sweet fruit full of tiny seeds

fruit [fruːt] the part of a plant that contains seeds, covered with a substance that you can often eat; *a piece of fruit*; *fresh fruit and vegetables*

grapefruit [ˈgreɪpfruːt] a large, round, yellow fruit that has a slightly sour taste

grapes [greɪps] small green or purple fruits that grow in bunches and are used to make wine; *a bunch of grapes*

lemon [ˈlemən] a yellow fruit with a very sour taste

mango [ˈmæŋgəʊ] a large, sweet, yellow or red fruit that grows on trees in hot countries; *a mango smoothie*

EXAMPLES
I always have a piece of fruit in my lunchbox.
He squeezed the lemon over his fish.
I like a slice of lemon in my tea.

melon	['melən]	a large fruit with soft, sweet flesh and a hard green or yellow skin
nectarine	['nektəriːn]	a red and yellow fruit with a smooth skin
orange	['ɒrɪndʒ]	a round, juicy fruit with a thick, orange-coloured skin
peach	[piːtʃ]	a round fruit with a soft red and orange skin
pear	[peə]	a juicy fruit that is narrow at the top and wider at the bottom. Pears have white flesh and green, yellow or brown skin.
peel	[piːl]	the skin of a fruit such as a lemon or an apple, especially when it has been removed
pineapple	['paɪnæpəl]	a large fruit with sweet, yellow flesh and thick, rough, brown skin
pip	[pɪp]	one of the small, hard seeds in a fruit such as an apple or an orange
plum	[plʌm]	a small, sweet fruit with a smooth purple, red or yellow skin and a large seed in the middle
raisin	['reɪzən]	a dried grape
raspberry	['rɑːzbri]	a small, soft, red fruit that grows on bushes; *raspberry jam*
rhubarb	['ruːbɑːb]	a plant with large leaves and long red stems that are cooked with sugar to make jam or desserts
skin	[skɪn]	the outer part that covers a fruit
stone	[stəʊn]	the large hard seed in the middle of a fruit such as a plum or a cherry; *a cherry stone*
strawberry	['strɔːbri]	a small soft red fruit that has a lot of very small seeds on its skin; *strawberries and cream*

EXAMPLES

I'd like a kilo of oranges, please.
It was a very sweet and juicy pear.
Can I have half a kilo of plums, please?

tomato	[tə'mɑːtəʊ]	a soft red fruit that you can eat raw in salads or cook like a vegetable; *sliced/ chopped tomatoes*; *sun-dried tomatoes*; *tomato sauce/soup/juice*; *tomato puree/ paste*; *tomato ketchup*

NUTS

brazil nut	[brə'zɪl nʌt]	a curved nut with a hard dark-brown shell with three sides
cashew nut	['kæʃuː nʌt]	a small curved nut that is often eaten salted
chestnut	['tʃesnʌt]	a reddish-brown nut with a shell that has points on it; *roasted chestnuts*
hazelnut	['heɪzəlnʌt]	a round nut with a hard shell
peanut	['piːnʌt]	a small round nut often eaten roasted and salted; *a packet of salted peanuts*
walnut	['wɔːlnʌt]	a nut that is hard and round, with a rough texture

VEGETABLES

aubergine	['əʊbəʒiːn]	a vegetable with a smooth, dark purple skin (*In American English, use* **eggplant**)
beans	[biːnz]	seeds or seed cases of a climbing plant, that are usually cooked before eating; *baked beans*; *green beans*; *broad beans*; *soya beans*
beet (*American English*)		*see* **beetroot**
beetroot	['biːtruːt]	a dark red root, eaten as a vegetable and in salads; *pickled beetroot* (*In American English, use* **beet**)
broccoli	['brɒkəli]	a vegetable with thick green stems and small green flowers on top
cabbage	['kæbɪdʒ]	a round vegetable with white, green or purple leaves; *red cabbage*; *spring cabbages*
carrot	['kærət]	a long, thin, orange-coloured vegetable; *grated carrot*; *raw carrot*; *carrot cake*

EXAMPLE
Add the fruit and sprinkle with the chopped hazelnuts.

cauliflower	['kɒliflaʊə]	a large, round, white vegetable surrounded by green leaves; *cauliflower cheese*
celery	['seləri]	a vegetable with long, pale-green sticks that you can cook or eat raw; *a stick of celery*; *celery sticks/stalks*
courgette	[kʊə'ʒet]	a long, thin vegetable with a dark green skin (*In American English, use* **zucchini**)
cucumber	['kjuːkʌmbə]	a long dark-green vegetable that you eat raw; *sliced cucumber*; *tomatoes and cucumber*; *cucumber sandwiches*
eggplant (*American English*)		*see* **aubergine**
garlic	['gɑːlɪk]	a plant like a small onion with a strong flavour, that you use in cooking; *garlic bread*; *chopped/crushed garlic*
herb	[hɜːb]	a plant whose leaves are used in cooking to add flavour to food; *dried/fresh herbs*; *mixed herbs*
leek	[liːk]	a long, thin vegetable that is white at one end and has long green leaves
lentils	['lentɪlz]	round flat seeds that are dried and then soaked and cooked before eating; *red/green lentils*; *lentil soup*
lettuce	['letɪs]	a plant with large green leaves that is eaten mainly in salads; *lettuce leaves*
mushroom	['mʌʃruːm]	a plant with a short stem and a round top that you can eat; *sliced mushrooms*; *wild mushrooms*; *button mushrooms*
olive	['ɒlɪv]	a small green or black fruit with a bitter taste; *olive oil*; *green/black olives*
onion	['ʌnjən]	a round vegetable with many layers, that has a strong, sharp smell and taste; *sliced/chopped onion*; *fried onion*; *red onions*; *pickled onions*

EXAMPLES

When the oil is hot, add a clove of garlic.

Fry the mushrooms in a little olive oil and add the chopped herbs.

parsley	[ˈpɑːsli]	a herb with small green leaves that you use in cooking; *chopped parsley*
peas	[piːz]	very small round green seeds that grow in long narrow cases (called pods) and are cooked and eaten as a vegetable; *frozen green peas*
pepper	[ˈpepə]	a hollow green, red or yellow vegetable with seeds inside it; *chopped/roasted peppers; sweet/chilli peppers*
potato	[pəˈteɪtəʊ]	a hard, round, white vegetable with brown or red skin, that grows under the ground; *roast potatoes; baked/jacket potatoes; mashed/boiled/fried potatoes*
pumpkin	[ˈpʌmpkɪn]	a large, round, orange vegetable with a thick skin; *pumpkin seeds; pumpkin pie; pumpkin soup*
spinach	[ˈspɪnɪdʒ]	a vegetable with large dark green leaves
squash	[skwɒʃ]	a large vegetable with thick skin and hard flesh
sweetcorn	[ˈswiːtkɔːn]	a long round vegetable covered in small yellow seeds. The seeds are also called sweetcorn.
turnip	[ˈtɜːnɪp]	a round white vegetable that grows under the ground
vegetable	[ˈvedʒtəbəl]	a plant that you can cook and eat; *roasted vegetables; fruit and vegetables; vegetable oil*
zucchini (*American English*)		*see* **courgette**

ADJECTIVES

ripe	[raɪp]	used for describing fruit that is ready to eat
vegetarian	[ˌvedʒɪˈteəriən]	not containing meat or fish; *a vegetarian diet/dish/meal*

EXAMPLES
Thinly slice two red or green peppers.
Choose firm but ripe fruit.

health

NOUNS

accident	['æksɪdənt]	an occasion when something bad happens to a person by chance, causing injury or death
A&E	[eɪ ənd 'iː]	short for 'Accident and Emergency': the part of a hospital where people who have severe injuries or sudden illness go for emergency treatment
ache	[eɪk]	a steady pain in a part of your body
AIDS	[eɪdz]	a disease that destroys the body's ability to fight other diseases
ambulance	['æmbjʊləns]	a vehicle for taking people to hospital; *call an ambulance*
appointment	[ə'pɔɪntmənt]	an arrangement to see someone such as a doctor at a particular time
aspirin	['æspɪrɪn]	a mild drug that reduces pain; *take an aspirin*
bandage	['bændɪdʒ]	a long piece of cloth that is wrapped around an injured part of your body to protect or support it
bruise	[bruːz]	a purple mark that appears on a part of your body when you injure it
cancer	['kænsə]	a serious disease that makes groups of cells in the body grow when they should not
chickenpox	['tʃɪkɪnpɒks]	a disease that gives you a high temperature and red spots that itch
cold	[kəʊld]	an illness that makes liquid flow from your nose, and makes you cough

---

EXAMPLES

The boy was injured in an accident at a swimming pool.

She made an appointment with her doctor.

How did you get that bruise on your arm?

She was diagnosed with breast cancer.

I've got a cold.

condom	['kɒndɒm]	a rubber covering that a man wears on his penis during sex to stop a woman from becoming pregnant and to protect against disease; *use a condom*
cough	[kɒf]	an illness that makes you cough
crutch	[krʌtʃ]	a stick that you put under your arm to help you to walk if you have hurt your leg or your foot
dentist	['dentɪst]	a person whose job is to examine and treat people's teeth
the dentist's	[ðə 'dentɪsts]	the place where a dentist works
diarrhoea	[ˌdaɪə'riːə]	an illness that makes all the waste products come out of your body as liquid
diet	['daɪət]	the type of food that you regularly eat; *a balanced diet*; *a healthy diet*
doctor	['dɒktə]	a person whose job is to treat people who are ill or injured
the doctor's	[ðə 'dɒktəz]	the place where a doctor works
drug	[drʌg]	a chemical that is used as a medicine
earache	['ɪəreɪk]	a pain inside your ear
first aid kit	[fɜːst 'eɪd kɪt]	a collection of bandages and medicines for giving first aid when someone has an injury
flu	[fluː]	short for 'influenza': an illness that is like a very bad cold
germ	[dʒɜːm]	a very small living thing that can cause disease or illness
headache	['hedeɪk]	a pain in your head
health	[helθ]	the condition of a person's body; *in good health*; *health problems*

EXAMPLES

I've got a bad cough.
I can walk without crutches now.
I'm going to the dentist's after work.
I went to the doctor's today.
This chemical is used for killing germs.
I've got a headache.

heart attack	[ˈhɑːt ə,tæk]	an occasion when someone's heart begins to beat irregularly or stops completely; *have a heart attack*
hospital	[ˈhɒspɪtəl]	a place where doctors and nurses care for people who are ill or injured
illness	[ˈɪlnəs]	**1** a particular disease or a period of bad health **2** the state of being ill
injection	[ɪnˈdʒekʃən]	medicine that is put into your body using a special type of needle; *have an injection*
measles	[ˈmiːzəlz]	an illness that gives you a high fever and red spots on your skin
medicine	[ˈmedsən]	**1** the treatment of illness and injuries by doctors and nurses; *a career in medicine* **2** a substance that you use to treat or cure an illness; *take medicine*
nurse	[nɜːs]	a person whose job is to care for people who are ill or injured
ointment	[ˈɔɪntmənt]	a smooth, thick substance that you put on sore or damaged skin
operation	[ˌɒpəˈreɪʃən]	the process of cutting open a patient's body in order to remove, replace or repair a part
pain	[peɪn]	an unpleasant feeling that you have in a part of your body, because of illness or an injury; *chest/back pain*
patient	[ˈpeɪʃənt]	a person who receives medical treatment from a doctor
pharmacy	[ˈfɑːməsi]	a place where you can get medicines
pill	[pɪl]	a small, solid, round piece of medicine that you swallow; *take a pill*
plaster	[ˈplɑːstə]	a piece of sticky material used for covering small cuts on your body

EXAMPLES

She is recovering from a serious illness.
He was away from work because of illness.
The medicine saved his life.
Where do you feel the pain?

poison	['pɔɪzən]	a substance that harms or kills people if they swallow or touch it
pregnancy	['pregnənsi]	the condition of having a baby or babies developing in your body
prescription	[prɪ'skrɪpʃən]	a piece of paper on which a doctor writes an order for medicine
pulse	[pʌls]	the regular beat of your heart that you can feel when you touch your wrist
scar	[skɑ:]	a mark that is left on the skin by an old wound
scratch	[skrætʃ]	a small cut made by a sharp object
sling	[slɪŋ]	a piece of cloth that you wear around your neck and arm, to hold up your arm when it is broken or injured
sore throat	[sɔ: 'θrəʊt]	a pain in your throat
splinter	['splɪntə]	a thin, sharp piece of wood or glass that has broken off from a larger piece
spoonful	['spu:nfəl]	an amount of food that a spoon holds; *a spoonful of medicine*
stomach-ache	['stʌməkeɪk]	a pain in your stomach
stress	[stres]	an unpleasant feeling of worry caused by difficulties in life; *suffer from stress*
sunburn	['sʌnbɜ:n]	pink sore skin caused by too much time in the sun; *suffer sunburn*
surgery	['sɜ:dʒəri]	a process in which a doctor cuts open a patient's body in order to repair, remove or replace a diseased or damaged part; *knee surgery*; *heart surgery*

EXAMPLES

We keep a record of your weight gain during pregnancy.
Press very gently until you can feel the pulse.
She's got her arm in a sling.
I've got a sore throat.
I've got a splinter in my toe.
I've got a stomach-ache.
I had a terrible stomach-ache.
It will need surgery.

tablet	['tæblət]	a small solid piece of medicine that you swallow; *take a sleeping tablet*
temperature	['temprətʃə]	how hot someone's body is
thermometer	[θə'mɒmɪtə]	an instrument that measures your body's temperature
wheelchair	['wiːltʃeə]	a chair with wheels that you use if you cannot walk very well
wound	[wuːnd]	damage to part of your body caused by a gun or something sharp like a knife; *head wounds*
X-ray	['eksreɪ]	**1** a process in which a picture is taken of the bones or organs inside your body.; *have an X-ray* **2** a picture of the bones or organs inside your body

VERBS

be ill		to not be in good health
be on a diet		to eat special types of food, or eat less food than usual
bleed	[bliːd]	if a part of your body bleeds, you lose blood from it
break	[breɪk]	to make a bone in your body separate into pieces, by hitting it or falling on it
breathe	[briːð]	to take air into your lungs and let it out again
bruise	[bruːz]	to injure a part of your body so that a purple mark appears there
burn	[bɜːn]	if you burn a part of your body, you injure it with something hot

EXAMPLES
The baby's temperature continued to rise.
The wound is healing well.
I was too ill to go to work.
His nose was bleeding heavily.
He's broken his arm.
I've burnt myself.

catch cold/catch a cold		to become ill with a cold
cough	[kɒf]	to suddenly force air out of your throat with a noise
cure	[kjʊə]	to make someone become well again
cut	[kʌt]	if you cut a part of your body, you injure it with something sharp, such as a knife
die	[daɪ]	to stop living
faint	[feɪnt]	to become unconscious for a short time
feel better		to feel less ill than before
feel sick		to feel as if you are going to vomit
get better		to recover from an illness
have a temperature		to have a temperature that is higher than it should be
hurt	[hɜːt]	to damage a part of your body, causing pain
itch	[ɪtʃ]	to have an unpleasant feeling on your skin that makes you want to scratch it
look after someone		to take care of someone who is ill
lose weight		to become thinner
pass out		to become unconscious for a short time
put on weight		to become fatter
rest	[rest]	to spend some time relaxing after doing something tiring
scratch	[skrætʃ]	to rub your fingernails against the skin on a part of your body

---

EXAMPLES
Dry your hair so you don't catch cold.
I cut my finger when I was preparing vegetables.
He is feeling much better today.
The thought of food made him feel sick.
Doctors have said that he may not get better.
I fell over and hurt myself.
Ouch! That hurts!
I put on a lot of weight and my symptoms got worse.

sneeze	[sni:z]	to suddenly take in your breath and then blow it down your nose noisily, for example, because you have a cold
take someone's temperature		to use a thermometer to measure the temperature of someone's body
treat	[tri:t]	to try to make a patient well again
twist	[twɪst]	to injure a part of your body by turning it too suddenly
vomit	['vɒmɪt]	if you vomit, food and drink comes up from your stomach and out through your mouth

ADJECTIVES

bleeding	['bli:dɪŋ]	losing blood as a result of injury or illness; *bleeding gums*
cold	[kəʊld]	feeling uncomfortable because you are not warm enough
feverish	['fi:vərɪʃ]	feeling ill and very hot
fit	[fɪt]	healthy and strong; *keep fit*
healthy	['helθi]	1 well, and not often ill 2 good for your health
ill	[ɪl]	not in good health
injured	['ɪndʒəd]	if you are injured, part of your body is damaged
in plaster	[ɪn 'plɑ:stə]	with a hard white cover around your leg or arm to protect a broken bone
off sick	[ɒf 'sɪk]	not at work because you are ill
painful	['peɪnfʊl]	causing pain; *painful joints*
pregnant	['pregnənt]	having a baby or babies developing in your body

EXAMPLES

Doctors treated the boy for a minor head wound.
He twisted an ankle playing football.
The headache was accompanied by nausea and vomiting.
People need to exercise to be healthy.
Try to eat a healthy diet.
No one was seriously injured.
I had my arm in plaster for two months.

sick	[sɪk]	ill; *a sick child*
sore	[sɔ:]	painful and uncomfortable
sweaty	['sweti]	covered with sweat (= liquid that forms on your body when you are hot)
tired	[taɪəd]	feeling that you want to rest or sleep
uncomfortable	[ʌn'kʌmftəbəl]	feeling slight pain or discomfort
unconscious	[ʌn'kɒnʃəs]	not awake and not aware of what is happening around you because of illness or a serious injury
wounded	['wu:ndɪd]	injured by an attack

IDIOMS

(as) right as rain	completely well or healthy again after an illness
off-colour	slightly ill; *feel off-colour*
on the mend	recovering from an illness or injury
under the weather	feeling slightly ill

EXAMPLES

I sometimes feel uncomfortable after eating in the evening.
The baby had been poorly but seemed to be on the mend.
I was still feeling a bit under the weather.

hotels

NOUNS

alarm call [əˈlɑːm kɔːl] a telephone call that is intended to wake you up

baggage [ˈbægɪdʒ] same as **luggage**

bar [bɑː] a place where you can buy and drink alcoholic drinks; *the hotel bar*

bath [bɑːθ] a long container that you fill with water and sit or lie in to wash your body; *I'd like a room with a bath.* (In American English, use **bathtub**)

bathroom [ˈbɑːθruːm] a room that contains a bath, a washbasin and often a toilet

bathtub (American English) *see* **bath**

bed and breakfast [bed ənd ˈbrekfəst] **1** a small hotel offering rooms and breakfast, but not lunch or dinner
2 if the price at a hotel includes bed and breakfast, it includes breakfast, but not lunch or dinner

bellhop (American English) *see* **porter**

bill [bɪl] a document that shows how much money you must pay for something

breakfast [ˈbrekfəst] the first meal of the day

chambermaid [ˈtʃeɪmbəmeɪd] a woman who cleans and tidies the bedrooms in a hotel

complaint [kəmˈpleɪnt] when you say that you are not satisfied; *make a complaint*

deposit [dɪˈpɒzɪt] a part of the full price of something that you pay when you agree to buy it

---

EXAMPLES

Could I have an alarm call at 5.30 tomorrow morning, please?
Double rooms cost £180 per night for bed and breakfast.
We stayed in a small bed and breakfast by the sea.
They paid the bill and left the hotel.
What time is breakfast served?
The chambermaid came to clean the room.
No booking will be accepted unless the deposit is paid.

double room	[ˌdʌbəl 'ruːm]	a bedroom for two people
elevator (*American English*)		*see* **lift**
en-suite bathroom	[ɒn ˌswiːt 'bɑːθruːm]	a bathroom that is joined to a bedroom and can only be reached by a door in the bedroom
entrance	['entrəns]	the door or gate that you use to go into a place; *the main entrance*; *the hotel entrance*
facilities	[fə'sɪlɪtiz]	something such as rooms, buildings or pieces of equipment that are used for a particular purpose
fire escape	['faɪə ɪˌskeɪp]	a metal staircase on the outside of a building, which can be used to escape from the building if there is a fire
floor	[flɔː]	one of the levels of a building; *the ground/ first/second/third floor*
foyer	['fɔɪeɪ]	the large area inside the doors of a hotel where people meet or wait
full board	[fʊl 'bɔːd]	if the price at a hotel includes full board, it includes all your meals
guest	[gest]	someone who is staying in a hotel; *hotel guests*
guest house	['gest haʊs]	a small hotel; *stay in a guest house*
half board	[hɑːf 'bɔːd]	if the price at a hotel includes half board, it includes breakfast and evening meal, but not lunch
hotel	[həʊ'tel]	a building where people pay to sleep and eat meals

---

EXAMPLES

Would you like a single or a double room?

Every room has an en-suite bathroom.

The hotel has excellent sports facilities.

All rooms have tea and coffee-making facilities.

Our hotel room was on the third floor.

The price includes six nights' full board.

Prices start from £121 per person for half board.

Ali stayed the night in a small hotel near the harbour.

key	[kiː]	a specially shaped piece of metal that opens or closes a lock
key card	['kiː kɑːd]	a small plastic card that you can use instead of a key to open a door in some hotels
lift	[lɪft]	a machine that carries people or things up and down inside tall buildings; *take/use the lift* (*In American English, use* **elevator**)
luggage	['lʌɡɪdʒ]	the bags that you take with you when you travel
manager	['mænɪdʒə]	a person who controls all or part of a business or organization; *a hotel manager*
minibar	['mɪnibɑː]	a small fridge containing drinks in a hotel room
passport	['pɑːspɔːt]	an official document that you have to show when you enter or leave a country
porter	['pɔːtə]	a person whose job is to carry people's luggage (*In American English, use* **bellhop**)
price	[praɪs]	the amount of money that you have to pay for something
rate	[reɪt]	the amount of money that goods or services cost
reception	[rɪ'sepʃən]	the desk in a hotel that you go to when you first arrive
receptionist	[rɪ'sepʃənɪst]	in a hotel, a person whose job is to answer the telephone and deal with guests
restaurant	['restərɒnt]	a place where you can buy and eat a meal; *the hotel restaurant*
room	[ruːm]	a separate area inside a building that has its own walls

EXAMPLES

Do you have any luggage?
Is that price inclusive of VAT?
The hotel offers a special weekend rate.
I checked in at reception.
I'd prefer a room overlooking the sea.

room number	['ru:m ˌnʌmbə]	the number given to a bedroom in a hotel
room service	['ru:m ˌsɜ:vɪs]	in a hotel, a service that provides meals or drinks for guests in their room; *order room service*
safe	[seɪf]	a strong metal box with a lock, where you keep money or other valuable things
single room	[ˌsɪŋgəl 'ru:m]	a room for one person
stay	[steɪ]	a period of living in a place for a short time
suitcase	['su:tkeɪs]	a case for carrying your clothes when you are travelling
swimming pool	['swɪmɪŋ pu:l]	a large hole filled with water that people can swim in; *the hotel swimming pool*
tip	[tɪp]	money that you give someone to thank them for a job they have done for you
twin room	[twɪn 'ru:m]	a room containing two single beds
view	[vju:]	everything that you can see from a place
youth hostel	['ju:θ ˌhɒstəl]	a cheap place where people can stay when they are travelling

VERBS

book	[bʊk]	to arrange to stay in a hotel room
make a reservation		to make an arrangement for a room in a hotel to be kept for you
stay	[steɪ]	to live somewhere for a short time
tip	[tɪp]	to give someone some money to thank them for a job they have done for you

EXAMPLES

You are advised to deposit valuables in the hotel safe.
Please contact the hotel reception if you have any problems during your stay.
He handed the bellboy a tip.
From our hotel room we had a spectacular view of the sea.
I'd like to book a room.
Samir made a reservation for two rooms at the hotel.
Wolfgang stayed at The Park Hotel, Milan.
Anna tipped the porter.

ADJECTIVES

accessible	[æk'sesɪbəl]	easy for people to reach or enter
luxury	['lʌkʃəri]	comfortable, beautiful and expensive; *a luxury hotel*
three-/four-/five- etc. star		used for talking about the quality of a hotel, which is indicated by a number of star-shaped symbols

PHRASES

Do not disturb	if a sign on a hotel room door says 'Do not disturb', it means that the person inside does not want to be interrupted
Vacancies	if a sign outside a hotel says 'Vacancies', it means that there are some rooms available

EXAMPLES
The hotel is wheelchair accessible.
They own a three-star hotel.

houses and homes

NOUNS

accommodation [əˌkɒməˈdeɪʃən] buildings or rooms where people live or stay; *rented accommodation*

address [əˈdres] the number of the building, the name of the street, and the town or city where you live or work; *postal address*

apartment *(mainly American English)* see **flat**

apartment block *(mainly American English)* see **block of flats**

attic [ˈætɪk] a room at the top of a house, just under the roof

balcony [ˈbælkəni] a place where you can stand or sit on the outside of a building, above the ground

basement [ˈbeɪsmənt] a part of a building below ground level; *a basement flat*

bathroom [ˈbɑːθruːm] a room that contains a bath, a washbasin and often a toilet

bedroom [ˈbedruːm] a room that is used for sleeping in

block of flats [blɒk əv ˈflæts] a residential building consisting of several flats (*In American English, use* **apartment block**)

building [ˈbɪldɪŋ] a structure that has a roof and walls; *an office building*

ceiling [ˈsiːlɪŋ] the top inside part of a room; *low/high ceilings*

cellar [ˈselə] a room under a building; *a wine cellar*

chimney [ˈtʃɪmni] a pipe above a fire that lets the smoke travel up and out of the building

conservatory [kənˈsɜːvətri] a glass room built onto a house

cottage [ˈkɒtɪdʒ] a small house, usually in the country

detached house [dɪˈtætʃt ˌhaʊs] a house that is not joined to any other building

dining room [ˈdaɪnɪŋ ruːm] the room in a house where people have their meals

---

EXAMPLES

Please give your full name and address.

'What's your address?' — 'It's 24 Cherry Road, Cambridge, CB1 5AW'.

door	[dɔː]	a piece of wood, glass or metal that fills an entrance
doorbell	['dɔːbel]	a button next to a door that makes a noise when you press it to tell the people inside that you are there
doorstep	['dɔːstep]	a step in front of a door outside a building
driveway	['draɪvweɪ]	a small road that leads from the street to the front of a building
elevator (American English)		see **lift**
entrance	['entrəns]	the door or gate where you go into a place
estate agent	[ɪ'steɪt ˌeɪdʒənt]	someone who works for a company selling houses and land (In American English, use **realtor**)
flat	[flæt]	a set of rooms for living in, usually on one floor and part of a larger building (In American English, use **apartment**)
floor	[flɔː]	**1** the part of a room that you walk on **2** all the rooms that are on a particular level of a building; the ground/first/second floor
front door	[frʌnt 'dɔː]	the main door of a house or other building, that is usually in the wall that faces a street
garage	['gærɑːʒ]	a building where you keep a car
garden	['gɑːdən]	the part of the land by your house where you grow flowers and vegetables; the front/back garden (In American English, use **yard**)
gate	[geɪt]	a type of door that you use to enter the area around a building
hall	[hɔːl]	the area inside the main door of a house that leads to other rooms
home	[həʊm]	the house or flat where someone lives

EXAMPLES

I knocked at the front door, but there was no answer.
The doorbell rang.
I went and sat on the doorstep.
They are renting a two-bedroom flat.
There were no seats, so we sat on the floor.
The bathroom was on the second floor.
They have a lovely home in the Scottish countryside.

house	[haʊs]	a building where people live
kitchen	[ˈkɪtʃɪn]	a room that is used for cooking
landing	[ˈlændɪŋ]	the flat area at the top of the stairs in a house
landlady	[ˈlændleɪdi]	a woman who owns a building and allows people to live there in return for rent
landlord	[ˈlændlɔːd]	a man who owns a building and allows people to live there in return for rent
lavatory	[ˈlævətri]	[FORMAL] a toilet
lift	[lɪft]	a machine that carries people or things up and down inside tall buildings (*In American English, use* **elevator**)
living room	[ˈlɪvɪŋ ruːm]	a room where people sit together and talk or watch television
owner	[ˈəʊnə]	the person that something belongs to; *property owners*
patio	[ˈpætiəʊ]	a flat area next to a house, where people can sit and relax or eat
porch	[pɔːtʃ]	a covered area with a roof and sometimes walls at the entrance to a building
property	[ˈprɒpəti]	a building and the land around it; *buy/sell property*; *private property*
realtor (*American English*)		*see* **estate agent**
rent	[rent]	money that you pay to live in a house or flat that is owned by someone else
roof	[ruːf]	the top surface that covers a building
room	[ruːm]	a separate area inside a building that has its own walls
semi-detached house	[semidɪˈtætʃt ˌhaʊs]	a house that is joined to another house on one side by a shared wall
shutters	[ˈʃʌtəz]	wooden or metal covers fitted on the outside of a window; *open/close the shutters*

EXAMPLES

I live in a three-bedroom house.
I'm having a party at my house tomorrow night.
We have meals on the patio in the summer.
She worked hard to pay the rent on the flat.

sitting room	['sɪtɪŋ ruːm]	same as **living room**
spare room	[speə 'ruːm]	a bedroom that is kept especially for visitors to sleep in
stairs	[steəz]	a set of steps inside a building that go from one level to another; *climb the stairs*
step	[step]	a raised flat surface that you put your feet on in order to walk up or down to a different level; *go up/down the steps*
storey	['stɔːri]	one of the different levels of a building; *the top storey*
study	['stʌdi]	a room in a house that is used for reading, writing and studying
tenant	['tenənt]	someone who pays money to use a house
terraced house	[terɪst 'haʊs]	one of a row of houses that are joined together by both of their side walls
wall	[wɔːl]	one of the sides of a building or a room
window	['wɪndəʊ]	a space in the wall of a building that has glass in it
yard (American English)		*see* **garden**

VERBS

decorate	['dekəreɪt]	to put paint or paper on the walls of a room
live	[lɪv]	to have your home in a particular place
move house		to change the place where you live
own	[əʊn]	to have something that belongs to you
rent	[rent]	to pay the owner of a house or flat in order to be able to live in it yourself

EXAMPLES

Houses must not be more than two storeys high.
They were decorating Claude's bedroom.
Where do you live?
When Dad got a new job, we had to move house.
He owns a flat in Paris.
She rents a house with three other women.

ADJECTIVES

downstairs	['daʊnsteəz]	on a lower floor of a building; *a downstairs toilet*
furnished	['fɜːnɪʃt]	containing furniture; *a furnished flat*; *elegantly furnished rooms*
homeless	['həʊmləs]	having nowhere to live; *homeless people*
residential	[ˌrezɪ'denʃəl]	containing houses rather than offices or shops; *a residential area*
upstairs	['ʌpsteəz]	on a higher floor of a building; *an upstairs window*

ADVERBS

at home	[ət 'həʊm]	in the place where you live
downstairs	[daʊn'steəz]	on or to a lower floor of a building
home	[həʊm]	in or to the house or flat where you live
next door	[nekst 'dɔː]	in the next room or building
upstairs	[ʌp'steəz]	on or to a higher floor of a building

PHRASES

Make yourself at home	used for telling someone that you want them to relax and feel comfortable in your home
There's no place like home.	used for saying that your home is the place where you feel happiest and most comfortable

EXAMPLES

At least 100,000 people were left homeless by the earthquake.
She wasn't at home.
Nobody lives downstairs.
She went downstairs to the kitchen.
She wasn't feeling well and she wanted to go home.
Hi Mum! I'm home!
Who lives next door?
The children are upstairs.
He went upstairs and changed his clothes.

in the home

FURNITURE

armchair	[ˈɑːmtʃeə]	a big comfortable chair that supports your arms
bed	[bed]	a piece of furniture that you lie on when you sleep; *a double/single bed*
bookcase	[ˈbʊkkeɪs]	a piece of furniture with shelves that you keep books on
chair	[tʃeə]	a piece of furniture for one person to sit on, with a back and four legs
chest of drawers	[tʃest əv ˈdrɔːəz]	a piece of furniture with drawers in which you keep clothes
cot	[kɒt]	a bed for a baby; *a travel cot*
cupboard	[ˈkʌbəd]	a piece of furniture with doors and shelves for storing things like food or dishes; *a kitchen cupboard*
desk	[desk]	a table that you sit at to write or work
drawer	[ˈdrɔːə]	the part of a desk, for example, that you can pull out and put things in; *open/close a drawer*; *a kitchen drawer*; *a desk drawer*
fireplace	[ˈfaɪəpleɪs]	the place in a room where you can light a fire
furniture	[ˈfɜːnɪtʃə]	large objects in a room such as tables, chairs or beds; *a piece of furniture*
lampshade	[ˈlæmpʃeɪd]	a covering that is fitted round an electric light bulb
mattress	[ˈmætrəs]	the thick, soft part of a bed that you lie on
shelf	[ʃelf]	a long flat piece of wood on a wall or in a cupboard that you can keep things on
sofa	[ˈsəʊfə]	a long, comfortable seat with a back, that two or three people can sit on
stool	[stuːl]	a seat with legs and no support for your arms or back

EXAMPLES

We went to bed at about 10 p.m.
Ana was already in bed.
Francine rearranged all the furniture.

table	['teɪbəl]	a piece of furniture with a flat top that you put things on; *a wooden table*; *a kitchen table*; *a dining table*
wardrobe	['wɔːdrəʊb]	a cupboard where you hang your clothes

APPLIANCES

appliance	[ə'plaɪəns]	a machine that you use to do a job in your home; *a kitchen appliance*
computer	[kəm'pjuːtə]	an electronic machine that can store and deal with large amounts of information; *computer software*
cooker	['kʊkə]	a piece of kitchen equipment that is used for cooking food; *an electric cooker*; *a gas cooker*
dishwasher	['dɪʃwɒʃə]	a machine that washes and dries dishes; *load/unload the dishwasher*
freezer	['friːzə]	a large container used for freezing food
fridge	[frɪdʒ]	a large container that is used for keeping food cool and fresh
hairdryer	['heədraɪə]	a machine that you use to dry your hair
heater	['hiːtə]	a piece of equipment that is used for making a room warm; *an electric heater*; *a gas heater*
iron	['aɪən]	a piece of electrical equipment with a flat metal base that you heat and move over clothes to make them smooth
ironing board	['aɪənɪŋ bɔːd]	a long board covered with cloth on which you iron clothes
kettle	['ketəl]	a metal container with a lid and a handle, that you use for boiling water; *put the kettle on*
lamp	[læmp]	a light that works using electricity or by burning oil or gas; *a bedside lamp*

EXAMPLES
He shut the dishwasher and switched it on.
James put the kettle on for a cup of tea.
He switched on the lamp.

in the home

microwave oven	['maɪkrəuweɪv ˌʌvən]	an oven that cooks food very quickly using electric waves
oven	['ʌvən]	a piece of equipment for cooking that is like a large metal box with a door
phone	[fəʊn]	same as **telephone**; *The phone rang.*; *make a phone call*; *a phone number*
radio	['reɪdiəʊ]	a piece of equipment that you use in order to listen to radio programmes; *listen to the radio*; *a radio programme*
stereo	['steriəʊ]	a machine that plays music, with two parts (= speakers) that the sound comes from
telephone	['telɪˌfəʊn]	a piece of equipment that you use for speaking to someone who is in another place
television	['telɪˌvɪʒən]	a piece of electrical equipment with a screen on which you watch moving pictures with sound; *a television programme*; *a television show*
tumble-dryer	[ˌtʌmbəl 'draɪə]	a machine that uses hot air to dry clothes
vacuum cleaner	['vækjuːm ˌkliːnə]	an electric machine that sucks up dust and dirt from carpets
washing machine	['wɒʃɪŋ məˌʃiːn]	a machine that you use for washing clothes

OTHER THINGS IN THE HOME

bath	[bɑːθ]	a long container that you fill with water and sit or lie in to wash your body; *a hot bath* (*In American English, use* **bathtub**)
bathtub (*American English*)		*see* **bath**
bin	[bɪn]	a container that you put rubbish in

EXAMPLES
Put the potatoes in the oven for thirty minutes.
He never answers his phone.
Can I use your phone?
She's always on the phone.
What's on television tonight?
I took the letter and threw it in the bin.

blanket	['blæŋkɪt]	a large, thick piece of cloth that you put on a bed to keep you warm
blinds	[blaɪndz]	pieces of cloth or other material that you can pull down over a window to cover it; *close/open the blinds*
brush	[brʌʃ]	an object with a lot of bristles or hairs attached to it that you use for cleaning things
bucket	['bʌkɪt]	a round metal or plastic container with a handle, used for holding water; *a plastic bucket*
carpet	['kɑːpɪt]	a thick, soft covering for the floor; *a patterned carpet*
central heating	[ˌsentrəl 'hiːtɪŋ]	a heating system in which water or air is heated and passed round a building through pipes and radiators; *gas central heating*
clock	[klɒk]	an object that shows you what time it is
curtain	['kɜːtən]	a piece of material that hangs from the top of a window to cover it at night; *open/close the curtains*
cushion	['kʊʃən]	a bag of soft material that you put on a seat to make it more comfortable
dust	[dʌst]	a fine powder of dry earth or dirt
duster	['dʌstə]	a cloth that you use for removing dust from furniture
duvet	['duːveɪ]	a thick warm cover for a bed
key	[kiː]	a specially shaped piece of metal that opens or closes a lock; *a door key*
laundry	['lɔːndri]	**1** clothes and other things that you are going to wash; *dirty laundry* **2** clothes and other things that you have just washed; *clean laundry*

EXAMPLES

The blinds were drawn to shut out the sun.

He filled the bucket with water.

She could hear the hall clock ticking.

She closed her bedroom curtains.

Fold the laundry neatly after washing and drying it.

laundry liquid	['lɔːndri ˌlɪkwɪd]	liquid soap for washing laundry
light	[laɪt]	something such as an electric lamp that produces light; *switch on/off the light*
light bulb	['laɪt bʌlb]	the round glass part of an electric light that light shines from
lock	[lɒk]	the part of a door or a container that you use to make sure that no-one can open it. You can open a lock with a key.
mirror	['mɪrə]	a flat piece of special glass that you can see yourself in; *look in the mirror*; *a full-length mirror*
ornament	['ɔːnəmənt]	an attractive object that you use to decorate your home
pillow	['pɪləʊ]	a soft object that you rest your head on when you are in bed
plug	[plʌg]	**1** the plastic object with metal pins that connects a piece of electrical equipment to the electricity supply **2** a round object that you use to block the hole in a bath or a sink
radiator	['reɪdieɪtə]	a metal object that is full of hot water or steam, and is used for heating a room
rubbish	['rʌbɪʃ]	things you do not want any more (*In American English, use* **trash**)
rug	[rʌg]	a piece of thick cloth that you put on a small area of a floor
sheet	[ʃiːt]	a large piece of cloth that you sleep on or cover yourself with in bed
shower	['ʃaʊə]	a piece of equipment that covers you with water when you stand under it to wash yourself

EXAMPLES

She turned on all the lights and drew the curtains.
I turned the key in the lock.
She put the plug in and turned on the taps.

sink	[sɪŋk]	a large fixed container in a kitchen or a bathroom that you can fill with water; *a kitchen sink; a bathroom sink*
soap	[səʊp]	a substance that you use with water for washing yourself or for washing clothes; *Wash with soap and water.*
socket	['sɒkɪt]	a small hole in a wall where you can connect electrical equipment to the power supply
switch	[swɪtʃ]	a small control for turning electricity on or off
tablecloth	['teɪbəlklɒθ]	a cloth that you use to cover a table
tap	[tæp]	an object that controls the flow of a liquid or a gas from a pipe; *turn on/off a tap*
tea towel	['tiː ˌtaʊəl]	a cloth that you use to dry dishes after they have been washed
toilet	['tɔɪlət]	a large bowl with a seat that you use when you want to get rid of waste from your body; *go to the toilet*
toothpaste	['tuːθpeɪst]	a thick substance that you put on a toothbrush and use for cleaning your teeth
toy	[tɔɪ]	an object that children play with
trash (*American English*)		*see* **rubbish**
tray	[treɪ]	a flat piece of wood, plastic or metal that is used for carrying and serving food and drinks
vase	[vɑːz]	a container that is used for holding flowers
wallpaper	['wɔːlpeɪpə]	coloured or patterned paper that is used for decorating the walls of rooms
washing-up liquid	[ˌwɒʃɪŋˈʌp ˌlɪkwɪd]	liquid soap for cleaning dirty dishes

VERBS

clean	[kliːn]	to remove the dirt from something; *clean the windows*

EXAMPLES

I turned the bath taps on.
He brought soapy water and brushes to clean the floor.

in the home

do housework	to do work in your home such as cleaning, washing and ironing
do the laundry	to wash dirty clothes, towels, etc.
draw the curtains	to pull the curtains across a window in order to open or close them
dust [dʌst]	to remove dust from furniture with a cloth
have/take a bath	to sit or lie in a bath filled with water to wash your body
have/take a shower	to wash yourself by standing under the water that comes from a shower
iron [ˈaɪən]	to make clothes smooth using an iron; *an ironed shirt*
lock [lɒk]	to close a door or a container with a key
plug something in	to connect a piece of electrical equipment to the electricity supply
sweep [swiːp]	to push dirt away from an area using a brush with a long handle; *sweep the floor*
switch something off	to stop electrical equipment from working by operating a switch
switch something on	to make electrical equipment start working by operating a switch
throw something in the bin	to get rid of something that you do not want by putting it in the bin
tidy things away	to organize a place by putting things in their proper places
vacuum [ˈvækjuːm]	to clean a room or a surface using a piece of electrical equipment that sucks up dirt (called a vacuum cleaner)

EXAMPLES
Men are doing more housework nowadays.
She got out of bed and drew the curtains.
They had forgotten to lock the front door.
She plugged in the telephone.
She switched off the television.
He switched on the TV.
It's time for the children to tidy away their toys.

industry

assembly line	[əˈsembli laɪn]	an arrangement of workers and machines in a factory where a product passes from one worker to another until it is finished
banking	[ˈbæŋkɪŋ]	the business activity of banks and similar institutions
call centre	[ˈkɔːl ˌsentə]	an office where people work answering or making telephone calls for a company
catering	[ˈkeɪtərɪŋ]	the activity or business of providing food for people; *a catering business*
clothing industry	[ˈkləʊðɪŋ ˌɪndəstri]	an industry that makes and sells clothes
construction	[kənˈstrʌkʃən]	the business of building things such as houses, roads and bridges
engineering	[ˌendʒɪˈnɪərɪŋ]	the business of designing and constructing machines or structures such as roads and bridges
export	[ˈekspɔːt]	a product that one country sells to another country
factory	[ˈfæktri]	a large building where people use machines to make goods
farming	[ˈfɑːmɪŋ]	the business of growing crops or keeping animals on a farm
film industry	[ˈfɪlm ˌɪndəstri]	an industry that produces and sells films
fishing	[ˈfɪʃɪŋ]	the business of catching fish
forestry	[ˈfɒrɪstri]	the science of growing trees in forests
goods	[ɡʊdz]	things that you can buy or sell

EXAMPLES

He works on an assembly line.

She wants a career in banking.

Italy's clothing industry is one of the most successful in the world.

Jason was an engineer with a large construction company.

Ghana's main export is cocoa.

They invested £1 million in the British film industry.

Money can be exchanged for goods or services.

industry

heavy industry	[ˌhevi ˈɪndəstri]	industry that uses large machines to produce raw materials or to make large objects
hospitality industry	[hɒspɪˈtælɪti ˌɪndəstri]	an industry that provides food, drink and entertainment
import	[ˈɪmpɔːt]	a product bought from another country for use in your own country
industrial sector	[ɪnˈdʌstriəl ˌsektə]	the part of a country's economy that produces things from raw materials
industry	[ˈɪndəstri]	**1** the work of making things in factories; *Industry is growing.* **2** all the people and activities involved in making a particular product or providing a particular service; *the Scottish tourist industry*
insurance industry	[ɪnˈʃʊərəns ˌɪndəstri]	an industry that provides insurance (= money given to someone if something bad happens to them, in return for regular payments)
invention	[ɪnˈvenʃən]	**1** something that someone has invented; *a new invention* **2** an occasion when something is invented; *the invention of the telephone*
leisure industry	[ˈleʒə ˌɪndəstri]	an industry that provides activities for people to do when they are not working
light industry	[ˌlaɪt ˈɪndəstri]	industry in which only small items are made, for example household goods and clothes
machinery	[məˈʃiːnəri]	large pieces of electrical equipment that do a particular job

EXAMPLES

John works in the hospitality industry.

Farmers are angry about cheap imports of grain.

Antigua has a small industrial sector producing clothing and electronic equipment.

The insurance industry lost billions of pounds because of the floods.

manufacturer	[ˌmænjʊ 'fæktʃərə]	a company that makes large amounts of things
manufacturing	[ˌmænjʊ 'fæktʃərɪŋ]	the business of making things in factories
mass production	[ˌmæs prə'dʌkʃən]	the production of something in large quantities, usually using machinery
mining	['maɪnɪŋ]	the business of getting valuable substances such as coal and gold from the ground; *coal mining*
oil drilling	['ɔɪl drɪlɪŋ]	the business of getting oil from under the ground by making deep holes in the bottom of the sea
output	['aʊtpʊt]	the amount that a person or a thing produces
plant	[plɑːnt]	**1** a factory; *a clothes manufacturing plant* **2** a place where power is produced; *a nuclear power plant*
private sector	[ˌpraɪvɪt 'sektə]	the part of a country's economy that the government does not control or own
processing	['prəʊsesɪŋ]	the business of preparing raw materials before they are sold
product	['prɒdʌkt]	something that you make or grow in order to sell it
production	[prə'dʌkʃən]	**1** the process of making or growing something in large amounts; *the production of oil* **2** the quantity of goods that you make or grow; *the volume of production*
production line	[prə'dʌkʃən ˌlaɪn]	an arrangement of machines in a factory where the products pass from one machine to another until they are finished
public sector	[ˌpʌblɪk 'sektə]	the part of a country's economy that the government controls or gives money to

EXAMPLES

He works for the world's largest doll manufacturer.

During the 1980s, 300,000 workers in the manufacturing industry lost their jobs.

This equipment allows the mass production of baby food.

Industry output has decreased.

raw materials	[ˌrɔːməˈtɪəriəlz]	substances that have not been processed
research and development	[rɪˌsɜːtʃ ənd dɪˈveləpmənt]	the activity of improving products and making new products
retailing	[ˈriːteɪlɪŋ]	the activity of selling goods directly to the public
service	[ˈsɜːvɪs]	something that the public needs, such as transport, hospitals or energy supplies
service sector	[ˈsɜːvɪs ˌsektə]	the part of a country's economy that provide services
shipping	[ˈʃɪpɪŋ]	the business of transporting goods, especially by ship; *the international shipping industry*
supplier	[səˈplaɪə]	a company that sells something such as goods or equipment to customers
textile industry	[ˈtekstaɪl ˌɪndəstri]	an industry that makes cloth
tourism	[ˈtʊərɪzəm]	the business of providing hotels, restaurants, and activities for people who are on holiday
trade	[treɪd]	the activity of buying and selling goods
transportation	[ˌtrænspɔːˈteɪʃən]	the activity of taking goods or people somewhere in a vehicle

VERBS

assemble	[əˈsembəl]	to fit the different parts of something together
deliver	[dɪˈlɪvə]	to take something to a particular place
export	[ɪkˈspɔːt]	to sell products to another country

EXAMPLES

We import raw materials and export industrial products.
We are campaigning for better nursery and school services.
They are one of the U.K.'s biggest food suppliers.
Another 75,000 jobs will be lost in the textile industry.
Tourism is very important for the Spanish economy.
Workers were assembling aeroplanes.
Canada exports beef to the U.S.

import	[ɪmˈpɔːt]	to buy goods from another country for use in your own country
invent	[ɪnˈvent]	to be the first person to think of something or to make it
manufacture	[ˌmænjʊ ˈfæktʃə]	to make something in a factory
produce	[prəˈdjuːs]	to make or grow something
provide	[prəˈvaɪd]	to make available something that people need or want
ship	[ʃɪp]	to send goods somewhere
subcontract	[sʌbkənˈtrækt]	to pay another company to do part of the work that you have been employed to do; *subcontract work to someone*
supply	[səˈplaɪ]	to give someone an amount of something

ADJECTIVES

corporate	[ˈkɔːprət]	relating to large companies; *the corporate sector*
domestic	[dəˈmestɪk]	happening or existing within one particular country
economic	[ˌiːkəˈnɒmɪk]	relating to the organization of the money and industry of a country
financial	[faɪˈnænʃəl]	relating to money
foreign	[ˈfɒrɪn]	coming from a country that is not your own; *a foreign import*
industrial	[ɪnˈdʌstriəl]	**1** relating to industry; *industrial machinery* **2** used to describe a city or a country in which industry is very important; *an industrial country*

EXAMPLES
The U.S. imports over half of its oil.
The company produces about 2.3 billion tons of steel a year.
We provide a wide range of products and services.
They supply many cities with gas.
We need to increase domestic oil production.

international	[ˌɪntəˈnæʃənəl]	involving different countries; *international trade*
modern	[ˈmɒdən]	new, or relating to the present time
private	[ˈpraɪvɪt]	not owned by the government; *a private company*
public	[ˈpʌblɪk]	owned or controlled by the government; *a public company*

jobs and careers

accountant [ə'kaʊntənt] someone whose job is to keep financial records

architect ['ɑːkɪtekt] someone whose job is to design buildings

attorney (*American English*) *see* **lawyer**

builder ['bɪldə] someone whose job is to build or repair houses and other buildings

businessman ['bɪznɪsmən] a man who works in business
(PL) **businessmen** ['bɪznɪsmən]

businesswoman ['bɪznɪswʊmən] a woman who works in business
(PL) **businesswomen** ['bɪznɪswɪmɪn]

carer ['keərə] someone whose job is to look after another person

carpenter ['kɑːpɪntə] someone whose job is to make and repair wooden things

cashier [kæ'ʃɪə] someone whose job is to take customers' money in shops or banks

chef [ʃef] someone whose job is to cook in a restaurant

cleaner ['kliːnə] someone whose job is to clean the rooms and furniture inside a building

clerk [klɑːk] someone whose job is to work with numbers or documents in an office

cook [kʊk] someone who prepares and cooks food

decorator ['dekəreɪtə] someone whose job is to paint houses and put wallpaper on walls

dentist ['dentɪst] someone whose job is to examine and treat people's teeth

doctor ['dɒktə] someone whose job is to treat people who are ill or injured

editor ['edɪtə] someone whose job is to check and correct texts

electrician [ɪlek'trɪʃən, ˌelek-] someone whose job is to repair electrical equipment

EXAMPLES
McDowell won the Businesswoman of the Year award in 2011.
Henry Harris is head chef at The Fifth Floor Restaurant in London.
She is a doctor.

engineer	[ˌendʒɪˈnɪə]	someone who designs, builds and repairs machines, or structures such as roads, railways and bridges
factory worker	[ˈfæktri wɜːkə]	someone who works in a factory (= a large building where machines are used to make things)
farmer	[ˈfɑːmə]	someone who owns or works on a farm
firefighter	[ˈfaɪəfaɪtə]	someone whose job is to put out fires
hairdresser	[ˈheədresə]	someone whose job is to cut and style people's hair
housewife (PL) **housewives**	[ˈhaʊswaɪf] [ˈhaʊswaɪvz]	a woman who does not have a paid job, but spends most of her time looking after her house and family
journalist	[ˈdʒɜːnəlɪst]	someone whose job is to write about news stories for newspapers, magazines, television or radio
judge	[dʒʌdʒ]	the person in a court of law who decides how criminals should be punished
lawyer	[ˈlɔɪə]	someone whose job is to advise people about the law and to represent them in court (*In American English, use* **attorney**)
lecturer	[ˈlektʃərə]	a teacher at a university or college
librarian	[laɪˈbreəriən]	someone who works in a library (= a place where people can borrow books)
mailman, (PL) **mailmen** (*American English*)		*see* **postman**
manager	[ˈmænɪdʒə]	someone who controls all or part of a business or organization
mechanic	[mɪˈkænɪk]	someone whose job is to repair machines and engines, especially car engines
miner	[ˈmaɪnə]	someone whose job is to work underground to obtain materials such as coal
monk	[mʌŋk]	a member of a group of religious men who live together in a special building
musician	[mjuːˈzɪʃən]	someone who plays a musical instrument
nanny	[ˈnæni]	someone whose job is to look after children in the children's own home

nun	[nʌn]	a member of a group of religious women who often live together in a special building
nurse	[nɜːs]	someone whose job is to care for people who are ill or injured
optician	[ɒpˈtɪʃən]	someone whose job is to make and sell glasses
painter	[ˈpeɪntə]	**1** someone whose job is to paint walls, doors or other parts of buildings **2** an artist who paints pictures
pilot	[ˈpaɪlət]	someone whose job is to control an aircraft
plumber	[ˈplʌmə]	someone whose job is to put in and repair things like water and gas pipes, toilets and baths
police officer	[pəˈliːs ˈɒfɪsə]	a member of the police force
porter	[ˈpɔːtə]	someone whose job is to carry things, for example, people's luggage
postman (PL) **postmen**	[ˈpəʊstmən] [ˈpəʊstmən]	a man who collects and delivers letters and packages (In American English, use **mailman**)
priest	[priːst]	someone who has religious duties in a place where people worship
programmer	[ˈprəʊɡræmə]	someone whose job is to write programs for computers
publisher	[ˈpʌblɪʃə]	someone whose job is to prepare and print copies of books, newspapers or magazines
rabbi	[ˈræbaɪ]	a Jewish religious leader
receptionist	[rɪˈsepʃənɪst]	someone in a hotel or a large building whose job is to answer the telephone and deal with visitors
sales clerk (American English)		see **shop assistant**
sales representative [ˈseɪlz ˌreprɪˈzentətɪv]		someone whose job is to travel around an area and sell the goods of a particular company
salesman (PL) **salesmen**	[ˈseɪlzmən] [ˈseɪlzmən]	a man whose job is to sell things
saleswoman (PL) **saleswomen**	[ˈseɪlzwʊmən] [ˈseɪlzwɪmɪn]	a woman whose job is to sell things

secretary	['sekrətri]	someone whose job is to type letters, answer the telephone, and do other office work
shop assistant	[ˌʃɒp ə'sɪstənt]	someone who works in a shop selling things to customers (*In American English, use* **sales clerk**)
social worker	['səʊʃəl ˌwɜːkə]	someone whose job is to give help and advice to people who have serious family problems or financial problems
soldier	['səʊldʒə]	a member of an army
solicitor	[sə'lɪsɪtə]	a lawyer who gives legal advice, prepares legal documents, and arranges for people to buy and sell land
surgeon	['sɜːdʒən]	a doctor who is specially trained to perform operations
surveyor	[sə'veɪjə]	someone whose job is to examine the condition of a house, usually in order to give information to people who want to buy the house
teacher	['tiːtʃə]	someone whose job is to teach (= give lessons on a subject), usually in a school
technician	[tek'nɪʃən]	someone who works with scientific or medical equipment or machines
vet	[vet]	someone whose job is to treat ill or injured animals
waiter	['weɪtə]	a man whose job is to serve food in a restaurant
waitress	['weɪtrəs]	a woman whose job is to serve food in a restaurant
writer	['raɪtə]	someone whose job is to write books, stories or articles

EXAMPLE
I was a teacher for 20 years.

law

NOUNS

accident	['æksɪdənt]	an occasion when something bad happens to a person by chance, sometimes causing injury or death
assault	[ə'sɔːlt]	a physical attack on a person
attorney *(American English)*		*see* **lawyer**
burglar	['bɜːglə]	someone who enters a building by force in order to steal things
burglary	['bɜːgləri]	the crime of entering a building by force and stealing things
charge	[tʃɑːdʒ]	a formal accusation that someone has committed a crime
corpse	[kɔːps]	a dead body
court	[kɔːt]	a place where a judge and a jury decide if someone has done something wrong (*In American English, use* **courthouse**)
courthouse *(American English)*		*see* **court**
crime	[kraɪm]	an illegal act; *commit a crime*
criminal	['krɪmɪnəl]	someone who does something illegal
drug	[drʌg]	a type of illegal substance that some people take because they enjoy its effects
drug dealer	[ˌdrʌg 'diːlə]	someone who sells illegal drugs
evidence	['evɪdəns]	information that is used in a court in order to try to show that something really happened
fault	[fɔːlt]	if something bad is your fault, you made it happen
fine	[faɪn]	money that someone has to pay because they have done something wrong; *pay a fine*

EXAMPLES

The police say the man's death was an accident.
At the police station, he was charged with assault.
They faced charges of murder.
She will appear in court later this month.
There is no evidence that he stole the money.
It's not my fault.
He got a fine for speeding.
She got a 100-euro fine.

fraud	[frɔːd]	the crime of getting money by not telling the truth
gang	[gæŋ]	an organized group of criminals
gun	[gʌn]	a weapon that shoots bullets
homicide (mainly American English)		*see* **murder**
hostage	['hɒstɪdʒ]	someone who is kept as a prisoner by someone who refuses to let them go until they get what they want
identity	[aɪ'dentɪti]	who you are
jail	[dʒeɪl]	same as **prison**
judge	[dʒʌdʒ]	the person in a court who decides how criminals should be punished
jury	['dʒʊəri]	the group of people in a court who listen to the facts about a crime and decide if a person is guilty or not
law	[lɔː]	**1** a system of rules that a society or government develops to deal with things like crime; *break the law* **2** one of the rules in a system of law; *a new law*
lawyer	['lɔɪə]	someone whose job is to advise people about the law and to represent them in court (*In American English, use* **attorney**)
murder	['mɜːdə]	the crime of deliberately killing a person (*In American English, use* **homicide**)
murderer	['mɜːdərə]	someone who deliberately kills a person
passport	['pɑːspɔːt]	an official document that you have to show when you enter or leave a country
police	[pə'liːs]	**1** the organization that is responsible for making sure that people obey the law **2** men and women who are members of the police

---

EXAMPLES

He used a different name to hide his identity.
Driving too fast is against the law.
The police are looking for the stolen car.

police officer	[pə'liːs ˌɒfɪsə]	a member of the police force
police station	[pə'liːs ˌsteɪʃən]	the local office of a police force in a particular area
prison	['prɪzən]	a building where criminals are kept as punishment; *send someone to prison*
prisoner	['prɪzənə]	someone who is in prison
proof	[pruːf]	something that shows that something else is true
reward	[rɪ'wɔːd]	something that someone gives you because you have done something good
robbery	['rɒbəri]	the crime of stealing money or property from a place
sentence	['sentəns]	the punishment that a person receives in a law court
shoplifter	['ʃɒplɪftə]	someone who steals money from a shop
solicitor	[sə'lɪsɪtə]	a lawyer who gives legal advice, prepares legal documents, and arranges for people to buy and sell land
spy	[spaɪ]	someone whose job is to find out secret information about another country or organization
statement	['steɪtmənt]	something that you say or write that gives information in a formal way; *make a statement*
suspect	['sʌspekt]	someone who the police think may be guilty of a crime
terrorism	['terəˌrɪzəm]	the use of violence to force a government to do something
terrorist	['terərɪst]	someone who uses violence to achieve their aims
theft	[θeft]	the crime of stealing

EXAMPLES

There wasn't enough proof to charge them.

The firm offered a £10,000 reward for information about the killer.

He was given a four-year sentence.

Three suspects were arrested in connection with the assault.

thief	[θiːf]	someone who steals something from
(PL) **thieves**	[θiːvz]	another person
trial	['traɪəl]	a formal meeting in a court, at which people decide whether someone is guilty of a crime
vandal	['vændəl]	someone who deliberately damages property
victim	['vɪktɪm]	someone who has been hurt or killed
will	[wɪl]	a legal document that says who will receive someone's money when they die
witness	['wɪtnəs]	someone who appears in a court to say what they know about a crime or other event

VERBS

arrest	[ə'rest]	to take someone to a police station, because they may have broken the law
assault	[ə'sɔːlt]	to attack a person physically
break the law		to do something illegal
burglarize (American English)		see **burgle**
burgle	['bɜːgəl]	to enter a building by force and steal things (In American English, use **burglarize**)
charge	[tʃɑːdʒ]	to formally tell someone that they have done something wrong
commit	[kə'mɪt]	to do something illegal; commit a crime; commit murder
confess	[kən'fes]	to admit that you have done something wrong
convict	[kən'vɪkt]	to find someone guilty of a crime in a court

EXAMPLES

He is on trial for murder.
The driver apologised to the victim's family.
Police arrested five young men in connection with the robbery.
Our house was burgled last year.
Police charged Mr Bell with murder.
He confessed to seventeen murders.
He was convicted of manslaughter.

escape	[ɪˈskeɪp]	to manage to get away from a place; *escape from prison*
fine	[faɪn]	to order someone to pay a sum of money because they have done something illegal
forge	[fɔːdʒ]	to make illegal copies of paper money, a document or a painting in order to cheat people
hold something up		to point a gun at someone in a place such as a bank or a shop, in order to get their money; *hold up a bank*
kidnap	[ˈkɪdnæp]	to take someone away by force and keep them as a prisoner, often until their friends or family pay a ransom (= a large amount of money)
mug	[mʌg]	to attack someone and steal their money
murder	[ˈmɜːdə]	to kill someone deliberately
prove	[pruːv]	to show that something is true
rape	[reɪp]	to force someone to have sex when they do not want to
rob	[rɒb]	to steal money or property from someone
sentence	[ˈsentəns]	to say in court what a person's punishment will be
solve	[sɒlv]	to find out who committed a crime; *solve a crime*
steal	[stiːl]	to take something from someone without their permission
suspect	[səˈspekt]	to believe that someone probably did something wrong
vandalize	[ˈvændəˌlaɪz]	to damage something on purpose
witness	[ˈwɪtnəs]	to see something happen

EXAMPLES

She was fined £300.
She was sentenced to nine years in prison.
Someone has stolen my wallet!
Police suspect him of fraud.
Anyone who witnessed the attack should call the police.

ADJECTIVES

criminal	['krɪmɪnəl]	connected with a crime; *criminal charges*
guilty	['gɪlti]	having committed a crime or an offence
illegal	[ɪ'liːgəl]	not allowed by law
innocent	['ɪnəsənt]	not guilty of a crime
legal	['liːgəl]	**1** used for describing things that relate to the law; *the legal system* **2** allowed by law
violent	['vaɪələnt]	using physical force to hurt or kill other people

EXAMPLES
He was found guilty.
He was proved innocent.
Is this legal?

materials

NOUNS

acrylic [æ'krɪlɪk] a soft artificial material that feels like wool

aluminium [,ælu:'mɪnɪəm] a light metal used for making things such as cooking equipment and cans for food and drink (*In American English, use* **aluminum**)

aluminum (*American English*) *see* **aluminium**

brass [brɑːs] a yellow-coloured metal

brick [brɪk] a rectangular block used in the building of walls; *a brick wall*

bronze [brɒnz] a yellowish-brown metal that is a mixture of copper and tin

canvas ['kænvəs] a strong, heavy material that is used for making tents and bags

cardboard ['kɑːdbɔːd] thick, stiff paper that is used for making boxes; *a cardboard box*

cement [sɪ'ment] a grey powder that is mixed with sand and water in order to make concrete

china ['tʃaɪnə] a hard white substance that is used for making expensive cups and plates

clay [kleɪ] a type of earth that is soft when it is wet and hard when it is dry. Clay is used for making things such as pots and bricks.; *a clay pot*

coal [kəʊl] a hard black substance that comes from under the ground and is burned to give heat

concrete ['kɒŋkriːt] a hard substance made by mixing cement with sand and water. Concrete is used for building.

copper ['kɒpə] a soft reddish-brown metal

cotton ['kɒtən] cloth or thread that is made from the soft fibres of a plant called a cotton plant

---

EXAMPLES
We ate from small bowls made of china.
He put some more coal on the fire.

crystal	['krɪstəl]	**1** a small, hard piece of a natural substance; *ice crystals* **2** a clear rock used in jewellery; *a crystal necklace* **3** high-quality glass; *a crystal vase*
denim	['denɪm]	a thick cotton cloth, usually blue, that is used for making clothes; *a denim jacket*
elastic	[ɪ'læstɪk]	a rubber material that stretches when you pull it, and then returns to its original size and shape
fabric	['fæbrɪk]	cloth that you use for making things like clothes and bags
fur	[fɜ:]	the thick hair that grows on the bodies of many animals; *a fur coat*
glass	[glɑːs]	a hard, transparent substance that is used for making things such as windows and bottles
glue	[gluː]	a sticky substance that is used for joining things together
gold	[gəʊld]	a valuable, yellow-coloured metal that is used for making jewellery, ornaments and coins
iron	['aɪən]	a hard, dark grey metal; *an iron gate*
lace	[leɪs]	a delicate cloth with a design made of fine threads; *lace curtains*
lead	[led]	a soft, grey, heavy metal; *a lead pipe*
leather	['leðə]	animal skin that is used for making shoes, clothes, bags and furniture
linen	['lɪnɪn]	a type of strong cloth
liquid	['lɪkwɪd]	a substance, for example water or oil, that flows and can be poured

EXAMPLES

The documents were rolled up and held together with an elastic band.
We sell our tablecloths in plain or printed fabric.
This ring is made of solid gold.
He was wearing a white linen suit.

marble	['mɑːbəl]	a type of very hard rock that people use to make parts of buildings or statues (= models of people)
material	[mə'tɪərɪəl]	1 any solid substance 2 cloth 3 the things that you need for a particular activity; *building materials*
metal	['metəl]	a hard, usually shiny substance such as iron, steel or gold
nylon	['naɪlɒn]	a strong, artificial substance that is used for making cloth and plastic
paper	['peɪpə]	a material that you write on or wrap things with; *a piece of paper*
plaster	['plɑːstə]	a substance that is used for making a smooth surface on the inside of walls and ceilings
plastic	['plæstɪk]	a light but strong material that is produced by a chemical process; *a plastic bag*
pottery	['pɒtəri]	pots, dishes and other objects made from clay
rubber	['rʌbə]	a strong substance that is used for making tyres, boots and other products
satin	['sætɪn]	a smooth, shiny cloth that is made of silk or other materials
silk	[sɪlk]	a smooth, shiny cloth that is made from very thin threads from an insect called a silkworm
silver	['sɪlvə]	a valuable pale grey metal that is used for making jewellery
steel	[stiːl]	a very strong metal that is made mainly from iron
stone	[stəʊn]	1 a hard solid substance that is found in the ground and is often used for building; *a stone wall*

EXAMPLE
The thick material of her skirt was too warm for summer.

2 a piece of beautiful and valuable rock that is used in making jewellery; *a precious stone*

straw	[strɔː]	the dried, yellow stems of crops; *a straw hat*
string	[strɪŋ]	very thin rope that is made of twisted thread
textile	['tekstaɪl]	any type of cloth
thread	[θred]	a long, very thin piece of cotton, nylon or silk that you use for sewing
timber	['tɪmbə]	wood that is used for building and making things
tin	[tɪn]	a type of soft metal
velvet	['velvɪt]	soft cloth that is thick on one side; *velvet curtains*
wax	[wæks]	a solid, slightly shiny substance that is used for making candles (= sticks that you burn for light) and polish for furniture
wire	[waɪə]	a long, thin piece of metal; *a wire fence*
wood	[wʊd]	the hard material that trees are made of
wool	[wʊl]	a material made from the hair that grows on sheep and on some other animals

ADJECTIVES

hard	[hɑːd]	not easily bent, cut or broken
man-made	[mæn'meɪd]	created by people, rather than occurring naturally; *man-made fibres*
natural	['nætʃərəl]	existing in nature and not created by people
raw	[rɔː]	used for describing materials or substances that are in their natural state; *raw materials*
rough	[rʌf]	not smooth or even

EXAMPLE
She works in the textile industry.

smooth	[smuːð]	flat, with no rough parts, lumps or holes
soft	[sɒft]	1 pleasant to touch, and not rough or hard 2 changing shape easily when pressed
solid	['sɒlɪd]	1 hard; not like liquid or gas 2 with no holes or space inside; *solid rock*
synthetic	[sɪn'θetɪk]	made from chemicals or artificial substances rather than from natural ones
transparent	[træns'pærənt]	used for describing an object or a substance that you can see through
wooden	['wʊdən]	made of wood; *a wooden chair*
woollen	['wʊlən]	made from wool; *a woollen jumper*

EXAMPLES
Shoes made from synthetic materials can be washed easily.
He fell on the hard wooden floor.

maths

addition [əˈdɪʃən] the process of calculating the total of two or more numbers

algebra [ˈældʒɪbrə] a type of maths in which letters and signs are used to represent numbers

angle [ˈæŋgəl] the space between two lines or surfaces that meet in one place; *a 30° angle*

area [ˈeəriə] the amount of flat space that a surface covers, measured in square units

arithmetic [əˈrɪθmɪtɪk] basic number work, for example adding or multiplying

average [ˈævərɪdʒ] the result that you get when you add two or more amounts together and divide the total by the number of amounts you added together; *The average of 1, 2 and 6 is 3.*

axis [ˈæksɪs] one of the two lines on a graph on which you mark points to show measurements or amounts
  (PL) **axes** [ˈæksiːs]

bar chart [ˈbɑː ˌtʃɑːt] a chart that shows amounts as thick lines of different heights

bar graph [ˈbɑː ˌgrɑːf] same as **bar chart**

calculator [ˈkælkjʊˌleɪtə] a small electronic machine that you use to calculate numbers

chart [tʃɑːt] a diagram or graph that shows information

circle [ˈsɜːkəl] a round shape

circumference [səˈkʌmfrəns] the distance around the edge of a circle

column [ˈkɒləm] a section in a table that you read from top to bottom

compasses [ˈkʌmpəsɪz] a piece of equipment that you use for drawing circles; *a pair of compasses*

EXAMPLES
She can count to 100, and do simple addition problems.
What's the area of this triangle?
We can label the axes: time is on the vertical axis and money is on the horizontal one.

cone	[kəʊn]	a solid shape with one flat round end and one pointed end
cube	[kjuːb]	**1** a solid object with six square surfaces **2** the number that you get if you multiply a number by itself twice
cylinder	['sɪlɪndə]	a shape with circular ends and long straight sides
decimal	['desɪməl]	a part of a whole number that is written in the form of a dot followed by one or more numbers, for example 0.25 or 10.6
decimal point	['desɪməl ˌpɔɪnt]	the dot in front of a decimal
degree	[dɪ'griː]	**1** a unit for measuring temperatures that is often written as °; *180° Celsius* **2** a unit for measuring angles that is often written as °; *a 45° angle*
diameter	[daɪ'æmɪtə]	the length of a straight line that can be drawn across a round object, passing through the middle of it
digit	['dɪdʒɪt]	a written symbol for any of the ten numbers from 0 to 9
division	[dɪ'vɪʒən]	the process of dividing one number by another number
figure	['fɪgə]	**1** one of the symbols from 0 to 9 that you use to write numbers **2** an amount or a price expressed as a number
formula (PL) **formulas, formulae**	['fɔːmjʊlə] ['fɔːmjʊliː]	a group of letters, numbers or other symbols that represents a scientific rule
fraction	['frækʃən]	a part of a whole number, such as ½ or ⅓

EXAMPLES

The cube of 2 is 8.

The waiter forgot to put a decimal point in their £45.00 bill and they were charged £4500.

They put the figures in the wrong column.

The mathematical formula describes the distances of the planets from the Sun.

geometry	[dʒɪˈɒmɪtri]	a type of maths relating to lines, angles, curves and shapes
graph	[grɑːf]	a picture that shows information about sets of numbers or measurements
half (PL) **halves**	[hɑːf] [hɑːvz]	one of two equal parts of a number, an amount or an object
height	[haɪt]	the amount that something measures from the bottom to the top
hexagon	[ˈheksəgən]	a shape with six straight sides
length	[leŋθ]	the amount that something measures from one end to the other, along the longest side
math (American English)		*see* **maths**
mathematics	[ˌmæθəˈmætɪks]	same as **maths**
maths	[mæθs]	the study of numbers, quantities or shapes (*In American English, use* **math**)
multiplication	[ˌmʌltɪplɪˈkeɪʃən]	the process of calculating the total of one number multiplied by another
number	[ˈnʌmbə]	a word such as 'two', 'nine' or 'twelve' or a symbol such as 1, 3 or 47 that is used in counting
numeral	[ˈnjuːmərəl]	a written symbol that represents a number; *The Roman numeral for 7 is VII.*
oblong	[ˈɒblɒŋ]	a shape that has two long sides and two short sides
pentagon	[ˈpentəˌgɒn]	a shape with five straight sides
per cent	[pə ˈsent]	used for talking about an amount as part of 100, often written as %
percentage	[pəˈsentɪdʒ]	an amount of something, considered as part of 100

EXAMPLES

The graph shows that prices went up about 20 per cent last year.

More than half of all U.S. houses are heated with gas.

The table is about one metre in length.

Only ten per cent of our customers live in this city.

A large percentage of the population speaks English.

perimeter	[pə'rɪmɪtə]	the total distance around the edge of a flat shape
pie chart	['paɪ tʃɑːt]	a circle that is divided into sections to show something divided into different amounts
pyramid	['pɪrə,mɪd]	a solid shape with a flat base and flat sides that form a point where they meet at the top
quarter	['kwɔːtə]	one of four equal parts of something
radius (PL) **radiuses, radii** ['reɪdiaɪ]	['reɪdiəs]	the distance from the centre of a circle to its outside edge
ratio	['reɪʃiəʊ]	a relationship between two things when it is expressed in numbers or amounts
rectangle	['rektæŋgəl]	a shape with four straight sides and four 90° angles
right angle	['raɪt ,æŋgəl]	an angle of 90°
row	[rəʊ]	a section in a table that you read from one side to the other
ruler	['ruːlə]	a long, flat object that you use for measuring things and for drawing straight lines
scale	[skeɪl]	a set of levels or numbers that you use to measure things
semicircle	['semi,sɜːkəl]	one half of a circle
shape	[ʃeɪp]	something such as a circle, a square or a triangle
sphere	['sfɪə]	an object that is completely round, like a ball
square	[skweə]	a shape with four straight sides that are all the same length
square root	['skweə ,ruːt]	a number that you multiply by itself to produce another number; *The square root of 36 is 6.*

EXAMPLES

To work out the perimeter of a rectangle, you need to know its length and width.

A quarter of the residents are over 55 years old.

The adult to child ratio is one to six.

The earthquake measured 5.5 on the Richter scale.

subtraction	[səbˈtrækʃən]	the process of taking one number away from another number
sum	[sʌm]	**1** the number that you get when you add two or more numbers together; *Fourteen is the sum of six and eight.* **2** a simple calculation; *do a sum*
table	[ˈteɪbəl]	a set of numbers that you arrange in neat rows and columns
triangle	[ˈtraɪæŋgəl]	a shape with three straight sides
unit	[ˈjuːnɪt]	a fixed measurement such as a litre or a centimetre
volume	[ˈvɒljuːm]	the amount of space that an object contains
width	[wɪdθ]	the amount that something measures from one side to the other

VERBS

add	[æd]	to calculate the total of various numbers or amounts
calculate	[ˈkælkjʊleɪt]	to find out an amount by using numbers
count	[kaʊnt]	**1** to say all the numbers in order up to a particular amount; *count to 20* **2** to see how many there are in a group; *count the money*
divide	[dɪˈvaɪd]	to find out how many times one number can fit into another bigger number
equal	[ˈiːkwəl]	to be the same as a particular number or amount; *Nine minus two equals seven.*
multiply	[ˈmʌltɪˌplaɪ]	to add a number to itself a certain number of times; *If you multiply 3 by 4, you get 12.*
subtract	[səbˈtrækt]	to take one number away from another number; *If you subtract 3 from 5, you get 2.*

EXAMPLES

What is the volume of a cube with sides 3cm long?
Add all the numbers together, and divide by three.
Have you calculated the cost of your trip?
Measure the floor area and divide it by six.

take something away		same as **subtract**
work something out		same as **calculate**

ADJECTIVES

circular	['sɜːkjʊlə]	shaped like a circle
diagonal	[daɪ'ægənəl]	going from one corner of a square across to the opposite corner
even	['iːvən]	used for describing numbers that can be divided exactly by two, for example 4, 8 and 24
mathematical	[ˌmæθə'mætɪkəl]	involving numbers and calculating; *a mathematical formula*
negative	['negətɪv]	less than zero; *a negative number*
odd	[ɒd]	used for describing numbers such as 3 and 17, that cannot be divided exactly by two
parallel	['pærəlel]	used for describing two lines that are the same distance apart along their whole length; *parallel lines*
positive	['pɒzɪtɪv]	higher than zero; *a positive number*
rectangular	[rek'tæŋgjʊlə]	shaped like a rectangle
square	[skweə]	1 used for describing a shape that has four straight sides that are all the same length; *a square table* 2 used for talking about the area of something; *30 square metres*
triangular	[traɪ'æŋgjʊlə]	shaped like a triangle

EXAMPLES

Add up the bills for each month. Take this away from the income.
It took me some time to work out the answer to the sum.
The screen showed a pattern of diagonal lines.

PREPOSITIONS

minus   ['maɪnəs]   used when you are taking one number away from another number; *Ten minus two is eight.*

plus   [plʌs]   used for showing that one number is being added to another; *Three plus four equals seven.*

times   [taɪmz]   used when you are multiplying one number by another; *Five times two is ten.*

money

NOUNS

allowance	[əˈlaʊəns]	**1** money that is given regularly to someone **2** (*American English*) *see* **pocket money**
ATM (*mainly American English*)		*see* **cash machine**
balance	[ˈbæləns]	the amount of money you have in your bank account; *check your balance*
bank	[bæŋk]	a place where people can keep their money
bank account	[ˈbæŋk əkaʊnt]	an arrangement with a bank where they look after your money for you; *open/close a bank account*
bill	[bɪl]	a document that shows how much money you must pay for something; *pay the bill*
billfold (*American English*)		*see* **wallet**
breadwinner	[ˈbredwɪnə]	the person in a family who earns the money that the family needs
budget	[ˈbʌdʒɪt]	the amount of money that you have available to spend; *a low-budget film*
building society	[ˈbɪldɪŋ sə,saɪɪti]	a business that lends people money to buy houses and that provides savings accounts
cash	[kæʃ]	money in the form of notes and coins; *two thousand pounds in cash*
cashier	[kæˈʃɪə]	a person whose job is to take your money in a shop or a bank
cash machine	[ˈkæʃ mə,ʃiːn]	a machine, usually outside a bank, from which you can get money using a special plastic card (*In American English, use* **ATM**)
change	[tʃeɪndʒ]	**1** the money that you get back when you pay with more money than something costs **2** coins; *change for the parking meter*
change purse (*American English*) *see* **purse**		
charge	[tʃɑːdʒ]	an amount of money that you have to pay for a service; *a small charge*
checking account (*American English*)		*see* **current account**

EXAMPLES
They couldn't afford to pay their bills.
I've always paid the bills and been the breadwinner.

cheque	[tʃek]	a printed piece of paper from a bank that you write an amount of money on and use to pay for things; *pay by cheque*
chequebook	['tʃekbʊk]	a book containing cheques
coin	[kɔɪn]	a small round piece of metal money
cost	[kɒst]	the amount of money you need in order to buy, do, or make something; *the high cost of housing*
credit	['kredɪt]	an arrangement that allows someone to buy something and pay for it later; *They bought it on credit.*
credit card	['kredɪt kɑːd]	a plastic card that you use to buy goods on credit; *pay by credit card*
currency	['kʌrənsi]	the money that is used in a particular country; *pay in a different currency*
current account	[ˌkʌrənt ə'kaʊnt]	a bank account that you can take money out of at any time (*In American English, use* **checking account**)
debit card	['debɪt ˌkɑːd]	a bank card that you can use to pay for things; *pay by debit card*
debt	[det]	an amount of money that you owe someone; *get into debt*
deposit	[dɪ'pɒzɪt]	**1** a sum of money that is part of the full price of something, and that you pay when you agree to buy it; *a 10% deposit* **2** an amount of money that you put into a bank account; *make a deposit*
direct debit	[daɪˌrekt 'debɪt]	an arrangement that you make with a company, allowing them to take money that you owe them from your bank account every month

EXAMPLES

He gave me a cheque for £1500.
He counted out the coins into her hand.
The cost of a loaf of bread has gone up.
There will be an increase in the cost of posting a letter.
He is trying to pay off his debts.

economy	[ɪˈkɒnəmi]	the system for organizing the money and industry of the world, a country, or local government
expenses	[ɪkˈspensɪz]	money that you spend on things
income	[ˈɪnkʌm]	the money that a person earns or receives
inheritance	[ɪnˈherɪtəns]	money or property that you receive from someone who has died
insurance	[ɪnˈʃʊərəns]	an agreement that you make with a company in which you pay money to them regularly, and they pay you if something bad happens to you or your property; *travel insurance*
interest	[ˈɪntrəst, -tərest]	the extra money that you pay if you have borrowed money, or the extra money that you receive if you have money in some types of bank account
loan	[ləʊn]	an amount of money that you borrow
money	[ˈmʌni]	the coins or notes that you use to buy things
mortgage	[ˈmɔːgɪdʒ]	a loan of money that you get from a bank or building society in order to buy a house
payment	[ˈpeɪmənt]	**1** an amount of money that is paid to someone; *weekly payments* **2** the act of paying money or of being paid; *immediate payment*
pension	[ˈpenʃən]	money that you regularly receive from a business or the government after you stop working because of your age

EXAMPLES

The Indian economy is changing fast.

Her hotel expenses were paid by the company.

She used her inheritance to buy a house.

How much interest do you have to pay on the loan?

Do you earn much interest on that account?

I had to sell my home because I couldn't afford the mortgage payments.

PIN	[pɪn]	short for 'Personal Identification Number': a secret number that you can use, for example, with a bank card to get money from a cash machine; *key in your PIN*
pocket money	['pɒkɪt mʌni]	a small amount of money that parents regularly give their children (*In American English, use* **allowance**)
poverty	['pɒvəti]	the state of being very poor; *living in poverty*
price	[praɪs]	the amount of money that you have to pay in order to buy something
profit	['prɒfɪt]	the amount of money that you gain when you sell something for more than you paid for it
purse	[pɜːs]	a very small bag used for carrying money, especially by women (*In American English, use* **change purse**)
rent	[rent]	money that you pay to someone so that you can use something that belongs to them; *pay the rent*
salary	['sæləri]	the money that you earn from your employer
savings	['seɪvɪŋz]	all the money that you have saved, especially in a bank
savings account	['seɪvɪŋz əkaʊnt]	a bank account that gives you interest on your money
share	[ʃeə]	one of the equal parts that the value of a company is divided into, which people can buy so that they own a part of the company and have a part of its profit
standing order	[,stændɪŋ 'ɔːdə]	an instruction to your bank to pay a fixed amount of money to someone at regular times

EXAMPLES

To use the service you'll need a PIN number.
We have seen huge changes in the price of gas.
They expect house prices to rise.
The lawyer was paid a huge salary.
I bought shares in my brother's new company.

statement	['steɪtmənt]	a printed document showing how much money you have paid into, and taken out of, your bank account
tax	[tæks]	an amount of money that you have to pay to the government so that it can pay for public services such as roads and schools; *raise/lower taxes*
VAT	[ˌviː eɪ ˈtiː, væt]	short for 'value added tax': a tax that is added to the price of goods or services
wages	['weɪdʒɪz]	the amount of money that is paid to someone for the work that they do
wallet	['wɒlɪt]	a small case that you can keep money and cards in (*In American English, use* **billfold**)

VERBS

borrow	['bɒrəʊ]	to get money from someone and agree to pay it back some time in the future
buy	[baɪ]	to get something by paying money for it
charge	[tʃɑːdʒ]	to ask someone to pay money for something
cost	[kɒst]	to have as a price; *cost a lot*
deposit	[dɪ'pɒzɪt]	to put an amount of money into a bank account
donate	[dəʊ'neɪt]	to give something to an organization
earn	[ɜːn]	to receive money for work that you do
inherit	[ɪn'herɪt]	to receive money or property from someone who has died

EXAMPLES

His wages have gone up.
I've lost my wallet.
He could not afford to buy a house.
Lizzie bought herself a bike.
The driver charged us only £2 each.
How much do you charge for printing photos?
He often donates large amounts of money to charity.
He has no children to inherit his house.

invest	[ɪnˈvest]	to put money into a business or a bank, in order to try to make a profit from it
lend	[lend]	to give someone money that they must give back after a certain amount of time
make money		to get money for doing something
owe	[əʊ]	to have to pay money to someone
pay	[peɪ]	**1** to give someone an amount of money for something that you are buying; *pay for the food*
		2 to give someone an amount of money for something such as a bill or a debt; *pay the bill*
		3 to give someone money for the work that they do; *We can pay you every week.*
		4 to give someone the money that you owe them; *I haven't paid him back yet.*
pay something in		to put money into a bank account
pay up		to give someone the money that you owe them, even though you would prefer not to
save	[seɪv]	to gradually collect money by spending less than you get
sign	[saɪn]	to write your name on a document; *sign a cheque*
spend	[spend]	to pay money for things that you want or need; *spend money*
withdraw	[wɪðˈdrɔː]	to take money out of a bank account

EXAMPLES

He made a lot of money from his first book.
The company owes money to more than 60 banks.
Blake owed him £50.
Tim and Barbara are saving for a house.
I was saving money to go to college.

ADJECTIVES

bankrupt	['bæŋkrʌpt]	without enough money to pay your debts
cheap	[tʃi:p]	costing little money, or less than you expected
expensive	[ɪk'spensɪv]	costing a lot of money
generous	['dʒenərəs]	giving you more than you expect of something; *a generous gift*
mean	[mi:n]	not willing to spend much money
poor	[pʊə, pɔ:]	having very little money and few possessions
rich	[rɪtʃ]	having a lot of money or valuable possessions
thrifty	['θrɪfti]	saving money, not buying unnecessary things, and not wasting things
valuable	['væljʊəbəl]	worth a lot of money
wealthy	['welθi]	having a large amount of money, property, or valuable possessions

IDIOMS

be rolling in it	[INFORMAL] to have a lot of money
cheap and cheerful	[INFORMAL] not costing much, but pleasing or enjoyable
in the red	[INFORMAL] owing money to a bank
make ends meet	to manage to live on your income
money doesn't grow on trees	used for saying that money is not freely available
save something for a rainy day	to keep money to use if an unexpected need arises
tighten your belt	to spend less money than you usually do

EXAMPLES

I want to rent a cheap room near the university.
She was always dressed in the most expensive silk and cashmere.
My mother taught me to be thrifty.
Do not leave any valuable items in your hotel room.
The company is £5 million in the red.

music

music	['mjuːzɪk]	**1** the pleasant sound that you make when you sing or play instruments; *listen to music* **2** the symbols that you write on paper to tell people what to sing or play; *read music*

TYPES OF MUSIC

classical music		a traditional type of music, written in a standard form
country music	['kʌntri ˌmjuːzɪk]	a type of music in the style of the traditional music of the southern and western US
folk music	['fəʊk ˌmjuːzɪk]	music that is traditional or typical of a particular group of people or country
jazz	[dʒæz]	a style of music that has strong rhythms. It was invented by African-American musicians in the early part of the twentieth century.
pop music	['pɒp ˌmjuːzɪk]	modern popular music, usually with a strong rhythm and simple tunes
rap	[ræp]	a type of modern music in which the words are spoken
rock and roll	[ˌrɒk ənd 'rəʊl]	a type of pop music developed in the 1950s which has a strong beat for dancing

MUSICAL INSTRUMENTS

cello	['tʃeləʊ]	a musical instrument that is like a large violin. You sit behind it and rest it on the floor.
clarinet	[ˌklærɪ'net]	a musical instrument that you blow. It is a long black wooden tube with keys on it that you press, and a single reed (= small flat part that moves and makes a sound when you blow).

EXAMPLES
This is a collection of traditional folk music from nearly 30 countries.
The club plays live jazz on Sundays.
Elvis Presley was known as the King of Rock and Roll.

drum	[drʌm]	a simple musical instrument that you hit with sticks or with your hands
flute	[fluːt]	a musical instrument that you play by blowing. You hold it sideways to your mouth.
guitar	[gɪˈtɑː]	a musical instrument that has six strings and a long neck
harp	[hɑːp]	a large musical instrument that has strings stretched from the top to the bottom of a frame. You play the harp with your fingers.
horn	[hɔːn]	a musical instrument with a long metal tube that you play by blowing into it
keyboard	[ˈkiːbɔːd]	1 the set of black and white keys that you press when you play a piano 2 an electronic musical instrument that has a keyboard
musical instrument	[ˌmjuːzɪkəl ˈɪnstrəmənt]	an object such as a piano, guitar, or violin that you use for playing music
oboe	[ˈəʊbəʊ]	a musical instrument that you blow. It is a long black wooden tube with keys on it that you press, and a double reed (= small flat part that moves and makes a sound when you blow).
organ	[ˈɔːgən]	a large musical instrument that is like a piano
piano	[piˈænəʊ]	a large musical instrument that you play by pressing black and white bars (= keys)
recorder	[rɪˈkɔːdə]	a wooden or plastic musical instrument in the shape of a pipe. You play it by blowing down one end and covering holes with your fingers.
saxophone	[ˈsæksəˌfəʊn]	a musical instrument made of metal that you play by blowing into it
sitar	[sɪˈtɑː]	an Indian musical instrument with two layers of strings, a long neck, and a round body

EXAMPLE
Sam is a great guitar player.

tambourine	[ˌtæmbəˈriːn]	a round musical instrument that has small bells around its edge. You shake it or hit it with your hand.
trumpet	[ˈtrʌmpɪt]	a metal musical instrument that you blow
violin	[ˌvaɪəˈlɪn]	a musical instrument made of wood with four strings. You hold it under your chin, and play it by moving a long stick (= a bow) across the strings
xylophone	[ˈzaɪləˌfəʊn]	a musical instrument with a row of wooden bars of different lengths that you play with special hammers

PEOPLE

band	[bænd]	a group of people who play music together; *play in a band*
choir	[ˈkwaɪə]	a group of people who sing together
composer	[kəmˈpəʊzə]	a person who writes music
conductor	[kənˈdʌktə]	a person who stands in front of a group of musicians and directs their performance
drummer	[ˈdrʌmə]	a person who plays a drum or a drum kit
guitarist	[gɪˈtɑːrɪst]	a person who plays the guitar
musician	[mjuːˈzɪʃən]	a person who plays a musical instrument as their job or hobby
orchestra	[ˈɔːkɪstrə]	a large group of musicians who play different instruments together
pianist	[ˈpiːənɪst]	a person who plays the piano
singer	[ˈsɪŋə]	a person who sings, especially as a job

PIECES AND PARTS OF MUSIC

chord	[kɔːd]	a number of musical notes played or sung at the same time; *a chord of G major*
chorus	[ˈkɔːrəs]	a part of a song that you repeat several times
duet	[djuːˈet]	a piece of music performed by two people; *a duet for two guitarists*

EXAMPLE
He sang in his church choir for ten years.

harmony	[ˈhɑːməni]	the pleasant combination of different notes of music played at the same time; *play in harmony*
key	[kiː]	a particular scale of musical notes; *the key of C*
lyrics	[ˈlɪrɪks]	the words of a song
melody	[ˈmelədi]	a group of musical notes that make a tune
note	[nəʊt]	1 one particular musical sound; *a wrong note* 2 a symbol that represents this sound
octave	[ˈɒktɪv]	a series of eight notes in music, or the difference between the first and last notes in the series
piece of music	[piːs əv ˈmjuːzɪk]	a complete musical work; *an orchestral piece*
rhythm	[ˈrɪðəm]	a regular pattern of sounds or movements
scale	[skeɪl]	a set of musical notes that are played in a fixed order
solo	[ˈsəʊləʊ]	a piece of music performed by one person
song	[sɒŋ]	words and music sung together
verse	[vɜːs]	one of the groups of lines in a poem or song

RECORDING, PERFORMING AND LISTENING TO MUSIC

album	[ˈælbəm]	a collection of songs on a CD
CD	[ˌsiː ˈdiː]	short for 'compact disc': a disc for storing music
concert	[ˈkɒnsət]	a performance of music
iPod™	[ˈaɪpɒd]	a small piece of electronic equipment that stores music, photos, and movies
karaoke	[ˌkæriˈəʊki]	a form of entertainment in which a machine plays songs, and you sing the words

---

EXAMPLE
She has a deep voice so she can't sing high notes.
He raised his sticks and beat out the rhythm of the song.
The band released their new album on July 1.
The weekend began with an outdoor rock concert.

MP3 player	[ˌem piː ˈθriː ˈpleɪə]	a small piece of electronic equipment that stores and plays music
microphone	[ˈmaɪkrəˌfəʊn]	a piece of electronic equipment that you use to make sounds louder or to record them onto a machine
record	[ˈrekɔːd]	a round, flat piece of black plastic on which sound, especially music, is stored. A record can be played on a record player.

VERBS

compose	[kəmˈpəʊz]	to write a piece of music
conduct	[kənˈdʌkt]	to stand in front of musicians and direct their performance
perform	[pəˈfɔːm]	to play a piece of music in front of an audience
play	[pleɪ]	1 to produce music from a musical instrument 2 to put a CD into a machine and listen to it
practise	[ˈpræktɪs]	to do something regularly in order to do it better
record	[rɪˈkɔːd]	to store something such as a speech or a performance in a computer file or on a disk so that it can be heard or seen again later
sing	[sɪŋ]	to make music with your voice
tune	[tjuːn]	to adjust a musical instrument so that it produces the right notes

ADJECTIVES

| **acoustic** | [əˈkuːstɪk] | an acoustic musical instrument is one which is not electric; *an acoustic guitar* |
| **classical** | [ˈklæsɪkəl] | traditional in form, style, or content; *classical music* |

EXAMPLE

the Orchestra of Welsh National Opera conducted by Carlo Rizzi
They will be performing works by Bach and Scarlatti.
Nina was playing the piano.
She played her CDs too loudly.
My brother and I used to sing this song.

flat	[flæt]	used for describing a note that is slightly lower than another note
major	['meɪdʒə]	used for talking about a scale with half steps in sound between the third and fourth and the seventh and eighth notes; *a scale of G major*
minor	['maɪnə]	used in music for talking about a scale in which the third note is one half step lower that the related major scale
musical	['mjuːzɪkəl]	**1** relating to playing or studying music; *musical training* **2** having a natural ability and interest in music; *musical children*
sharp	[ʃɑːp]	used for describing a note that is slightly higher than another note

ADVERBS

in tune	[ˌɪn 'tjuːn]	singing or playing the correct musical notes; *sing in tune*
loudly	['laʊdli]	easily heard because the level of sound is very high; *playing loudly*
out of tune	[ˌaʊt əv 'tjuːn]	not singing or playing the correct musical notes; *sing out of tune*
softly	['sɒftli]	quietly or gently; *singing softly*

the office

NOUNS

binder ['baɪndə] a cover for holding loose sheets of paper together

briefcase ['briːfkeɪs] a small suitcase for carrying business papers in; *a leather briefcase*

bulletin board (American English) see **noticeboard**

business card ['bɪznɪs kɑːd] a small card printed with your name, job, business address, and other contact information; *give someone your business card*

calculator ['kælkjʊˌleɪtə] a small electronic machine that you use to calculate numbers

department [dɪˈpɑːtmənt] one of the sections in an organization

desk [desk] a table that you sit at to write or work

fax machine ['fæks məʃiːn] a special machine that you use to send and receive documents electronically

file [faɪl] **1** a box or a type of envelope that you keep papers in
2 a collection of information that you keep on your computer; *open a file; a computer file*

filing cabinet ['faɪlɪŋ kæbɪnɪt] a tall piece of office furniture with deep drawers for documents

folder ['fəʊldə] **1** a folded piece of cardboard or plastic that you keep papers in; *a work folder*
2 a group of files that are stored together on a computer

highlighter ['haɪlaɪtə] a brightly coloured pen that is used for marking important parts of a document

ink cartridge ['ɪŋk kɑːtrɪdʒ] a small container holding ink, that you put into a printer

meeting room ['miːtɪŋ ˌruːm] a room in an office building where people have meetings

notepad ['nəʊtpæd] **1** a pad of paper for writing notes on
2 a pocket-sized personal computer

EXAMPLES
She works in the accounts department.
The file contained letters and reports.

noticeboard	['nəʊtɪsˌbɔːd]	a board on a wall for notices giving information (*In American English, use* **bulletin board**)
office	['ɒfɪs]	a place where people work sitting at a desk; *work in an office*
overhead projector	[ˌəʊvəhed prə'dʒektə]	a piece of equipment that you use to make an image on a plastic sheet appear large on a screen
pair of scissors	[ˌpeə əv 'sɪzəz]	a small tool for cutting, with two sharp parts that are joined together
paperclips	['peɪpəklɪps]	small metal clips used for holding sheets of paper together
pen	[pen]	a long thin object that you use for writing with ink (= coloured liquid)
pencil	['pensəl]	a thin piece of wood with a black or coloured substance through the middle that you use to write or draw with
photocopier	['fəʊtəʊˌkɒpiə]	a machine that copies documents by photographing them
photocopy	['fəʊtəʊˌkɒpi]	a copy of a document that you make using a photocopier; *make a photocopy*
printer	['prɪntə]	a machine for printing copies of computer documents on paper
reception	[rɪ'sepʃən]	the desk in an office building that you go to when you first arrive
receptionist	[rɪ'sepʃənɪst]	a person who works in a reception
safe	[seɪf]	a strong metal box with a lock, where you keep money or other valuable things
sellotape™	['seləteɪp]	clear plastic sticky tape that is used for sticking things together; *a roll of sellotape*
stapler	['steɪplə]	a small piece of equipment that is used for attaching sheets of paper together with staples

EXAMPLE

Her telephone number was pinned to the noticeboard.

staples	['steɪpəlz]	pieces of thin wire that attach sheets of paper together
toner	['təʊnə]	a black or coloured powder used as ink in a printer or a photocopier
vending machine	['vendɪŋ məʃiːn]	a machine that you can buy small articles from, such as food, drinks, or cigarettes

VERBS

photocopy	['fəʊtəʊˌkɒpi]	to make a copy of a document using a photocopier; *photocopy a document*
scan	[skæn]	to make an electronic copy of a picture or a document using a special piece of equipment (called a scanner)
type	[taɪp]	to write something using a machine like a computer

personal items

NOUNS

billfold (American English)   see **wallet**

bracelet   ['breɪslɪt]   a piece of jewellery that you wear around your wrist; *a silver bracelet*

brush   [brʌʃ]   an object with a lot of hairs attached to it that you use for making your hair tidy

change purse (American English) see **purse**

comb   [kəʊm]   a thin piece of plastic or metal with narrow, pointed parts (called teeth). You use a comb to make your hair tidy.

cotton wool   ['kɒtən ˌwʊl]   soft fluffy cotton, often used for applying creams to your skin

dental floss   ['dentəl ˌflɒs]   a type of thread that is used to clean between your teeth

deodorant   [diˈəʊdərənt]   a substance that you can put on your skin to hide or prevent bad smells

diamond   ['daɪəmənd]   a hard, clear stone that is very expensive, and is used for making jewellery; *diamond earrings*

earring   ['ɪərɪŋ]   a piece of jewellery that you wear on your ear

face cream   ['feɪs ˌkriːm]   a thick substance that you can rub into your face to keep it soft

face powder   ['feɪs ˌpaʊdə]   a very fine soft powder that you can put on your face to make it look smoother

flannel   ['flænəl]   a small cloth that you use for washing yourself (*In American English, use* **washcloth**)

gel   [dʒel]   a thick substance like jelly, used for keeping your hair in a particular style or for washing your body; *shower gel*

hairdryer   ['heədraɪə]   a machine that you use to dry your hair

hairspray   ['heəspreɪ]   a sticky substance that you spray out of a can onto your hair in order to hold it in place

---

EXAMPLE
Rosalinda was wearing gold earrings.

handbag	['hændbæg]	a small bag that a woman uses for carrying things such as money and keys (*In American English*, use **purse**)
handkerchief	['hæŋkətʃɪf]	a small square piece of cloth that you use for blowing your nose
jewellery	['dʒuːəlri]	decorations that you wear on your body, such as a ring that you wear on your finger; *a jewellery box*
key-ring	['kiːrɪŋ]	a metal ring that you use to keep your keys together
lipstick	['lɪpstɪk]	a coloured substance that women sometimes put on their lips
make-up	['meɪkʌp]	the creams and powders that you can put on your face to make yourself look more attractive; *put on make-up*; *take off make-up*
mirror	['mɪrə]	a flat piece of special glass that you can see yourself in
mouthwash	['maʊθwɒʃ]	a liquid that you put in your mouth to clean it and make your breath smell pleasant
nail file	['neɪl ˌfaɪl]	a small rough strip that you rub across the ends of your nails to shorten them or shape them
nail varnish	['neɪl vɑːnɪʃ]	a thick liquid that you can paint on your nails
necklace	['neklɪs]	a piece of jewellery that you wear around your neck
perfume	['pɜːfjuːm]	a liquid with a pleasant smell that you put on your skin
purse	[pɜːs]	**1** a very small bag used for carrying money, especially by women (*In American English*, use **change purse**) **2** (*American English*) *see* **handbag**

EXAMPLE

Eva was wearing red lipstick.
Anna doesn't usually wear much make-up.
Dan looked at himself in the mirror.
The hall smelled of her mother's perfume.

razor	['reɪzə]	a tool that people use for shaving
ring	[rɪŋ]	a small circle of metal that you wear on your finger; *a wedding ring*
shampoo	[ʃæm'puː]	liquid soap that you use for washing your hair
soap	[səʊp]	a substance that you use with water for washing yourself; *a bar of soap*
sponge	[spʌndʒ]	a piece of a very light soft material with a lot of small holes in it, that you use for washing yourself
sun cream	['sʌn ˌkriːm]	a cream that you can put on your skin to protect it from the sun
tissue	['tɪʃuː, 'tɪsjuː]	a piece of thin, soft paper that you use to wipe your nose; *a packet of tissues*
toilet paper	['tɔɪlət ˌpeɪpə]	paper that you use to clean yourself after using the toilet
toilet roll	['tɔɪlət ˌrəʊl]	a roll of toilet paper
toiletries	['tɔɪlətriz]	the things that you use when you are washing or taking care of your body, such as soap and toothpaste
toothbrush	['tuːθbrʌʃ]	a small brush that you use for cleaning your teeth
toothpaste	['tuːθpeɪst]	a thick substance that you put on a toothbrush for cleaning your teeth
towel	['taʊəl]	a piece of thick soft cloth that you use to dry yourself; *a bath towel*
wallet	['wɒlɪt]	a small case in which you keep money and cards (*In American English, use* **billfold**)
washcloth (*American English*)		*see* **flannel**
watch	[wɒtʃ]	a small clock that you wear on your wrist

VERBS

brush	[brʌʃ]	to tidy something using a brush; *brush your hair*
carry	['kæri]	**1** to hold something in your hand and take it with you; *carry a handbag* **2** to always have something with you; *carry a passport*
comb	[kəʊm]	to use a comb to make your hair tidy; *comb your hair*
put something on		to place clothing or make-up on your body in order to wear it
take something off		to remove clothing or make-up
wear	[weə]	to have something such as clothes, shoes, or jewellery on your body

EXAMPLE
She put on her make-up.

plants, trees and gardens

NOUNS

ash	[æʃ]	a tree that has smooth grey bark and loses its leaves in winter
bark	[bɑːk]	the rough surface of a tree
beech	[biːtʃ]	a tree with a smooth grey trunk
birch	[bɜːtʃ]	a tall tree with thin branches
bird feeder	[ˈbɜːd ˌfiːdə]	a container that you fill with food for birds
blossom	[ˈblɒsəm]	the flowers that appear on a fruit tree; *cherry blossom*
border	[ˈbɔːdə]	a long area of ground along the edge of a garden that is planted with flowers; *border plants*
branch	[brɑːntʃ]	one of the parts of a tree that have leaves, flowers, and fruit
bud	[bʌd]	a new growth on a tree or plant that develops into a leaf or flower
bush	[bʊʃ]	a plant with leaves and branches that is smaller than a tree; *a rose bush*
buttercup	[ˈbʌtəkʌp]	a small wild plant with bright yellow flowers
compost	[ˈkɒmpɒst]	a mixture of dead plants and vegetables that is used to improve soil
daffodil	[ˈdæfədɪl]	a yellow flower with a long stem that appears in spring
daisy	[ˈdeɪzi]	a small wild flower with a yellow centre and white petals
dandelion	[ˈdændɪˌlaɪən]	a wild plant with yellow flowers that turn into balls of soft white seeds
elm	[elm]	a tree with broad leaves that it loses in autumn
fence	[fens]	a wooden or metal wall around a piece of land
fern	[fɜːn]	a plant that has long stems with leaves that look like feathers

EXAMPLES

We picked apples from the upper branches of a tree.
Small pink buds were beginning to form on the bushes.

fertilizer	[ˈfɜːtɪˌlaɪzə]	a substance that you put on soil to make plants grow well
fir tree	[ˈfɜː triː]	a tall evergreen tree that has thin needle-like leaves
flower	[ˈflaʊə]	the brightly coloured part of a plant; *a bunch of flowers*; *a flower bed*; *a flower pot*
forest	[ˈfɒrɪst]	a large area where trees grow close together; *a forest fire*
forget-me-not	[fəˈgetmɪˌnɒt]	a small plant with very small blue flowers
garden	[ˈgɑːdən]	**1** the part of the land by your house where you grow flowers and vegetables **2** places with plants, trees and grass, that people can visit
garden bench	[ˌgɑːdən ˈbenʃ]	a long seat of wood or metal that two or more people can sit on in a garden
garden centre	[ˈgɑːdən ˌsentə]	a shop, usually with an outdoor area, where you can buy plants and tools for your garden
gardener	[ˈgɑːdnə]	a person who works in a garden
gardening	[ˈgɑːdnɪŋ]	the activity of working in a garden
grass	[grɑːs]	a plant with thin, green leaves that cover the surface of the ground; *cut the grass*
greenhouse	[ˈgriːnhaʊs]	a glass building where you grow plants to protect them from bad weather
ground	[graʊnd]	the soil on the Earth's surface in which you can grow plants
grounds	[graʊndz]	the garden or area of land around a large or important building
hedge	[hedʒ]	a row of small trees growing close together around a garden or a field

EXAMPLES
She has a beautiful garden.
The gardens are open from 10.30 a.m. until 5.00 p.m.
Mrs Daly employs a gardener.
My favourite hobby is gardening.
We walked around the palace grounds.

hoe	[həʊ]	a tool with a long handle and a small square blade that you use to break up the surface of the soil
holly	['hɒli]	a plant that has hard, shiny leaves with sharp points, and red berries in winter
hose	[həʊz]	a long rubber or plastic pipe that you use to put water on plants; *a garden hose*
ivy	['aɪvi]	a dark-green plant that grows up walls or along the ground
jasmine	['dʒæzmɪn]	a climbing plant which has small white or yellow flowers with a pleasant smell
lawn	[lɔːn]	an area of short grass around a house or other building
lawnmower	['lɔːnməʊə]	a machine for cutting grass
leaf (PL) **leaves**	[liːf] [liːvz]	the parts of a tree or plant that are flat, thin, and usually green; *an oak leaf*
lily	['lɪli]	a plant with large sweet-smelling flowers
oak	[əʊk]	a type of large tree
orchard	['ɔːtʃəd]	an area of land where fruit trees grow; *a cherry orchard*
orchid	['ɔːkɪd]	a plant with brightly coloured, unusually shaped flowers
palm tree	['pɑːm ˌtriː]	a straight tree with a lot of long leaves at the top, which grows in tropical countries
path	[pɑːθ]	a long, narrow piece of ground that people walk along
patio	['pætiəʊ]	a flat area next to a house, where people can sit and relax or eat; *patio furniture*
petal	['petəl]	the thin coloured parts of a plant that form the flower; *rose petals*
pine	[paɪn]	a tall tree with long, thin leaves that it keeps all year

EXAMPLES
We had lunch on the lawn.
We followed the path through the grounds.

plant	[plɑːnt]	a living thing that grows in the earth and has a stem, leaves, and roots
poppy	['pɒpi]	a plant with large, delicate, red flowers
primrose	['prɪmrəʊz]	a wild plant with pale yellow flowers
rainforest	['reɪnfɒrɪst]	a thick forest of tall trees that grows in tropical areas where there is a lot of rain
rake	[reɪk]	a tool with a long handle, used for collecting loose grass or leaves
root	[ruːt]	the part of a plant that grows under the ground
rose	[rəʊz]	a flower with a pleasant smell and sharp points (called thorns) on its stems
seed	[siːd]	the small, hard part of a plant from which a new plant grows
shade	[ʃeɪd]	an area where direct sunlight does not reach; *in the shade*
shed	[ʃed]	a small building where you store things
shrub	[ʃrʌb]	a small bush
soil	[sɔɪl]	the substance on the surface of the Earth in which plants grow
sprinkler	['sprɪŋklə]	a machine that spreads drops of water over an area of grass
stalk	[stɔːk]	the thin part of a flower, leaf, or fruit that joins it to the plant or tree
stem	[stem]	the long, thin part of a plant that the flowers and leaves grow on
sunflower	['sʌnflaʊə]	a very tall plant with large yellow flowers
thorn	[θɔːn]	a sharp point on some plants and trees

EXAMPLES

Water each plant daily.
Plant the seeds in small plastic pots.
They grow well in sun or partial shade.
This book tells you how to choose shrubs for your garden.
The soil here is good for growing vegetables.
A single flower grows on each long stalk.
He cut the stem and gave her the flower.
He removed a thorn from his foot.

tree	[triː]	a tall plant that lives for a long time. It has a trunk, branches, and leaves; *apple trees*
trunk	[trʌŋk]	the large main stem of a tree from which the branches grow
tulip	[ˈtjuːlɪp]	a flower that grows in the spring and is shaped like a cup
vase	[vɑːz]	a container that is used for holding flowers
violet	[ˈvaɪəlɪt]	a small plant that has purple or white flowers in the spring
watering can	[ˈwɔtərɪŋ ˌkæn]	a container with a handle that is used to water plants
weed	[wiːd]	a plant that grows where you do not want it
weedkiller	[ˈwiːdkɪlə]	a substance that you put on your garden to kill weeds
weeping willow	[ˌwiːpɪŋ ˈwɪləʊ]	a type of tree with long thin branches that hang down to the ground
wheelbarrow	[ˈwiːlbærəʊ]	an open container with one wheel and two handles, that is used for moving things such as earth or plants
window box	[ˈwɪndəʊ ˌbɒks]	a long narrow container on a shelf at the bottom of a window that is used for growing plants
wood	[wʊd]	a large area of trees growing near each other
yew	[juː]	an evergreen tree with sharp leaves that are broad and flat, and red berries

VERBS

blossom	[ˈblɒsəm]	to produce flowers
cultivate	[ˈkʌltɪˌveɪt]	to grow plants on a piece of land
flower	[ˈflaʊə]	to produce flowers

EXAMPLES
There was a small vase of flowers on the table.
The garden was full of weeds.
Rain begins to fall and peach trees blossom.
These plants will flower soon.

grow	[grəʊ]	**1** to gradually become bigger **2** used for saying that a plant or a tree lives in a particular place **3** to put seeds or young plants in the ground and take care of them
mow	[məʊ]	to cut an area of grass using a machine (called a mower); *mow the lawn*
pick	[pɪk]	to take flowers, fruit, or leaves from a plant or tree
plant	[plɑːnt]	to put something into the ground so that it will grow
prune	[pruːn]	to cut out parts of a bush or tree in order to make it grow thicker and better
tend	[tend]	to look after your garden and the plants in it
water	['wɔːtə]	to pour water over plants in order to help them to grow
weed	[wiːd]	to remove the weeds from an area

ADJECTIVES

deciduous	[dɪ'sɪdʒʊəs]	a deciduous tree loses its leaves in autumn every year
evergreen	['evəgriːn]	an evergreen tree has green leaves all year
indoor	['ɪndɔː]	done or used inside a building; *indoor plants*
leafy	['liːfi]	**1** having a lot of leaves; *leafy trees* **2** you say that a place is leafy when there are a lot of trees and plants there
mature	[mə'tjʊə]	fully grown; *mature fruit trees*
outdoor	[,aʊt'dɔː]	happening outside and not in a building
overgrown	[,əʊvə'grəʊn]	thickly covered with plants that have not been looked after
shady	['ʃeɪdi]	not in direct sunlight

EXAMPLES

There were roses growing by the side of the door.
He plans to plant fruit trees.
Try not to walk on the flower beds while you are weeding.

PHRASE

Keep off the grass used on signs to tell people not to walk on the grass

IDIOMS

have a green thumb *see* **have green fingers**
(*American English*)

have green fingers to be good at making plants grow
(*In American English, use* **have a green thumb**)

reading and writing

NOUNS

alphabet ['ælfəbet] a set of letters that is used for writing words

article ['ɑːtɪkəl] a piece of writing in a newspaper or magazine; *a newspaper article*

author ['ɔːθə] the person who wrote a book or a document

Biro ['baɪərəʊ] a pen with a small metal ball at the tip

book [bʊk] a number of pieces of paper, usually with words printed on them, that are fastened together and fixed inside a cover

capitals ['kæpɪtəlz] letters in the form that is used at the beginning of sentences or names, for example 'T', 'B', and 'F', rather than 't', 'b', and 'f'.

chapter ['tʃæptə] a part of a book; *See chapter 4.*

character ['kærɪktə] one of the people in a story

colon ['kəʊlən] the punctuation mark (:) that you can use to join parts of a sentence

comic ['kɒmɪk] a magazine that contains stories told in pictures

comma ['kɒmə] the punctuation mark (,) that you use to separate parts of a sentence or items in a list

conclusion [kən'kluːʒən] the ending of a story

contents page ['kɒntents ˌpeɪdʒ] a list of chapters that is shown at the beginning of a book

correction fluid [kə'rekʃən ˌfluːɪd] a white liquid that you use to cover written mistakes

cover ['kʌvə] the outside part of a book or a magazine

EXAMPLES

The Russian alphabet has 31 letters.
Jill Phillips is the author of 'Give Your Child Music'.
Please write your name and address in capitals.
The main character in 'Great Expectations' is Pip.
Her photograph was on the front cover of 'Zoo' magazine.

diary	['daɪəri]	a book in which you record what happens in your life
dictionary	['dɪkʃənri]	a book in which the words and phrases of a language are listed, together with their meanings
document	['dɒkjəmənt]	an official piece of paper with important information on it
draft	[drɑːft]	a piece of writing that you have not finished working on; *a first draft*
e-book	['iːbʊk]	short for 'electronic book': a book that you can read on a computer screen
editor	['edɪtə]	someone whose job is to check and correct texts
encyclopedia [ɪn,saɪklə'piːdiə]		a book or a CD-ROM containing facts about many different subjects
eraser (*American English*)		*see* **rubber**
essay	['eseɪ]	a short piece of writing on a subject
exclamation mark [,eksklə'meɪʃən ,mɑːk]		the punctuation mark (!) that you use at the end of a sentence to show excitement or anger (*In American English, use* **exclamation point**)
exclamation point (*American English*) *see* **exclamation mark**		
fairy tale	['feəri ,teɪl]	a story for children about magic and fairies
fiction	['fɪkʃən]	books and stories about people and events that are not real
full stop	[,fʊl 'stɒp]	the punctuation mark (.) that you use at the end of a sentence (*In American English, use* **period**)
handwriting	['hændraɪtɪŋ]	your style of writing with a pen or a pencil
headline	['hedlaɪn]	the title of a newspaper story, printed in large letters

EXAMPLES

I have kept a diary since I was eleven.
She writes romantic fiction.
The address was in Anna's handwriting.
The headline read 'Government plans to build new hospitals'.

hero	['hɪərəʊ]	the main male character of a story
heroine	['herəʊɪn]	the main female character of a story
hyphen	['haɪfən]	the punctuation sign (-) that you use to join two words together, as in 'left-handed'
index	['ɪndeks]	a list at the back of a book that tells you what is in the book and on which pages you can find each item
ink	[ɪŋk]	the coloured liquid that you use for writing or printing
introduction	[ˌɪntrə'dʌkʃən]	the part at the beginning of a book that tells you what the book is about
journal	['dʒɜːnəl]	**1** a magazine or a newspaper that deals with a special subject; *an academic journal* **2** same as **diary**
journalist	['dʒɜːnəlɪst]	someone whose job is to collect news stories and write about them for newspapers, magazines, television or radio
language	['læŋgwɪdʒ]	**1** a system of sounds and written symbols that people of a particular country or region use in talking or writing; *the English language* **2** the use of a system of communication that has a set of sounds or written symbols; *improve your language skills*
legend	['ledʒənd]	a very old and popular story
letter	['letə]	**1** a message that you write or type on paper and send to someone; *send someone a letter* **2** a written symbol that represents a sound in a language; *the letters of the alphabet*
library	['laɪbrəri]	a place where books, newspapers, DVDs and music are kept for people to use or borrow
literature	['lɪtrətʃə]	books, plays and poetry that most people consider to be of high quality

EXAMPLES
The letter was written in blue ink.
Ayumi is studying English literature at Leeds University.

magazine	[ˌmægəˈziːn]	a thin book with stories and pictures that you can buy every week or every month
myth	[mɪθ]	an ancient story about gods and magic; *a Greek myth*
narrator	[nəˈreɪtə]	the person who tells the story in a book
newspaper	[ˈnjuːzpeɪpə]	a number of large sheets of folded paper, with news, advertisements and other information printed on them
nonfiction	[nɒnˈfɪkʃən]	writing that is about real people and events rather than imaginary ones
novel	[ˈnɒvəl]	a long written story about imaginary people and events
novelist	[ˈnɒvəlɪst]	someone who writes novels
page	[peɪdʒ]	one side of a piece of paper in a book, a magazine or a newspaper; *Turn to page 7.*
paper	[ˈpeɪpə]	1 a material that you write on; *a piece of paper* 2 a newspaper
paperback	[ˈpeɪpəˌbæk]	a book with a thin cardboard or paper cover
paragraph	[ˈpærəˌɡrɑːf]	a section of a piece of writing that begins on a new line and contains more than one sentence
pen	[pen]	a long thin object that you use for writing with ink
pencil	[ˈpensəl]	a long thin piece of wood with a black substance through the middle, that you use for writing
period (American English)		*see* **full stop**
play	[pleɪ]	a piece of writing performed in a theatre, on the radio or on television

---

EXAMPLES

I read about the fire in the newspaper.
The library contains both fiction and nonfiction.
My favourite novel is 'War and Peace'.
I'm going to the shop to buy a paper.
I'll buy the book when it comes out in paperback.
'Hamlet' is my favourite play.

plot	[plɒt]	a series of events that make up the story of a book
poem	[ˈpəʊɪm]	a piece of writing in which the words are chosen for their beauty and sound, and are arranged in short lines
poet	[ˈpəʊɪt]	someone who writes poems
poetry	[ˈpəʊɪtri]	the form of literature that consists of poems
punctuation	[ˌpʌŋktʃʊˈeɪʃən]	signs such as ( ), ! or ? that you use to divide writing into sentences and phrases
question mark	[ˈkwestʃən ˌmɑːk]	the punctuation mark (?) that is used in writing at the end of a question
quotation	[kwəʊˈteɪʃən]	a sentence or a phrase from a book, a poem, a speech or a play
quotation marks	[kwəʊˈteɪʃən ˌmɑːks]	the punctuation marks (' ') or (" ") that are used in writing to show where speech or a quotation begins and ends
report	[rɪˈpɔːt]	**1** a newspaper article that gives information about something that happened; *a newspaper report* **2** a piece of work that a student writes on a particular subject; *a book report*
rubber	[ˈrʌbə]	a small object that you use for removing marks you have made with a pencil (*In American English, use* **eraser**)
scene	[siːn]	a part of a play or a book in which all the events happen in the same place
script	[skrɪpt]	the written words that actors speak in a play
semicolon	[ˌsemiˈkəʊlɒn]	the mark (;) that you use in writing to separate different parts of a sentence

EXAMPLES
He told me the plot of his new novel.
We studied French poetry last term.
Check your spelling and punctuation.
The opening scene shows a mother and daughter having an argument.

sentence	['sentəns]	a group of words that tells you something or asks a question
story	['stɔːri]	a description of imaginary people and events, that is intended to entertain people
summary	['sʌməri]	a short description of something that gives the main points but not the details
thesaurus (PL) **thesauruses, thesauri**	[θɪ'sɔːrəs] [θɪ'sɔːraɪ]	a reference book in which words with similar meanings are grouped together
thriller	['θrɪlə]	an exciting book or play about a crime
title	['taɪtəl]	the name of something such as a book or a play
translation	[trænz'leɪʃən]	a piece of writing or speech that has been put into a different language
vocabulary	[vəʊ'kæbjʊləri]	1 all the words that someone knows in a particular language; *She has a large vocabulary.* 2 all the words in a language; *a new word in the English vocabulary* 3 the words that you use when you are talking about a particular subject; *technical vocabulary*
word	[wɜːd]	a unit of language with meaning
writer	['raɪtə]	someone whose job is to write books, stories or articles
writing	['raɪtɪŋ]	1 something that has been written or printed 2 any piece of written work; *a piece of writing* 3 the activity of writing, especially of writing books for money

---

EXAMPLES

Here is a short summary of the news.
The title of the novel is 'Jane Eyre'.
The Italian word for 'love' is 'amore'.
Lydia tried to read the writing on the next page.
Elizabeth Johnston teaches creative writing at Concordia University.

VERBS

copy ['kɒpi] to write something that is exactly like another thing

delete [dɪ'liːt] to put a line through something that has been written down

look something up to try to find something in a book such as a dictionary

print [prɪnt] 1 to use a machine to put words or pictures on paper; *print copies of a novel*
2 to write letters that are not joined together; *print your name*

publish ['pʌblɪʃ] to prepare and print copies of a book, a magazine or a newspaper

read [riːd] 1 to look at written words and understand them; *read a book*
2 to say words that you can see; *read someone a story*

rhyme [raɪm] to end with a very similar sound to another word; *'June' rhymes with 'moon'.*

rub something out to remove something such as writing or a mark; *rub out a mistake*

set [set] if a story is set in a particular place or time, the events in it take place in that place or time

skim [skɪm] to read something quickly

spell [spel] 1 to write or speak each letter of a word in the correct order; *How do you spell 'potato'?*
2 to have a good knowledge of the correct order of letters in words; *Many students cannot spell.*

translate [trænz'leɪt] to say or write something again in a different language

---

EXAMPLES

I didn't know what 'subscribe' meant, so I looked it up in the dictionary
HarperCollins will publish his new novel in March.
The novel is set in China in 1900.
He skimmed the pages quickly, then read them again more carefully.
Martin Luther translated the Bible into German.

type	[taɪp]	to write something using a machine such as a computer
write	[raɪt]	**1** to use a pen or a pencil to produce words, letters or numbers
		2 to create something such as a book or a poem
		3 to give someone information, ask them something, or express your feelings in a letter or an email; *write to someone*

EXAMPLES
Please write your name and address on the back of the photo.
She writes articles for French newspapers.

routines

NOUNS

chore	[tʃɔː]	a job that you have to do, for example, cleaning the house; *household chores*; *do the chores*
day off	[ˌdeɪ ˈɒf]	a day when you do not go to work; *have a day off*
free time	[friː ˈtaɪm]	time when you are not working or studying, when you can do things that you enjoy; *in your free time*
habit	[ˈhæbɪt]	something that you do often or regularly; *a bad habit*; *an old habit*
hobby	[ˈhɒbi]	an activity that you enjoy doing in your free time
housework	[ˈhaʊswɜːk]	the work that you do to keep a house clean and tidy; *do housework*
lie-in	[ˈlaɪɪn]	an occasion when you rest by staying in bed later than usual in the morning
lifestyle	[ˈlaɪfstaɪl]	the way someone has chosen to live and behave; *a healthy lifestyle*
lunch break	[ˈlʌntʃ breɪk]	the period in the middle of the day when you stop work in order to have a meal; *have your lunch break*
routine	[ruːˈtiːn]	the usual activities that you do every day; *your daily routine*
rush hour	[ˈrʌʃ aʊə]	one of the periods of the day when most people are travelling to or from work; *rush-hour traffic*
time off	[ˌtaɪm ˈɒf]	a period of time when you do not work; *take time off*; *give someone time off*

EXAMPLES

She's always busy and has lots of hobbies.
Skiing is an expensive hobby.
I have a lie-in on Sundays.
I had to drive eight miles at rush hour.

VERBS

commute	[kəˈmjuːt]	to travel to work or school
shave	[ʃeɪv]	to remove hair from your face or body
do the shopping		to go to the shops to buy things
drop someone off		to take someone to a place in a car and leave them there
get dressed		to put clothes on yourself
get ready		to completely prepare yourself for something
get up		to get out of bed
go home		to return to the place where you live
go to bed		to lie down in your bed to sleep
go to sleep		to fall asleep
go to work		to go to the place where you do your job
have/take a bath		to sit or lie in a bath filled with water to wash your body
have/take a shower		to wash yourself by standing under the water that comes from a shower
have breakfast		to eat the first meal of the day
have dinner		to eat the main meal of the day, that is usually served in the evening
have lunch		to eat the meal that you have in the middle of the day
make dinner		to prepare the main meal of the day, that is usually served in the evening

EXAMPLES

Many women shave their legs.
He always shaves before breakfast.
Dad dropped me off at school on his way to work.
It takes her a long time to get ready for school.
They have to get up early in the morning.
We went to bed at about 10 p.m.
It was time to go to work.
Would you like to stay and have dinner?

pick someone up	to collect so... a car
set your alarm	to adjust an alarm clock so... wake you at a particular time
sleep in	to sleep until after the time you usually g... up in the morning
tidy up	to organize a place by putting things in their proper places
wake up	to stop sleeping

ADVERBS

at weekends	on Saturdays and Sundays
during the week	on any day from Monday to Friday
every day	on each day without exception
every week	at least one time each week
in the afternoon	during the part of the day that begins at lunchtime and ends at about six o'clock
in the evening	during the part of the day between the end of the afternoon and midnight
in the morning	during the part of the day between the time that people usually wake up and noon

EXAMPLES

I pick the children up from school at three o'clock.
Dad set the alarm for eight the next day.
It was cold and dark when I woke up at 6.30.
She was never at home at weekends.
He never goes out during the week.
They got up every day before dawn.
He phones his mother every week.
He's arriving in the afternoon.
We usually have dinner at seven in the evening.
The first thing people do in the morning is open the curtains.

...aries

IDIOMS

burn the candle at both ends	to stay up very late at night and get up very early in the morning
go out like a light	to fall asleep very quickly
on the go	always busy and active
rushed off your feet	very busy

EXAMPLE
I've been on the go all day.

school

NOUNS

assembly [ə'sembli] a meeting of all the teachers and pupils at the beginning of a school day; *a school assembly*

blackboard ['blækbɔːd] a big, dark-coloured board for writing on in a classroom (*In American English, use* **chalkboard**)

box lunch (*American English*) *see* **packed lunch**

break [breɪk] a period of time between lessons at school when pupils can play or eat; *lunch break*; *at break* (*In American English, use* **recess**)

bully ['bʊli] someone who uses their strength or power to frighten other people; *school bullies*

canteen [kæn'tiːn] a place in a school where pupils can buy and eat lunch; *the school canteen*

caretaker ['keəteɪkə] someone who looks after a school building and the area around it (*In American English, use* **janitor**); *a school caretaker*

chalkboard (*American English*) *see* **blackboard**

class [klɑːs] **1** a group of pupils who learn at school together
2 a time when you learn something at school

classroom ['klɑːsruːm] a room in a school where lessons take place

desk [desk] a table that you sit at to write or work

education [ˌedʒʊ'keɪʃən] teaching and learning; *secondary/primary education*; *higher/further education*; *sex/health education*

elementary school (*American English*) *see* **primary school**

EXAMPLES
We have assembly on Tuesday and Friday mornings.
After the first two lessons, we have break.
He spent six months in a class with younger pupils.
Classes start at 9 o'clock.
We do lots of reading in class.

essay	['eseɪ]	a short piece of writing on a subject; *write an essay*
exam	[ɪg'zæm]	a formal test that you take to show your knowledge of a subject; *take/sit an exam*; *pass/fail an exam*; *exam results*
examination	[ɪg,zæmɪ'neɪʃən]	[FORMAL] exam
exercise	['eksə,saɪz]	an activity that you do in order to practise a skill; *a writing exercise*; *an exercise book*
grade	[greɪd]	the mark that a teacher gives you to show how good your work is
gym	[dʒɪm]	a large room with equipment for doing physical exercises
head teacher	[,hed 'ti:tʃə]	a teacher who is in charge of a school
holidays	['hɒlɪdeɪz]	the time when children do not have to go to school; *the summer holidays*
homework	['həʊmwɜ:k]	school work that teachers give to pupils to do at home in the evening or at the weekend; *do your homework*
janitor *(American English)*		*see* **caretaker**
lesson	['lesən]	a time when you learn about a particular subject; *a history lesson*
lunchbox	['lʌntʃbɒks]	a small container for taking lunch to school
mark	[mɑ:k]	a number or letter on a pupil's work to show how good it is
mistake	[mɪ'steɪk]	something that is not correct
packed lunch	[,pækt 'lʌntʃ]	food that you take to school, and eat as your lunch; *take/have a packed lunch* (*In American English, use* **box lunch**)

EXAMPLES
She always got top grades.
the first day of the school holidays
I have homework every day.
I got a good mark.
Tony made three spelling mistakes in this essay.

PE	[ˌpiː ˈiː]	short for 'physical education': a school lesson in which pupils do physical exercises or sport
period	[ˈpɪəriəd]	one of the parts of the school day when lessons take place; *a free period*
playground	[ˈpleɪɡraʊnd]	a piece of land where children can play at school; *the school playground*
playtime	[ˈpleɪtaɪm]	the period of time between lessons at school when children can play outside
pre-school	[ˈpriːskuːl]	a school for children between the ages of two and five or six
primary school	[ˈpraɪməri ˌskuːl]	a school for children between the ages of five and 11 (*In American English, use* **elementary school**)
private school	[ˈpraɪvɪt ˌskuːl]	a school that parents have to pay for their children to go to
public school	[ˈpʌblɪk ˌskuːl]	**1** in Britain, a private school that provides secondary education which parents have to pay for **2** in the USA, Australia, and some other countries, a school that usually provides free education
pupil	[ˈpjuːpɪl]	one of the children who go to a school
recess (*American English*)		*see* **break**
register	[ˈredʒɪstə]	an official list of pupils in a class; *take the register*
result	[rɪˈzʌlt]	facts such as a score that you get at the end of a competition or a test; *exam results*
school	[skuːl]	a place where people go to learn; *a school bag; a school bus; school lunch*
school rules	[ˌskuːl ˈruːlz]	a list of things that pupils must do or must not do when they are at school; *obey school rules*

EXAMPLES

Friends in different classes can meet up at playtime.
He goes to a private school.

school uniform	[ˌskuːl ˈjuːnɪfɔːm]	the special clothes that some pupils wear at school; *wear/have a school uniform*
schoolchildren	[ˈskuːltʃɪldrən]	children who go to school
secondary school	[ˈsekəndri ˌskuːl]	a school for pupils between the ages of 11 or 12 and 17 or 18
smart board™	[ˈsmɑːt ˌbɔːd]	a large electronic board that can be used for teaching and learning
special education	[ˌspeʃəl ˌedʒʊˈkeɪʃən]	teaching for pupils who need extra help with their studies
state school	[ˈsteɪt ˌskuːl]	a government school that children can attend without having to pay; *go to a state school*
subject	[ˈsʌbdʒɪkt]	an area of knowledge that you study in school
teacher	[ˈtiːtʃə]	a person whose job is to give lessons in a subject at a school; *an English teacher*; *a science teacher*; *a primary/secondary school teacher*
term	[tɜːm]	one of the periods of time that a school year is divided into; *this/last term*
test	[test]	a series of questions that pupils must answer to show how much they know about a subject; *pass/fail a test*
textbook	[ˈtekstbʊk]	a book containing facts about a particular subject
timetable	[ˈtaɪmteɪbəl]	a list that shows the times in the week when particular subjects are taught; *an exam timetable*
tutor	[ˈtjuːtə]	someone who gives private lessons to one pupil or a very small group of pupils; *a private tutor*; *an English tutor*
whiteboard	[ˈwaɪtbɔːd]	a shiny, white board that teachers draw or write on, using special pens

EXAMPLES

Maths is my favourite subject.

The school's head teacher will retire at the end of the term.

(VERBS)

ask	[ɑːsk, æsk]	to say something in the form of a question; *ask a question*
answer	[ˈɑːnsə]	to write or say what you think is the correct answer to a question; *answer a question*
break up		to start the school holidays
bully	[ˈbʊli]	to use your strength or power to frighten other people
cheat	[tʃiːt]	to do something that is not honest or fair, often because you want to get something
correct	[kəˈrekt]	to look at a piece of writing and mark the mistakes in it; *correct pupils' work; correct mistakes*
expel	[ɪkˈspel]	to officially tell a pupil to leave a school permanently
fail	[feɪl]	not to pass an exam or a test; *fail an exam*
learn	[lɜːn]	to get knowledge or a skill by studying
mark	[mɑːk]	to write a number or letter on a pupil's work to show how good it is; *mark an essay*
pass	[pɑːs]	to succeed in an exam; *pass an exam*
punish	[ˈpʌnɪʃ]	to make someone suffer in some way because they have done something wrong
put up your hand		to raise your hand in the air in order to show that you want to answer a question
read	[riːd]	to look at written words and understand them; *learn to read and write*
repeat	[rɪˈpiːt]	to say or write the same thing that someone else has said or written
revise	[rɪˈvaɪz]	to study something again in order to prepare for an exam

EXAMPLES

The schools break up this weekend.
I think they were bullied in school.
Pupils sometimes cheated in order to get into top schools.
She was expelled for cheating in an exam.
I have to revise for my maths exam.

study	['stʌdi]	to spend time learning about a particular subject; *study history*
teach	[ti:tʃ]	to give lessons in a subject at a school
write	[raɪt]	to use a pen or a pencil to produce words, letters or numbers

ADJECTIVES

absent	['æbsənt]	not at school
correct	[kə'rekt]	right or true; *a correct answer*
difficult	['dɪfɪkəlt]	requiring a lot of effort; *a difficult question*
easy	['i:zi]	not difficult; *an easy task*
present	['prezənt]	at school; *be present*

ADVERB

| **off by heart** | | using only your memory |

EXAMPLES
Christine teaches biology at Piper High.
'Was he at school yesterday?' — 'No, he was absent.'
She's learnt the whole speech off by heart.

science

acid ['æsɪd] a chemical, usually a liquid, that can burn your skin and cause damage to other substances; *citric acid*

astronaut ['æstrənɔːt] a person who is trained for travelling in space

astronomy [ə'strɒnəmi] the scientific study of the stars, planets and other natural objects in space

atom ['ætəm] the very smallest part of a substance

axis ['æksɪs] **1** an imaginary line through the middle of
(PL) **axes** ['æksiːs] something; *the Earth's axis*
2 one of the two lines of a graph on which you mark points to show amounts; *the vertical/horizontal axis*

botany ['bɒtəni] the scientific study of plants

cell [sel] the smallest part of an animal or plant; *brain cells*

charge [tʃɑːdʒ] the amount or type of electrical force that something has; *an electrical charge*

chemical ['kemɪkəl] a substance that is used in a chemical process or made by a chemical process

chemist ['kemɪst] a scientist who studies chemistry

chemistry ['kemɪstri] the science of the structure of gases, liquids and solids, and how they change

circuit ['sɜːkɪt] a complete path that electricity can flow around; *an electrical circuit*

compound ['kɒmpaʊnd] a substance that is made from two or more elements, for example, carbon dioxide

current ['kʌrənt] a steady flow of water, air or energy

electricity [ɪlek'trɪsɪti, ,elek-] energy that is used for producing heat and light, and to provide power for machines

element ['elɪmənt] a basic chemical substance such as gold, oxygen or carbon

energy	[ˈenədʒi]	the power from electricity or the sun, for example, that makes machines work or provides heat
evolution	[ˌiːvəˈluːʃən, ˌev-]	a process in which animals or plants slowly change over many years
experiment	[ɪkˈsperɪmənt]	a scientific test that you do in order to discover what happens to something; *conduct an experiment*
force	[fɔːs]	the pulling or pushing effect that one thing has on another; *the Earth's gravitational force*
formula (PL) formulas, formulae	[ˈfɔːmjʊlə] [ˈfɔːmjʊliː]	1 a group of letters, numbers or other symbols that represents a scientific rule 2 a description of the chemical elements that a substance contains
fuse	[fjuːz]	a small wire in a piece of electrical equipment that stops it from working when too much electricity passes through it
gene	[dʒiːn]	the part of a cell that controls a person's, an animal's or a plant's physical characteristics, growth and development
genetics	[dʒɪˈnetɪks]	the study of how qualities are passed on from parents to children
gravity	[ˈgrævɪti]	the force that makes things fall to the ground
hormone	[ˈhɔːməʊn]	a chemical substance in your body that affects the way your body works
laboratory	[ləˈbɒrətri]	a building or a room where scientific work is done

EXAMPLES

The device converts energy from the sun into electrical energy.

He developed a mathematical formula describing the distances of the planets from the Sun.

The Earth's gravity pulls the oceans in daily tides.

lens	[lenz]	a thin, curved piece of glass or plastic used in things such as cameras and glasses. A lens makes things look larger, smaller or clearer
magnet	['mægnɪt]	a piece of special metal that attracts iron or steel towards it
microscope	['maɪkrəˌskəʊp]	a scientific instrument that makes very small objects look bigger
molecule	['mɒlɪˌkjuːl]	the smallest amount of a chemical substance that can exist by itself
organism	['ɔːgəˌnɪzəm]	a living thing
physics	['fɪzɪks]	the scientific study of things such as heat, light and sound
power	['paʊə]	energy that can be used for making electricity or for making machines work
radar	['reɪdɑː]	a way of discovering the position of objects when they cannot be seen, by using radio signals
science	['saɪəns]	the study of natural things
scientist	['saɪəntɪst]	someone whose job is to teach or do research in science
spacecraft	['speɪskrɑːft]	a vehicle that can travel in space
specimen	['spesɪmɪn]	an example or a small amount of something; *examine a specimen*
test tube	['test ˌtjuːb]	a small tube-shaped container made from glass. Test tubes are used in laboratories.
theory	['θɪəri]	an idea or a set of ideas that tries to explain something
volt	[vəʊlt]	a unit used for measuring electricity; *a 12-volt battery*
watt	[wɒt]	a unit for measuring electrical power; *a 60-watt light bulb*

EXAMPLES

The system creates enough power to run four lights.
The mystery objects showed up on the plane's radar.
Albert Einstein developed the Theory of Relativity.

VERBS

dilute	[daɪˈluːt]	to add water to another liquid
dissect	[daɪˈsekt, dɪ-]	to cut open a dead body in order to examine it
dissolve	[dɪˈzɒlv]	to become completely mixed with a liquid
evaporate	[ɪˈvæpəˌreɪt]	to change from a liquid into a gas
evolve	[ɪˈvɒlv]	to gradually develop over a period of time into something different
measure	[ˈmeʒə]	to find out the size of something
test	[test]	to use something to find out what condition it is in, or how well it works

ADJECTIVES

atomic	[əˈtɒmɪk]	relating to atoms or to power that is produced by splitting atoms
chemical	[ˈkemɪkəl]	relating to chemistry or chemicals; *a chemical reaction*
electric	[ɪˈlektrɪk]	**1** working using electricity; *an electric car* **2** carrying electricity; *electric cables*
nuclear	[ˈnjuːklɪə]	relating to the energy that is released when the central parts (= nuclei) of atoms are split or combined; *a nuclear power station*
scientific	[ˌsaɪənˈtɪfɪk]	relating to science; *a scientific experiment*

EXAMPLES
Dilute the fruit juice thoroughly.
Boil the water and sugar until the sugar has dissolved completely.
Water evaporates from the oceans into the atmosphere.
Humans have evolved with the power to hold things.
He spends a lot of time conducting scientific research.

shopping

NOUNS

baker's	['beɪkəz]	a shop where bread and cakes are sold
barcode	['bɑːkəʊd]	a set of lines on a product that tell the computer its price
bargain	['bɑːgɪn]	something that is sold at a lower price than usual
bookshop	['bʊkʃɒp]	a shop where books are sold (*In American English, use* **bookstore**)
bookstore (*American English*)		*see* **bookshop**
boutique	[buːˈtiːk]	a small shop that sells fashionable clothes, shoes or jewellery
butcher's	['bʊtʃəz]	a shop where meat is sold
carrier bag	['kæriə bæg]	a plastic or paper bag with handles that you use for carrying shopping
cash	[kæʃ]	coins and notes, rather than a cheque or bank card
catalogue	['kætəlɒg]	a list of things you can buy from a particular company
change	[tʃeɪndʒ]	the money that you get back when you pay with more money than something costs
checkout	['tʃekaʊt]	the place in a shop where you pay
chemist's	['kemɪsts]	a shop that sells medicines and beauty products
cheque	[tʃek]	a printed piece of paper from a bank that you write an amount of money on, and use to pay for things; *pay by cheque*
clothes shop	['kləʊðz ʃɒp]	a shop where you can buy clothes
complaint	[kəmˈpleɪnt]	when you say that you are not satisfied with the service or products you have received

EXAMPLES
I got these cakes from the baker's this morning.
If you go early, you could get a real bargain.
I'm afraid we only accept cash.
Here's your change.
I want to make a complaint.

credit card		a plastic card that you use to buy goods now and pay for them later; *pay by credit card*
customer	['kʌstəmə]	someone who buys something from a shop or a website
department	[dɪ'pɑːtmənt]	one of the sections in a department store; *the toy department*
department store	[dɪ'pɑːtmənt ˌstɔː]	a large shop that sells many different types of goods
discount	['dɪskaʊnt]	a reduction in the usual price of something
fishmonger's	['fɪʃmʌŋgəz]	a shop where fish is sold
florist's	['flɒrɪsts]	a shop where flowers are sold
fruit shop	['fruːt ʃɒp]	a shop where fruit is sold
gift shop	['gɪft ʃɒp]	a shop that sells things that people give as presents
goods	[gʊdz]	things that you can buy or sell; *electrical goods*
greengrocer's	['griːngrəʊsəz]	a shop where fruit and vegetables are sold
grocer's	['grəʊsəz]	a shop that sells food and other things that you need at home
jeweller's	['dʒuːələz]	a shop where jewellery is sold
line (American English)		*see* **queue**
mail order	[ˌmeɪl 'ɔːdə]	a system in which you choose goods from a catalogue and they are sent to you by post
market	['mɑːkɪt]	a place where people buy and sell goods on tables; *a farmers' market*
newsagent's	['njuːzeɪdʒəntz]	a shop where newspapers and magazines are sold
online store	['ɒnlaɪn ˌstɔː]	a website with photos and details of goods that customers can buy
opening hours	['əʊpənɪŋ aʊəz]	the hours that a shop is open
price	[praɪs]	the amount of money that you have to pay when you buy something

EXAMPLES
What are your opening hours?
The price of bread went up by 20 per cent last year.

queue	[kjuː]	a line of people who are waiting for something; *wait in a queue* (*In American English, use* **line**)
receipt	[rɪˈsiːt]	a piece of paper that shows that you have paid for something
refund	[ˈriːfʌnd]	money that is given back to you when you return goods to a shop
sale	[seɪl]	an occasion when a shop sells things at a lower price than usual
sales clerk (*American English*)		*see* **shop assistant**
shoe shop	[ˈʃuː ʃɒp]	a shop where shoes are sold
shop	[ʃɒp]	a place where you buy things (*In American English, use* **store**)
shop assistant	[ˈʃɒp əsɪstənt]	someone whose job is to deal with customers in a shop (*In American English, use* **sales clerk**)
shopping	[ˈʃɒpɪŋ]	the activity of going to shops to buy things; *go shopping*; *do the shopping*
shopping bag	[ˈʃɒpɪŋ bæg]	a large bag that is used for carrying things that you have bought
shopping cart (*American English*)		*see* **shopping trolley**
shopping centre	[ˈʃɒpɪŋ sentə]	an area in a town where there are a lot of shops
shopping list	[ˈʃɒpɪŋ lɪst]	a list of all the things that you want to buy
shopping trolley	[ˈʃɒpɪŋ trɒli]	a wire or plastic basket on wheels in which you put all the things that you want to buy in a particular shop (*In American English, use* **shopping cart**)
size	[saɪz]	how big or small something is
special offer	[ˌspeʃəl ˈɒfə]	a low price that is offered by a shop for a period of time

EXAMPLES

Please make sure you keep your receipt.
I'd like a refund.
I bought these jeans in the sale.
Do you have this in a smaller size?

stationer's	['steɪʃənəz]	a shop where you can buy things for writing such as paper, pens, and pencils
store	[stɔː]	**1** a large shop; *a furniture store* **2** (American English) see **shop**
supermarket	['suːpəmɑːkɪt]	a large shop that sells food and other products for the home
sweetshop	['swiːt ʃɒp]	a shop where sweets are sold
till	[tɪl]	a machine that holds money in a shop
toy shop	['tɔɪ ʃɒp]	a shop where toys are sold
window shopping	['wɪndəʊ ˌʃɒpɪŋ]	the activity of looking in shops without buying anything

VERBS

browse	[braʊz]	to look at things in a shop, without buying anything
buy	[baɪ]	to get something by paying money for it
close	[kləʊz]	when a shop closes, it stops being open, so that people cannot go in and buy things
cost	[kɒst]	to have as a price
open	['əʊpən]	when a shop opens, people can go in and buy things
pay	[peɪ]	to give someone an amount of money for something that you are buying
return	[rɪ'tɜːn]	to bring back something you have bought because you do not want it any more
sell	[sel]	to have something available for people to buy
spend	[spend]	to use money to buy things
try something on		to put a piece of clothing on in order to see if it fits

---

EXAMPLES
How much does it cost?
Can I pay with this card?
You may return any goods within 14 days.
Do you sell stamps?
Can I try this on?

ADJECTIVES

cheap	[tʃiːp]	**1** costing little money or less than you expected **2** costing less money than similar products but often of bad quality
closed	[kləʊzd]	a shop that is closed is not open, so people cannot go in and buy things
contactless	['kɒntæktləs]	contactless payment involves holding your payment card near a machine that reads the information on it
expensive	[ɪk'spensɪv]	costing a lot of money
in stock	[ɪn 'stɒk]	available for customers to buy in a shop
on sale	[ɒn 'seɪl]	**1** available for people to buy **2** available to buy at a lower price than usual
open	['əʊpən]	when a shop is open, people can go in and buy things
out of stock	[,aʊt əv 'stɒk]	no longer available for customers to buy
reduced	[rɪ'djuːst]	at a lower price than usual; *a reduced price*
second-hand	[,sekənd'hænd]	already used by another person; not new; *a second-hand car*
value-for-money	['væljuː fə ,mʌni]	not very expensive, but good; *a value-for-money clothing store*

PHRASES

Anything else?	used by a shop assistant to ask if there are any other things you would like to buy
Just looking.	used for telling a shop assistant that you do not need any help

EXAMPLES

I'd like something cheaper.
It's too expensive.
I'm afraid we don't have your size in stock.

society and politics

NOUNS

ambassador [æm'bæsədə] an important official person who lives in a foreign country and represents his or her own country there; *the British ambassador in Berlin*

army ['ɑːmi] a large group of soldiers who are trained to fight battles on land

asylum seeker [ə'saɪləm siːkə] someone who asks the government of a foreign country if they can live there, because they are in danger in their own country

capitalism ['kæpɪtəlɪzəm] an economic and political system in which property, business and industry are privately owned

capitalist ['kæpɪtəlɪst] someone who supports the ideas of capitalism

caste [kɑːst, kæst] one of the social classes into which people in a Hindu society are divided

ceasefire ['siːsfaɪə] an agreement to stop fighting for a period of time; *declare a ceasefire*

citizen ['sɪtɪzən] **1** a person who legally belongs to a particular country
2 a person who lives in a town or a city

civil war [ˌsɪvəl 'wɔː] a war that is fought between different groups of people living in the same country

civilian [sɪ'vɪliən] a person who is not a member of the armed forces

class [klɑːs] a group of people with the same economic and social position in a society

communism ['kɒmjʊˌnɪzəm] an economic and political system in which property, business and industry are owned by the state

---

EXAMPLES
Prince Charlie's army marched on Edinburgh in 1745.
The number of asylum seekers entering Britain fell last month.
Ten civilians died in the attack.

communist	[ˈkɒmjʊnɪst]	someone who supports the ideas of communism
community	[kəˈmjuːnɪti]	a group of people who are similar in some way, or have similar interests; *the Muslim community*
council	[ˈkaʊnsəl]	a group of people who are chosen to control a particular area; *the local council*
country	[ˈkʌntri]	an area of the world with its own government and people
culture	[ˈkʌltʃə]	the way of life, the traditions and beliefs of a particular group of people
democracy	[dɪˈmɒkrəsi]	a system of government in which people choose their leaders by voting for them in elections
dictator	[dɪkˈteɪtə]	a ruler who uses force to keep power in a country
election	[ɪˈlekʃən]	a process in which people vote in order to choose a person who will hold an official position; *a presidential election*
embassy	[ˈembəsi]	**1** a group of officials, headed by an ambassador, who represent their government in a foreign country **2** the building in which these people work
emperor	[ˈempərə]	a man who rules an empire
empire	[ˈempaɪə]	several separate nations that are all controlled by the ruler of one particular country
globalization [ˌgləʊbəlaɪˈzeɪʃən]		the idea that the world is developing a single economy as a result of modern technology and communications
government	[ˈgʌvənmənt]	the group of people who control and organize a country, a state or a city
human rights	[ˌhjuːmən ˈraɪts]	the rights that all people in a society should have

EXAMPLES

The embassy has confirmed the report.
A police officer was guarding the embassy.
The country has a poor human rights record.

immigrant	[ˈɪmɪgrənt]	a person who comes to live in a country from another country
independence	[ˌɪndɪˈpendəns]	a situation in which one country is not controlled by another country
king	[kɪŋ]	a man from a royal family, who is the head of state of that country
kingdom	[ˈkɪŋdəm]	a country that is ruled by a king or a queen
the middle class	[ðə ˌmɪdəl ˈklɑːs]	the people in a society who are well educated, and who have professional jobs, for example, teachers, doctors, and lawyers
monarchy	[ˈmɒnəki]	a system in which a country has a king or a queen
MP	[ˌem ˈpiː]	short for 'Member of Parliament': in Britain, a person in the government who has been elected to represent the people from a particular area
nation	[ˈneɪʃən]	an individual country, its people and its social and political structures
nationality	[ˌnæʃəˈnælɪti]	**1** the state of being a legal citizen of a particular country; *Polish nationality* **2** a group of people who have the same race, culture, or language
parliament	[ˈpɑːləmənt]	the group of people who make or change the laws of some countries
party	[ˈpɑːti]	a political organization whose members have similar aims and beliefs; *the Conservative Party*
peace	[piːs]	a situation where there is not a war
politics	[ˈpɒlɪtɪks]	the activities and ideas that are concerned with government
population	[ˌpɒpjʊˈleɪʃən]	all the people who live in a country or an area
president	[ˈprezɪdənt]	the person who is in charge of a country that has no king or queen

---

EXAMPLES
Biafra declared independence in May 1967.
We have several different nationalities in our team.
NATO forces were sent to Kosovo to keep the peace.

prime minister	[ˌpraɪm ˈmɪnɪstə]	the leader of a government in some countries
queen	[kwiːn]	**1** a woman from a royal family who rules a country **2** the wife of a king
refugee	[ˌrefjuːˈdʒiː]	a person who has been forced to leave their home or their country, because it is too dangerous for them there
republic	[rɪˈpʌblɪk]	a country with no king or queen, where the people choose their government
revolution	[ˌrevəˈluːʃən]	an attempt by a group of people to change their country's government by using force
ruler	[ˈruːlə]	the person who rules a country
slave	[sleɪv]	a person who belongs to another person and who is forced to work for them without being paid
soldier	[ˈsəʊldʒə]	a member of an army
state	[steɪt]	**1** a country, especially when it is considered politically; *E.U. member states* **2** a smaller area that some large countries such as the United States are divided into; *the state of Michigan* **3** the government of a country; *a state-owned bank*
territory	[ˈterətri]	all the land that a particular country owns
terrorism	[ˈterəˌrɪzəm]	the use of violence to force a government to do something
terrorist	[ˈterərɪst]	a person who uses violence to achieve political aims
the upper class	[ðiː ˌʌpə ˈklɑːs]	the people in a society who have the highest position in society
volunteer	[ˌvɒlənˈtɪə]	someone who works without being paid
war	[wɔː]	a period of fighting between countries or groups

EXAMPLE
In 1818, Argentina was at war with Spain.

the working class	[ðə ˌwɜːkɪŋ ˈklɑːs]	the people in a society who are less educated, and who have less money than other people

VERBS

assassinate	[əˈsæsɪneɪt]	to murder someone for political reasons
break out		when war breaks out, it begins
conquer	[ˈkɒŋkə]	to take complete control of the land of another country or group of people
elect	[ɪˈlekt]	to choose a person to do a particular job by voting for them; *elect a president*
govern	[ˈgʌvən]	to officially control and organize a country
invade	[ɪnˈveɪd]	to attack and enter a country
reign	[reɪn]	to rule a country as king or queen
volunteer	[ˌvɒlənˈtɪə]	to work without being paid
vote	[vəʊt]	to show your choice officially in an election; *vote in an election*

ADJECTIVES

armed	[ɑːmd]	carrying a weapon, usually a gun; *armed forces*
capitalist	[ˈkæpɪtəlɪst]	relating to or supporting capitalism
communist	[ˈkɒmjʊnɪst]	relating to or supporting communism
democratic	[ˌdeməˈkrætɪk]	**1** having or relating to a political system in which the leaders are elected by the people they govern; *democratic elections* **2** based on the idea that everyone has equal rights and should be involved in making important decisions; *a democratic decision*
global	[ˈgləʊbəl]	relating to the whole world; *the global economy*

EXAMPLES
The president was assassinated and the army took over.
Victoria reigned for over 60 years.

international	[ˌɪntəˈnæʃənəl]	involving different countries
local	[ˈləʊkəl]	in or relating to the area where you live
national	[ˈnæʃənəl]	**1** relating to the whole of a country or nation; *a national newspaper* **2** typical of the people or traditions of a particular country or nation; *a national pastime*
patriotic	[ˌpætriˈɒtɪk, ˌpeɪt-]	feeling love and loyalty towards your country
public	[ˈpʌblɪk]	**1** relating to all the people in a country or a community; *public opinion* **2** for everyone to use; *a public swimming pool*
social	[ˈsəʊʃəl]	relating to society
socialist	[ˈsəʊʃəlɪst]	relating to socialism
voluntary	[ˈvɒləntri]	voluntary work is done by people who are not paid

IDIOMS

| **the grass roots** | the ordinary people in a society, rather than the leaders |
| **win by a landslide** | to win an election by a very large number of votes |

sports

sport [spɔːt] a game or other activity that needs physical effort and skill

TYPES OF SPORT

aerobics [eəˈrəʊbɪks] a form of exercise that makes your heart and lungs stronger; *do aerobics*

American football [əˌmerɪkən ˈfʊtbɔːl] a game in which two teams of eleven players try to get an oval (= egg-shaped) ball to their opponents' end of the field (*In American English, use* **football**)

badminton [ˈbædmɪntən] a game in which two or four players stand either side of a high net, and get points by hitting a small object (called a shuttlecock) across it using a racket; *play badminton*

baseball [ˈbeɪsbɔːl] a game in which two teams of nine players get points by hitting a ball with a bat and running around four bases in a large field; *play baseball*

basketball [ˈbɑːskɪtbɔːl] a game in which two teams of five players each try to throw a large ball through a round net hanging from a high metal ring; *play basketball*

boxing [ˈbɒksɪŋ] a sport in which two people fight following special rules

cricket [ˈkrɪkɪt] a game played by two teams who try to score points by hitting a ball with a wooden bat; *play cricket*

darts [dɑːts] a game in which you throw darts (= small pointed objects) at a round board that has numbers on it; *play darts*

EXAMPLE
What's your favourite sport?

football	['fʊtbɔːl]	**1** a game in which two teams of eleven players try to win points by kicking the ball into an area at their opponent's end of the field; *play football* (*In American English, use* **soccer**)
		2 (*American English*) *see* **American football**
golf	[gɒlf]	a game in which you use long sticks (called golf clubs) to hit a small, hard ball into a hole in the ground; *play golf*
gymnastics	[dʒɪm'næstɪks]	a sport that consists of physical exercises that develop your strength and your ability to move easily; *do gymnastics*
hockey	['hɒki]	a sport in which two teams of eleven players use long curved sticks to hit a small hard ball; *play hockey*
horse racing	['hɔːs ˌreɪsɪŋ]	a sport in which riders (called jockeys) race against each other on horses
horse-riding	['hɔːsˌraɪdɪŋ]	the sport of riding on a horse; *go horse-riding* (*In American English, use* **horseback riding**)
horseback riding (*American English*)		*see* **horse-riding**
ice-skating	['aɪsˌskeɪtɪŋ]	the sport of moving around on ice wearing ice skates; *go ice skating*
jogging	['dʒɒgɪŋ]	the sport of running slowly; *go jogging*
judo	['dʒuːdəʊ]	a sport in which two people try to throw each other to the ground; *do judo*
karate	[kə'rɑːti]	a Japanese sport in which people fight using their hands, feet, and legs; *do karate*
rugby	['rʌgbi]	a game in which two teams try to get a ball past a line at the end of the field; *play rugby*
skiing	['skiːɪŋ]	the sport of travelling over snow on skis; *go skiing*

EXAMPLE

Terry was the captain of Chelsea Football Club.

snooker	['snuːkə]	a game that is played on a special table. Players use a long stick to hit a white ball so that it knocks coloured balls into holes around the edge of the table.; *play snooker*
soccer (*American English*)		*see* **football**
squash	[skwɒʃ]	a game in which two players hit a small rubber ball against the walls of a court; *play squash*
swimming	['swɪmɪŋ]	the sport of moving through water using your arms and legs; *go swimming*
tennis	['tenɪs]	a game for two or four players, who use rackets (= special bats) to hit a ball across a net between them; *a game of tennis*; *play tennis*
volleyball	['vɒliˌbɔːl]	a game in which two teams hit a large ball over a high net with their arms or hands; *play volleyball*
windsurfing	['wɪndˌsɜːfɪŋ]	a sport in which you move across water on a long narrow board with a sail on it; *go windsurfing*
Zumba™	['zʊmbə]	a dance programme based on Latin American music that people do as a form of exercise; *a Zumba fitness class*
PEOPLE		
athlete	['æθliːt]	someone who is good at physical sports, exercise or games, especially in competitions
captain	['kæptɪn]	the leader of a sports team
champion	['tʃæmpiən]	the winner of a sports competition or game; *the world champion*
coach	[kəʊtʃ]	someone who is in charge of teaching a person or a sports team
fan	[fæn]	someone who likes a particular sport, team, or player very much; *football fans*
opponent	[ə'pəʊnənt]	the person who is against you in a sports competition

EXAMPLE
She praised her opponent's ability.

player	['pleɪə]	a person who takes part in a sport or game
referee	[ˌrefə'riː]	the person who makes sure that players do not break the rules in a match
spectator	[spek'teɪtə]	someone who is watching a sports event
team	[tiːm]	a group of people who play a sport against other groups of people
umpire	['ʌmpaɪə]	someone who watches a game such as tennis or cricket to make sure that the players do not break the rules
winner	['wɪnə]	the person who wins a prize, a race or a competition

PLACES

boxing ring	['bɒksɪŋ ˌrɪŋ]	a square area with ropes around it, where boxing matches take place
court	[kɔːt]	an area for playing a game such as tennis or basketball; *a tennis court*
golf course	['gɒlf ˌkɔːs]	an area of land where people play golf
gymnasium	[dʒɪm'neɪziəm]	a room or hall with equipment for doing physical exercise
ice rink	['aɪs ˌrɪŋk]	an area of ice that people can skate on
pitch	[pɪtʃ]	an area of ground that is used for playing a game such as football; *a football pitch*
racetrack	['reɪstræk]	a track that is used for races
stadium	['steɪdiəm]	a large sports field with rows of seats all around it; *a football stadium*
swimming pool	['swɪmɪŋ ˌpuːl]	a place that has been built for people to swim in

EQUIPMENT AND CLOTHING

| **ball** | [bɔːl] | a round object that you kick, throw or hit in some sports and games |

EXAMPLES
She was a good golfer and tennis player.
The referee blew his whistle to end the game.
The umpire's decision is final.

basket	[ˈbɑːskɪt]	the net that you throw the ball through in basketball
bat	[bæt]	a long piece of wood that is used for hitting the ball in games such as cricket or baseball; *a cricket/baseball bat*
golf club	[ˈgɒlf klʌb]	a long, thin, metal stick that you use to hit the ball in golf
kit	[kɪt]	a set of clothes and equipment that is used for a particular sport; *football kit*
net	[net]	**1** in tennis, and some other sports, the piece of material across the centre of the court that the ball has to go over **2** in football, the material that is attached to the back of the goal **3** in basketball, the loose material that hangs from the ring
racket	[ˈrækɪt]	a thing with a long handle and a round part with strings stretched across it, used for hitting the ball in some games; *a tennis/badminton racket*
skis	[skiːz]	long, flat, narrow pieces of wood, metal or plastic that you fasten to your boots so that you can move easily over snow

COMPETITIONS

championship	[ˈtʃæmpiənʃɪp]	a competition to find the best player or team in a particular sport or game
competition	[ˌkɒmpɪˈtɪʃən]	an event in which people try to show that they are best at an activity
final	[ˈfaɪnəl]	the last game or race in a series, that decides who is the winner; *play in the final*
foul	[faʊl]	an action that breaks the rules of a particular sport

EXAMPLE
She's competing in the women's basketball championship this month.

game	[geɪm]	**1** an activity or a sport in which you try to win **2** one particular occasion when you play a game
goal	[gəʊl]	**1** the place, in games such as football, where the players try to put the ball in order to win a point for their team **2** a point that is scored when the ball goes into the goal in games such as football
half-time	[ˌhɑːʃˈtaɪm]	the short period between the two parts of a game when the players can rest
match	[mætʃ]	a sports game between two people or teams; *a tennis match*
medal	[ˈmedəl]	a piece of metal that is give to the person who wins a race or competition; *a gold/silver/bronze medal*
point	[pɔɪnt]	a mark that you win in a game or a sport
race	[reɪs]	a competition to see who is the fastest
score	[skɔː]	the result of a game
tie	[taɪ]	an occasion when both teams have the same number of points at the end of a game
tournament	[ˈtʊənəmənt]	a sports competition in which each player who wins a game plays another game, until just one person or team (the winner) remains
the World Cup	[ðə ˌwɜːld ˈkʌp]	an international football tournament that is held every four years in a different country

EXAMPLES
Football is such a great game.
a game of tennis
Liverpool are in the lead by 2 goals to 1.
The score at half-time was two all.
What's the score?

VERBS

beat	[biːt]	to defeat someone in a race or competition
catch	[kætʃ]	to take and hold a ball that is moving through the air
defend	[dɪˈfend]	to try to stop the other team from getting points
draw	[drɔː]	to finish a game with the same number of points as the other player or team
hit	[hɪt]	to bat a ball with a lot of force
jump	[dʒʌmp]	to bend your knees, push against the ground with your feet, and move quickly upwards into the air
kick	[kɪk]	to hit a ball with your foot
lose	[luːz]	to not win a game
miss	[mɪs]	to not manage to hit or catch something
practise	[ˈpræktɪs]	to do a sport regularly in order to do it better
run	[rʌn]	to move very quickly on your legs
save	[seɪv]	to stop the ball from going into the goal in a sports game; *save a goal*
score	[skɔː]	to get a goal or a point in a sports competition
serve	[sɜːv]	to hit the ball to start part of a game in a tennis match
ski	[skiː]	to move over snow or water on skis
swim	[swɪm]	to move through water by making movements with your arms and legs
throw	[θrəʊ]	to use your hand to make a ball move through the air

EXAMPLES
Switzerland beat the United States two-one.
England drew with Ireland in the first game.
He scored four of the goals but missed a penalty.
Federer is serving for the title.
Can you swim?

tie	[taɪ]	if two teams tie, they have the same number of points at the end of a game
train	[treɪn]	to prepare for a sports competition; *train for a match*
win	[wɪn]	to do better than everyone else in a race or a game; *win a game*

[ADJECTIVES]

in the lead	[ˌɪn ðə ˈliːd]	in front of all the other people in a race
professional	[prəˈfeʃənəl]	doing a particular activity as a job rather than just for pleasure

EXAMPLE
Ben Johnson in the lead. Can he hang on? Yes, he's done it!

telephone, post and communications

NOUNS

address [ə'dres] the number of the building, the name of the street, and the town where you live or work; *name and address*; *postal address*

Android™ ['ændrɔɪd] an operating system used by some mobile phones and tablets; *an Android phone*

area code *(American English)* *see* **dialling code**

call [kɔːl] an occasion when you phone someone; *a phone call*

cellphone *(mainly American English)* *see* **mobile phone**

delivery [dɪ'lɪvəri] an occasion when someone brings letters, packages or other goods to a particular place; *mail delivery*

dialling code ['daɪəlɪŋ ˌkəʊd] the series of numbers that you have to dial before a phone number if you are making a call from a different area; *the dialling code for an area* (In American English, use **area code**)

emoji [ɪ'məʊdʒi] a symbol that you use in an email or text message to show how you feel

envelope ['envələʊp] the paper cover in which you put a letter before you send it to someone; *a brown envelope*; *a self-addressed envelope*

extension [ɪk'stenʃən] a phone that connects to the main phone line in a building

fax [fæks] a copy of a document that you send or receive using a fax machine; *send/receive a fax*

fax machine ['fæks məʃiːn] a special machine that you use to send and receive documents electronically

form [fɔːm] a piece of paper with questions on it and spaces where you should write the answers; *fill in a form*

EXAMPLES
What is your address?
Please allow 28 days for delivery of your order.
Can I have extension forty-six please?

hashtag	['hæʃtæg]	a word with the symbol [#] before it, used in messages on social media websites to help other people to search for messages on that topic
international call	[ɪntə,næʃənəl 'kɔːl]	a phone call made between different countries; *make an international call*
landline	['lændlaɪn]	a phone connection that uses wires, in contrast to a mobile phone
letter	['letə]	a message that you write or type on paper and send to someone; *open a letter; write/ send a letter*
letterbox	['letəbɒks]	a hole in a door through which letters are delivered; *put something through the letterbox (In American English, use* **mailbox**)
line	[laɪn]	a phone connection or wire
local call	[,ləʊkəl 'kɔːl]	a phone call to a place that is near; *make a local call*
mail	[meɪl]	**1** (*American English*) see **post** **2** the email that you receive; *a mail server*
mailbox (*American English*)		*see* **letterbox**; **post box**
mailman (PL) **mailmen** (*American English*)		*see* **postman**
mailwoman (PL) **mailwomen** (*American English*)		*see* **postwoman**
message	['mesɪdʒ]	a piece of information that you send or give to someone; *a phone message; a voice message; send/receive a message; leave/take a message*
mobile	['məʊbaɪl]	same as **mobile phone**
mobile phone	[,məʊbaɪl 'fəʊn]	a phone that you can carry with you and use wherever you are (*In American English, use* **cell phone**)

EXAMPLES

You can add a hashtag to your message so that it reaches more people.
I'll call you later on your landline.
I received a letter from a friend.
Suddenly the telephone line went dead.
She isn't here yet. Do you want to leave a message?
Call me on my mobile.

operator	[ˈɒpəˌreɪtə]	a person who connects phone calls in a place such as an office or a hotel
P&P	[ˌpiː ənd ˈpiː]	short for 'postage and packing': the cost of wrapping an item and sending it by post
package	[ˈpækɪdʒ]	something that is wrapped in paper so that it can be sent by post
parcel	[ˈpɑːsəl]	same as **package**
phone	[fəʊn]	a piece of equipment that you use to talk to someone else in another place; *answer the phone; a pay phone; Can I use the phone?*
phone number	[ˈfəʊn nʌmbə]	the number of a particular phone, that you use when you make a call to it
post	[pəʊst]	the letters and packages that you receive (*In American English, use* **mail**)
post box	[ˈpəʊst ˌbɒks]	a box with a hole in it where you put letters that you want to send (*In American English, use* **mailbox**)
post office	[ˈpəʊst ɒfɪs]	a building where you can buy stamps and post letters
postage	[ˈpəʊstɪdʒ]	the money that you pay for sending post
postcard	[ˈpəʊstkɑːd]	a thin card, often with a picture on one side, that you can write on and post to someone without using an envelope; *send someone a postcard*
postcode	[ˈpəʊstkəʊd]	a series of numbers and letters at the end of an address (*In American English, use* **zip code**)
postman (PL) **postmen**	[ˈpəʊstmən] [ˈpəʊstmən]	a man who collects and delivers letters and packages (*In American English, use* **mailman**)
postwoman (PL) **postwomen**	[ˈpəʊstwʊmən] [ˈpəʊstwɪmɪn]	a woman who collects and delivers letters and packages (*In American English, use* **mailwoman**)

EXAMPLES
Price £12.95 plus £1.95 P&P.
They cost £24.95 including P&P.
Two minutes later the phone rang.
There has been no post in three weeks.
All prices include postage.

reply	[rɪ'plaɪ]	something that you say or write as an answer
retweet	['riːtwiːt]	a message on the social media website Twitter that repeats a message that another person sent
ringtone	['rɪŋtəʊn]	the sound that your mobile phone makes when someone calls you
selfie	['selfi]	a photo that you take of yourself, especially to show on a social media website; *take a selfie*
signature	['sɪgnətʃə]	your name, written in your own special way
SIM card	['sɪm ˌkɑːd]	a small piece of electronic equipment in a mobile phone that connects it to a particular phone network
smartphone	['smɑːtfəʊn]	a type of mobile phone that is also a small computer, allowing the user to connect to the internet
social media	[ˌsəʊʃəl 'miːdiə]	websites and programs that people use for sharing information, pictures, etc. with other people; *to share a photo on social media*
stamp	[stæmp]	a small piece of paper that you stick on an envelope before you post it
telephone	['telɪˌfəʊn]	same as **phone**
text message	['tekst mesɪdʒ]	a message that you send using a mobile phone; *send/receive a text message*
tweet	[twiːt]	a message on the social media website Twitter
voicemail	['vɔɪsmeɪl]	an electronic system that records spoken messages; *a voicemail message*
writing paper	['raɪtɪŋ peɪpə]	paper for writing letters on
zip code (*American English*)		*see* **postcode**

EXAMPLES
My wedding announcement got 250 retweets!
She put a stamp on the corner of the envelope.
Did you see Sam's tweet from the concert last night?

VERBS

answer	['ɑːnsə]	to pick up the phone when it rings
call	[kɔːl]	to telephone someone
call someone back		to phone someone in return for a call they made to you
deliver	[dɪ'lɪvə]	to take something to a particular place
dial	['daɪəl]	to press the buttons on a phone in order to call someone; *dial a number*
hang up		to end a phone call
hold the line		to wait for a short time when you are making a phone call
mail (American English)	[meɪl]	*see* **post**
phone	[fəʊn]	to contact someone and speak to them by phone; *Did anybody phone?*; *I phoned the police.*
post	[pəʊst]	to send a letter or a package somewhere by post (*In American English, use* **mail**)
reply	[rɪ'plaɪ]	to write an answer to something that someone writes to you
retweet	[riː'twiːt]	to send a message on the website Twitter that repeats a message that another person sent
send	[send]	to make a message or a package go to someone
sign	[saɪn]	to write your name on a document; *sign your name*; *sign a letter*

EXAMPLES

She didn't answer the phone.
Would you call me as soon as you find out?
Only 90% of first-class post is delivered on time.
I dialled her number, but there was no reply.
Don't hang up on me!
Could you hold the line, please?
I posted a letter to Stanley.
I'm posting you a cheque.
That's really funny. I'm going to retweet it.

text	[tekst]	to send someone a text message on a mobile phone
tweet	[twiːt]	to send a message on the social media website Twitter; *Sara tweeted a photo of herself in Florida.*
write	[raɪt]	to give someone information, ask them something or express your feelings in a letter or an email; *write a letter/an email*

ADJECTIVES

busy	['bɪzi]	same as **engaged**
dead	[ded]	if a phone line is dead it is no longer working
engaged	[ɪn'geɪdʒd]	if a phone line is engaged, it is already being used by someone else; *The line is engaged.*
first-class	[ˌfɜːst'klɑːs]	used for describing the fastest and most expensive way of sending letters; *a first-class letter*
second-class	[ˌsekənd'klɑːs]	used for describing the slower and cheaper way of sending letters; *a second-class stamp*

PHRASES

best wishes	used at the end of a letter or email, before your name, to someone you know who is not a very close friend
love from	used at the end of a letter or email, before your name, to a friend or relative
sincerely yours (American English)	*see* **yours sincerely**

EXAMPLES

Mary texted me when she got home.
Everyone's tweeting about the election results.
She wrote to her aunt asking for help.
I answered the phone and the line went dead.
We tried to call you back but you were engaged.

yours faithfully

used at the end of a formal letter, before your name, when you start the letter with the words 'Dear Sir' or 'Dear Madam'

yours sincerely

used at the end of a formal letter, before your name, when you have addressed it to someone by their name (*In American English, use* **sincerely yours**)

television and radio

NOUNS

ad (*American English*)   *see* **advert**

advert   ['ædvɜ:t]   a short film on television or short article on radio that tells you about something such as a product or an event (*In American English, use* **ad**)

adverts   ['ædvɜ:ts]   a short interruption in a television or radio programme when adverts are shown; *TV adverts* (*In American English, use* **commercial break**)

aerial   ['eəriəl]   a piece of equipment that receives television or radio signals (*In American English, use* **antenna**)

antenna,   *see* **aerial**
   (PL) **antennae, antennas**
   (*American English*)

Blu-ray™   ['blu:reɪ]   a type of computer disc that stores large amounts of high quality pictures and sound; *a Blu-ray disc player*

cable television   [ˌkeɪbəl 'telɪvɪʒən]   a television system in which signals travel along wires

cartoon   [kɑːˈtuːn]   a film that uses drawings instead of real people or objects

catch-up TV   [ˌkætʃʌp ti: 'vi:]   a system for watching television programmes after they have been shown, using a computer or phone that is connected to the internet; *watch a programme on catch-up TV*

celebrity   [sɪˈlebrɪti]   someone who is famous; *a TV celebrity*; *a celebrity guest*

channel   ['tʃænəl]   a television station; *change channels*; *What channel is it on?*

EXAMPLES
Have you seen that new advert for Pepsi?
We don't have cable TV.
We watched children's cartoons on TV.
There is a huge number of television channels in America.

chat show	['tʃæt ˌʃəʊ]	a television or radio show in which an interviewer talks to guests in a friendly informal way about different topics (*In American English, use* **talk show**)
clip	[klɪp]	a short piece of a film that is shown separately; *a video clip*
commercial break (*American English*)		*see* **adverts**
DJ	['di: ˌdʒeɪ]	short for 'disc jockey': someone whose job is to play music and talk on the radio; *a radio DJ*
DVD	[di: vi: 'di:]	short for 'digital video disk': a disk on which a film or music is recorded; *a DVD player*
documentary	[ˌdɒkjə'mentri]	a television programme that provides information about a particular subject; *a wildlife documentary*
game show	['geɪm ˌʃəʊ]	a television programme in which people compete to win prizes; *a television game show*
media	['mi:diə]	television, radio, newspapers and magazines
news	[nju:z]	information about recent events that is reported on the radio or television; *watch/ listen to the news*
presenter	[prɪ'zentə]	someone who introduces the different parts of a television or radio programme; *a TV/radio presenter*; *a sports presenter*
prime time	['praɪm ˌtaɪm]	the time when most people are watching television; *prime-time TV*
programme	['prəʊɡræm]	a television or radio show; *a television/ radio programme*

EXAMPLES

Did you see that documentary on TV last night?

A lot of people in the media have asked me that question.

Here are some of the top stories in the news.

He wants to watch his favourite TV programme.

quiz show	['kwɪz ˌʃəʊ]	a television or radio programme in which people compete in a quiz
radio	['reɪdiəʊ]	a piece of equipment that you use in order to listen to radio programmes; *listen to the radio*; *on the radio*; *FM/digital radio*
reality TV	[ri'ælɪti ti: vi:]	a type of television that aims to show how ordinary people behave in everyday life,
remote control	[rɪˌməʊt kən'trəʊl]	the device that you use to control a television or video recorder from a distance
satellite	['sætəˌlaɪt]	a piece of electronic equipment that is sent into space in order to receive and send back information; *satellite television/radio*; *a satellite dish*
screen	[skri:n]	a flat surface on a television, where you see pictures or words; *a TV screen*
series (PL) **series**	['sɪəri:z]	a set of radio or television programmes
set	[set]	a piece of equipment that receives television or radio signals; *a TV set*
sitcom	['sɪtkɒm]	short for 'situation comedy': a series in which a set of characters is involved in various amusing situations; *a TV sitcom*
soap opera	['səʊp ɒpərə]	a television drama serial about the daily lives of a group of people
station	['steɪʃən]	a company that broadcasts programmes on radio or television; *a local radio station*
subtitles	['sʌbtaɪtəlz]	the translation of the words of a foreign film or television programme that is shown at the bottom of the picture
talk show (*American English*)		*see* **chat show**

EXAMPLES

She reached for the remote control to switch on the news.
The long-running TV series is filmed in Manchester.
The dialogue is in Spanish, with English subtitles.

television	['telɪˌvɪʒən]	**1** a piece of electrical equipment with a screen on which you watch moving pictures with sound; *We bought a new television.* **2** the moving pictures and sounds that you watch and listen to on a television; *What's on television tonight?*
TV	[ˌtiː ˈviː]	[INFORMAL] television; *watch TV*
video	['vɪdiəʊ]	a film that you can watch at home
volume	['vɒljuːm]	how loud or quiet the sound is on a television or radio
wavelength	['weɪvleŋθ]	the size of a radio wave that a particular radio station uses to broadcast its programmes

[VERBS]

broadcast	['brɔːdkɑːst]	to send out a programme so that it can be heard on the radio or seen on television
fast-forward	[ˌfɑːstˈfɔːwəd]	to make a recording go forwards quickly
record	[reˈkɔːd]	to put sounds or images onto a CD, DVD, tape, or video so that they can be heard or seen again later
rewind	[ˌriːˈwaɪnd]	to make a recording go back to the beginning
switch something off		to stop electrical equipment from working by operating a switch; *switch off the radio/television*
switch something on		to make electrical equipment start working by operating a switch; *switch on the radio/television*

EXAMPLES

I prefer going to the cinema to watching television.
You can rent a video for £3 and watch it at home.
He turned the volume up on the radio.
She found the station's wavelength on her radio.
The concert will be broadcast live on television and radio.
Can you record the film for me?

tune	[tjuːn]	to adjust a radio or television so that it receives a particular station or programme
tune in		to listen to a radio programme or watch a television programme
turn something off		to make a piece of electrical equipment stop working; *turn off the radio/television*
turn something on		to make a piece of electrical equipment start working; *turn on the radio/television*
watch	[wɒtʃ]	to look at a television for a period of time

ADJECTIVES

animated	['ænɪmeɪtɪd]	an animated film is one in which puppets or drawings appear to move
digital	['dɪdʒɪtəl]	using information in the form of thousands of very small signals
on-demand	[ˌɒndɪ'mɑːnd]	available whenever needed

ADVERBS

live	[laɪv]	used for describing a television or radio programme that you watch at the same time that it happens; *watch something live*
on the air	[ˌɒn ði: 'eə]	on radio or television

IDIOMS

channel surfing	a way of watching television in which you keep changing from one channel to another using a remote control
couch potato	a person who spends a lot of time sitting watching television

EXAMPLES

The radio was tuned to the CBC.
They tuned in to watch the game.
I stayed up late to watch the film.
Enjoy 50 high-quality channels with our new digital TV package.
On-demand services like BBC iPlayer™ allow you to watch a show you have missed.
The show went on the air live at 8 o'clock.

theatre and cinema

NOUNS

actor	['æktə]	someone whose job is acting in plays or films; *a famous actor*
actress	['æktrəs]	a woman whose job is acting in plays or films
audience	['ɔːdiəns]	all the people who are watching or listening to a performance or a film; *a cinema audience*
audition	[ɔːˈdɪʃən]	a short performance that an actor gives so that someone can decide if they are good enough to be in a play or a film
ballet	['bæleɪ]	a performance of a type of dancing that tells a story; *go to the ballet*
Bollywood	['bɒliwʊd]	the Indian film industry; *a Bollywood film*; *a Bollywood actor*
box office	['bɒks ɒfɪs]	**1** the place in a theatre or cinema where the tickets are sold **2** used to refer to the success of a film or play in terms of the number of people who go to see it
cast	[kɑːst]	all the people who act in a play or a film
character	['kærɪktə]	one of the people in a story
cinema	['sɪnɪmɑː]	**1** a building where people go to watch films (*In American English, use* **movie theater**) **2** films in general
circus	['sɜːkəs]	a group of people and animals that travels around to different places and performs shows in a big tent

EXAMPLES

She's a really good actress.
They are holding final auditions for presenters.
They collected their tickets at the box office.
The film was a huge box-office success.
He plays the main character in the film.
I can't remember the last time we went to the cinema.
I always wanted to work as a clown in a circus.

comedian	[kə'mi:diən]	a person whose job is to make people laugh
comedy	['kɒmədi]	a play or film that is intended to make people laugh
costume	['kɒstju:m]	a set of clothes that someone wears in a performance; *the costumes and scenery*
curtain	['kɜ:tən]	the large piece of material that hangs at the front of the stage in a theatre; *the curtain rises/falls*
director	[daɪ'rektə, dɪr-]	the person who tells actors what to do; *a film director; a theatre director*
drama	['drɑ:mə]	a serious play or film
epic	['epɪk]	a long film about important events
film	[fɪlm]	a story that is told using moving pictures on the television or at a cinema; *to make/direct a film; to watch a film* (*In American English, use* **movie**)
film star	['fɪlm stɑ:]	a famous actor or actress who appears in films (*In American English, use* **movie star**)
full house	[ˌfʊl 'haʊs]	an occasion when there are no empty seats in a theatre; *playing to a full house*
Hollywood	['hɒliwʊd]	the American film industry; *Hollywood film stars; a Hollywood film*
horror film	['hɒrə ˌfɪlm]	a type of film that is very frightening
intermission (*American English*)		*see* **interval**
interval	['ɪntəvəl]	a short break between two parts of a film, concert, or show; *during the interval* (*In American English, use* **intermission**)
make-up	['meɪkʌp]	the creams and powders that actors put on their faces to change their appearance; *wear/apply make-up; a make-up artist; costumes and make-up*
matinee	['mætɪneɪ]	a performance of a play or a showing of a film in the afternoon; *a matinee performance*

EXAMPLES
The film is a romantic comedy.
I'm going to see a film tonight.

movie (*American English*)   *see* **film**

movie star (*American English*)   *see* **film star**

movie theater (*American English*)   *see* **cinema**

multiplex	['mʌltɪpleks]	a cinema with several screens; *a multiplex cinema*
musical	['mjuːzɪkəl]	a play or a film that uses singing and dancing in the story; *a stage musical*
opera	['ɒpərə]	a play with music in which all the words are sung; *an opera singer*; *an opera house*
Oscar™	['ɒskə]	a prize given to actors, directors and other people in the film industry; *get an Oscar*; *She has three Oscars.*
part	[pɑːt]	one character's words and actions in a play or film
performance	[pə'fɔːməns]	the activity of entertaining an audience by singing, dancing or acting; *a concert performance*
play	[pleɪ]	a piece of writing performed in a theatre, on the radio or on television
playwright	['pleɪraɪt]	a person who writes plays
plot	[plɒt]	a series of events that make up the story of a film
producer	[prə'djuːsə]	a person whose job is to produce plays or films; *a film producer*
production	[prə'dʌkʃən]	a play or other show that is performed in a theatre; *a theatre/stage production*; *a film production*
programme	['prəʊɡræm]	a small book or sheet of paper that tells you about a play or concert
review	[rɪ'vjuː]	a report that gives an opinion about something such as a play or a film

---

EXAMPLES

He played the part of 'Hamlet'.

They were giving a performance of Bizet's 'Carmen'.

'Hamlet' is my favourite play.

Tonight our class is going to see a production of 'Othello'.

The show received excellent reviews in all the papers.

romance	[rə'mæns, 'rəʊmæns]	a film or a play about a romantic relationship
rom-com	['rɒmkɒm]	short for 'romantic comedy': a humorous film in which the main story is about a romantic relationship
scene	[si:n]	a part of a play or a film that happens in the same place; *film/shoot a scene; a love scene*
science fiction	[ˌsaɪəns 'fɪkʃən]	stories and films about events that take place in the future or in other parts of the universe; *a science fiction film*
screen	[skri:n]	the flat area on the wall of a cinema, where you see the film; *the cinema screen*
script	[skrɪpt]	the written words that actors speak in a play or a film
seat	[si:t]	something that you can sit on in a theatre or cinema
sequel	['si:kwəl]	a film that continues the story of an earlier film
set	[set]	the place where a film is made or the scenery that is on the stage when a play is being performed; *a movie/film set*
show	[ʃəʊ]	a performance in a theatre; *a comedy show*
soundtrack	['saʊndtræk]	the music that is played during a film; *a film/movie soundtrack*
spotlight	['spɒtlaɪt]	a powerful light in a theatre that can be directed so that it lights up a small area
stage	[steɪdʒ]	the area in a theatre where people perform; *come on stage; a concert stage; on stage and screen; a stage play*
star	[stɑ:]	a famous actor or actress; *a movie/film star*

EXAMPLES

This is the opening scene of 'Hamlet'.

Watching a film on the television is not the same as seeing it on the big screen.

We had front-row seats at the concert.

The place looked like the set of a James Bond movie.

How about going to see a show tomorrow?

subtitles	['sʌbtaɪtəlz]	the translation of the words of a foreign film that are shown at the bottom of the picture
theatre	['θiːətə]	a place where you go to see plays or shows; *go to the theatre*
thriller	['θrɪlə]	an exciting film or play about a crime
ticket	['tɪkɪt]	a small piece of paper that shows that you have paid to go to see a film or a play; *theatre/cinema tickets*
tragedy	['trædʒɪdi]	a type of serious play, that usually ends with the death of the main character
trailer	['treɪlə]	a set of short pieces from a film that are shown to advertise it

VERBS

act	[ækt]	to have a part in a play or a film
book	[bʊk]	to buy tickets for a film or show that you will go to later
clap	[klæp]	to hit your hands together to show that you like something
dance	[dɑːns]	to move your body to music
play	[pleɪ]	to perform the part of a particular character in a play or film
shoot	[ʃuːt]	to make a film
sing	[sɪŋ]	to make music with your voice
star	[stɑː]	**1** to have a famous actor or actress in one of the most important parts in a play or film **2** to have one of the most important parts in a play or film
watch	[wɒtʃ]	to look at someone or something for a period of time; *watch a film/play*

EXAMPLES

The dialogue is in Spanish, with English subtitles.
He acted in many films, including 'Reds'.
You can book tickets for the cinema over the phone.
He played Mr Hyde in the film.
He'd love to shoot his film in Cuba.
The movie stars Brad Pitt.
She stars in the West End play.

ADJECTIVES

black-and-white [ˌblækənd'waɪt] showing everything in black, white, and grey; *old black-and-white film footage*

classic ['klæsɪk] of very good quality, and popular for a long time; *a classic film*

dubbed [dʌbd] having a different soundtrack added with actors speaking in a different language; *cartoons dubbed in Chinese*

low-budget [ˌləʊ'bʌdʒɪt] made spending very little money; *a low-budget movie*

sold out ['səʊld ˌaʊt] used to describe a performance for which all the tickets have been sold

subtitled ['sʌbtaɪtəld] with a translation of the words shown at the bottom of the picture; *a subtitled film*

THINGS YOU CAN SHOUT

bravo! [ˌbrɑː'vəʊ] an audience shouts 'bravo!' to show how much they have enjoyed a performance

encore! ['ɒŋkɔː] an audience shouts 'encore!' at the end of a concert to ask for a short extra performance

IDIOMS

it'll be all right on the night used to say that a performance will be successful even if the preparations for it have not gone well

bring the house down to make everyone laugh or cheer at a performance in the theatre

keep you on the edge of your seat to make you give your full attention to something

steal the show to attract more attention and praise than other people

EXAMPLE
The film kept everyone on the edge of their seats.

time

NOUNS

GENERAL

time	[taɪm]	**1** something that we measure in minutes, hours, days and years; *in a week's time*; *Time passed.* **2** used when you are talking about a particular point in the day, that you describe in hours and minutes
past	[pɑːst]	the time before the present, and the things that happened then; *in the past*
present	['prezənt]	the period of time that is happening now; *live in the present*
future	['fjuːtʃə]	the time that will come after now; *in the future*

HOURS, SECONDS AND MINUTES

half an hour	[ˌhɑːf ən 'aʊə]	a period of thirty minutes
hour	[aʊə]	a period of sixty minutes
minute	['mɪnɪt]	a unit for measuring time. There are sixty seconds in one minute, and there are sixty minutes in one hour.
moment	['məʊmənt]	a very short period of time; *a few moments later*
quarter of an hour	[ˌkwɔːtə əv ən 'aʊə]	a period of fifteen minutes
second	['sekənd]	a measurement of time. There are sixty seconds in one minute.

EXAMPLES

I've known Mr Martin for a long time.

What time is it?

Have you got the time?

He was making plans for the future.

I only slept about half an hour last night.

They waited for about two hours.

The pizza will take twenty minutes to cook.

In a moment he was gone.

For a few seconds nobody spoke.

TIMES OF THE DAY

dawn	[dɔːn]	the time when the sky becomes light in the morning; *Dawn was breaking.*
sunrise	['sʌnraɪz]	the time in the morning when the sun first appears in the sky; *at sunrise*
morning	['mɔːnɪŋ]	the part of each day between the time that people usually wake up and noon; *tomorrow morning*; *in the morning*; *on Sunday morning*
noon	[nuːn]	twelve o'clock in the middle of the day; *at noon*
midday	[ˌmɪd'deɪ]	same as **noon**
afternoon	[ˌɑːftə'nuːn]	the part of each day that begins at lunchtime and ends at about six o'clock; *in the afternoon*; *yesterday afternoon*
evening	['iːvnɪŋ]	the part of each day between the end of the afternoon and midnight; *yesterday evening*; *in the evening*
sunset	['sʌnset]	the time in the evening when the sun goes down; *at sunset*
dusk	[dʌsk]	the time just before night when it is not completely dark; *at dusk*
night	[naɪt]	**1** the time when it is dark outside, and most people sleep; *during the night* **2** the period of time between the end of the afternoon and the time that you go to bed; *last night*; *ten o'clock at night*
midnight	['mɪdnaɪt]	twelve o'clock in the middle of the night; *at midnight*

DAYS AND WEEKS

day	[deɪ]	a period of twenty-four hours from one midnight to the next midnight; *every day*

EXAMPLES
Nancy woke at dawn.
He stayed in his room all afternoon.
What day is it?

date	[deɪt]	a particular day and month or a particular year
fortnight	['fɔ:tnaɪt]	a period of two weeks
week	[wi:k]	a period of seven days; *last week*
weekday	['wi:kdeɪ]	any of the days of the week except Saturday and Sunday
weekend	[,wi:k'end]	Saturday and Sunday; *at the weekend*

DAYS OF THE WEEK

Monday	['mʌndeɪ, -di]	the day after Sunday and before Tuesday; *a week on Monday*
Tuesday	['tju:zdeɪ, -di]	the day after Monday and before Wednesday; *next Tuesday*
Wednesday	['wenzdeɪ, -di]	the day after Tuesday and before Thursday; *on Wednesday*
Thursday	['θɜ:zdeɪ, -di]	the day after Wednesday and before Friday; *every Thursday morning*
Friday	['fraɪdeɪ, -di]	the day after Thursday and before Saturday; *Friday 6 November*
Saturday	['sætədeɪ, -di]	the day after Friday and before Sunday; *every Saturday*
Sunday	['sʌndeɪ, -di]	the day after Saturday and before Monday; *on Sunday*

MONTHS

month	[mʌnθ]	one of the twelve parts that a year is divided into
January	['dʒænjəri]	the first month of the year
February	['febjʊəri]	the second month of the year
March	[mɑ:tʃ]	the third month of the year
April	['eɪprɪl]	the fourth month of the year
May	[meɪ]	the fifth month of the year

EXAMPLES

What's the date today?
What is he doing here on a weekday?
I had dinner with Tim last weekend.
We go on holiday next month.
We always have snow in January.

June	[dʒuːn]	the sixth month of the year; *on June 7*
July	[dʒʊˈlaɪ]	the seventh month of the year
August	[ˈɔːɡəst]	the eighth month of the year
September	[sepˈtembə]	the ninth month of the year
October	[ɒkˈtəʊbə]	the tenth month of the year
November	[nəʊˈvembə]	the eleventh month of the year
December	[dɪˈsembə]	the twelfth and last month of the year

SEASONS

season	[ˈsiːzən]	a part of the year that has its own typical weather conditions; *the rainy season*
spring	[sprɪŋ]	the season between winter and summer when the weather becomes warmer and plants start to grow again
summer	[ˈsʌmə]	the season between spring and autumn, when the weather is usually warm or hot; *a summer's day*
autumn	[ˈɔːtəm]	the season between summer and winter when the weather becomes cooler and the leaves fall off the trees; *in the autumn*; *last/ next autumn*; *autumn leaves* (In American English, use **fall**)
fall (*American English*)		*see* **autumn**
winter	[ˈwɪntə]	the season between autumn and spring, when the weather is usually cold

YEARS

century	[ˈsentʃəri]	one hundred years; *in the 21st century*
decade	[ˈdekeɪd]	a period of ten years
leap year	[ˈliːp ˌjɪə]	a year, happening every four years, that has 366 days including February 29 as an extra day

---

EXAMPLES
She was born on 6th September, 1970.
Autumn is my favourite season.
They are getting married next spring.
The plant flowers in late summer.

| year | [jɪə] | **1** a period of twelve months, beginning on the first of January and ending on the thirty-first of December; *next/last year*; *a calendar year*
2 any period of twelve months; *three times a year*; *the academic year* |

MEASURING TIME

alarm clock	[əˈlɑːm klɒk]	a clock that makes a noise so that you wake up at a particular time; *set the alarm clock*
calendar	[ˈkælɪndə]	a list of days, weeks and months for a particular year
clock	[klɒk]	a piece of equipment that shows you what time it is
watch	[wɒtʃ]	a small clock that you usually wear on your wrist

ADJECTIVES

annual	[ˈænjʊəl]	happening once every year; *an annual meeting*
daily	[ˈdeɪli]	appearing or happening every day; *a daily newspaper*; *a daily routine*
early	[ˈɜːli]	before the usual time; *an early start*
following	[ˈfɒləʊɪŋ]	used for describing the day, week or year after the one you have just mentioned; *the following morning*
last	[lɑːst]	the most recent; *last July*
late	[leɪt]	after the time that something should start or happen
monthly	[ˈmʌnθli]	happening every month; *monthly rent*
next	[nekst]	used for talking about the first day, week or year that comes after this one or the previous one; *the next day*
weekly	[ˈwiːkli]	happening once a week or every week; *a weekly meeting*

EXAMPLES

He didn't come home last night.
The train was 40 minutes late.
The magazine is published monthly.

ago	[ə'gəʊ]	in the past; before now; *two days ago*; *a while ago*
at the moment	[ət ðə 'məʊmənt]	now
early	['ɜːli]	before the usual time; *get up/arrive early*
immediately	[ɪ'miːdiətli]	happening without any delay
late	[leɪt]	after the time that something should start or happen
later	['leɪtə]	used for talking about a time that is after the one that you have been talking about; *two days later*
now	[naʊ]	used for talking about the present time
nowadays	['naʊə,deɪz]	now generally, and not in the past
once	[wʌns]	happening one time only
on time	[ɒn 'taɪm]	arriving at the expected time, and not late; *The train arrived on time.*
soon	[suːn]	after a short time
today	[tə'deɪ]	used when you are talking about the actual day on which you are speaking or writing
tomorrow	[tə'mɒrəʊ]	the day after today
twice	[twaɪs]	two times; *twice a week*
yesterday	['jestə,deɪ, -di]	used for talking about the day before today

EXAMPLES

She's busy at the moment.
'Call the police immediately!' she shouted.
It started forty minutes late.
I must go now.
Children watch a lot of TV nowadays.
I met Miquela once, at a party.
I'll call you soon.
How are you feeling today?
She left yesterday.

tools

axe	[æks]	a tool with a heavy metal blade and a long handle that is used for cutting wood
battery	['bætəri]	a small object that provides electricity for things such as radios
blade	[bleɪd]	the flat, sharp edge of a knife that is used for cutting; *a knife blade*
bolt	[bəʊlt]	a long piece of metal that you use with a nut to fasten things together; *nuts and bolts*
bucket	['bʌkɪt]	a round metal or plastic container with a handle, used for holding water; *a bucket of water*
drill	[drɪl]	a tool for making holes; *an electric drill*
file	[faɪl]	a tool that you use for rubbing rough objects to make them smooth
flashlight *(American English)*		*see* **torch**
glue	[glu:]	a sticky substance used for joining things together
hammer	['hæmə]	a tool that is made from a heavy piece of metal attached to the end of a handle, that is used for hitting nails into wood; *a hammer and nails*
handle	['hændəl]	the part of a tool that you hold; *a tool handle*
knife	[naɪf]	a sharp flat piece of metal with a handle, that you can use to cut things; *a sharp knife*
ladder	['lædə]	a piece of equipment made of two long pieces of wood or metal with short steps between them, that is used for reaching high places; *climb a ladder*
machine	[mə'ʃi:n]	a piece of equipment that uses electricity or an engine to do a particular job

---

EXAMPLES
The game requires two AA batteries.
You will need scissors and a tube of glue.

nail	[neɪl]	a thin piece of metal with one pointed end and one flat end that you hit with a hammer in order to fix things together
needle	['niːdəl]	a small, thin metal tool with a sharp point that you use for sewing; *a needle and thread*
nut	[nʌt]	a thick metal ring that you put onto a bolt, that is used for holding heavy things together
paint	[peɪnt]	a coloured liquid that you put onto a surface with a brush
paintbrush	['peɪntbrʌʃ]	a brush that you use for painting
pliers	['plaɪəz]	a tool with two handles at one end and two flat metal parts at the other that is used for holding or pulling things; *a pair of pliers*
rope	[rəʊp]	a type of very thick string that is made by twisting together several strings or wires; *a piece of rope*
saw	[sɔː]	a metal tool for cutting wood; *a saw blade*
scaffolding	['skæfəldɪŋ]	a frame of metal bars that people can stand on when they are working on the outside of a building; *put up/take down scaffolding*
screw	[skruː]	a small metal object with a sharp end, that you use to join things together
screwdriver	['skruːdraɪvə]	a tool that you use for turning screws
shovel	['ʃʌvəl]	a flat tool with a handle that is used for lifting and moving earth or snow
spade	[speɪd]	a tool that is used for digging; *a garden spade*
spanner	['spænə]	a metal tool that you use for turning nuts to make them tighter (*In American English, use* **wrench**)

EXAMPLES

If you want to repair the wheels, you must remove the four nuts.
Each shelf is attached to the wall with screws.
I'll need the coal shovel.

spring	[sprɪŋ]	a long piece of metal that goes round and round; *a coiled spring*
stepladder	['steplædə]	a short ladder that you can fold
tape measure	['teɪp meʒə]	a strip of metal, plastic, or cloth with marks on it, used for measuring
tool	[tu:l]	anything that you hold in your hands and use to do a particular type of work
toolbox	['tu:lbɒks]	a box or container for keeping tools in
torch	[tɔ:tʃ]	a small electric light that you carry in your hand (*In American English, use* **flashlight**)
varnish	['vɑ:nɪʃ]	a thick, clear liquid that is painted onto things to give them a shiny surface
wire	[waɪə]	a long, thin piece of metal; *a piece of wire; a wire fence*
workshop	['wɜ:kʃɒp]	a place where people make or repair things
wrench (*mainly American English*)		*see* **spanner**

VERBS

build	[bɪld]	to make something by joining different things together; *build a house/road*
cut	[kʌt]	to use something sharp to remove part of something, or to break it
drill	[drɪl]	to make holes using a drill
fix	[fɪks]	**1** to repair something **2** to attach something firmly or securely to a particular place
hammer	['hæmə]	to hit nails into wood using a hammer
measure	['meʒə]	to find out the size of something

EXAMPLES
They cut a hole in the roof and put in a piece of glass.
You'll need to drill a hole in the wall.
This morning, a man came to fix my washing machine.
The clock is fixed to the wall.
She hammered a nail into the window frame.
Measure the length of the table.

mend	[mend]	to repair something
paint	[peɪnt]	to cover a wall or an object with paint; *paint a wall*
screw	[skruː]	to join one thing to another thing using a screw

ADJECTIVES

blunt	[blʌnt]	not sharp or pointed; *a blunt knife*
electric	[ɪ'lektrɪk]	**1** working using electricity; *an electric light/motor* **2** carrying electricity; *an electric plug/switch*
manual	['mænjʊəl]	**1** used for describing work in which you use your hands or your physical strength **2** operated by hand, rather than by electricity or a motor; *a manual pump*
sharp	[ʃɑːp]	very thin and able to cut through things very easily; *a sharp knife/blade*

EXAMPLES

I screwed the shelf on the wall.
He began his career as a manual worker.

towns and cities

NOUNS

bank	[bæŋk]	a place where people can keep their money; *high street banks*
beltway *(American English)*		*see* **ring road**
bench	[bentʃ]	a long seat made of wood or metal; *a park bench*
bin	[bɪn]	a container that you put rubbish in; *put your rubbish in the bin* (In American English, use **trash can**)
bridge	[brɪdʒ]	a structure that is built over a river or a road so that people or vehicles can cross from one side to the other; *a railway bridge*
building	[ˈbɪldɪŋ]	a structure that has a roof and walls; *new/old buildings*; *public buildings*; *an office building*
bus station	[ˈbʌs steɪʃən]	a place in a town or a city where a lot of buses stop
bus stop	[ˈbʌs stɒp]	a place at the side of a road, marked by a sign, where a bus stops
café	[kæfeɪ]	a place where you can buy drinks and small meals
capital	[ˈkæpɪtəl]	the city where the government of a country meets; *a capital city*
car park	[ˈkɑː pɑːk]	an area or building where people can leave their cars (In American English, use **parking lot**)
castle	[ˈkɑːsəl]	a large building with thick, high walls that was built in the past to protect people during battles
cathedral	[kəˈθiːdrəl]	a large and important church
church	[tʃɜːtʃ]	a building where Christians go to pray; *go to church*
citizen	[ˈsɪtɪzən]	a person who lives in a town or city

EXAMPLES
He crossed the bridge to get to school.
Berlin is the capital of Germany.
His father goes to church every day.

city	['sɪti]	a large town; *a big/large/major city*; *the city centre*
crosswalk *(American English)*		*see* **pedestrian crossing**
crowd	[kraʊd]	a large group of people who have gathered together
directions	[daɪˈrekʃənz, dɪr-]	instructions that tell you how to get somewhere
district	['dɪstrɪkt]	a particular area of a city or town; *a business/shopping district*
fire station	['faɪə steɪʃən]	a building where fire engines and equipment for stopping fires are kept
guided tour	[ˌgaɪdɪd 'tʊə]	a short journey around a place of interest with a person who tells you about what you are seeing
high street	['haɪ striːt]	the main street of a town where most of the shops are; *high street shops/stores/banks*
hotel	[ˌhəʊ'tel]	a building where people pay to sleep and eat meals; *a luxury/cheap hotel*; *a five-star hotel*; *a hotel room*; *stay in a hotel*
launderette™	[ˌlɔːndə'ret]	a place where people pay to use machines to wash and dry their clothes
leaflet	['liːflət]	a piece of paper containing information about a particular subject
library	['laɪbrəri]	a place where books are kept for people to use or borrow; *the public/local library*
litter	['lɪtə]	paper or rubbish that people leave lying on the ground in public places
map	[mæp]	a drawing of a city, that shows things like roads and important buildings; *a road map*; *a map of the city*

EXAMPLES

A huge crowd gathered in the town square.
She stopped the car to ask for directions.
During the afternoon there's a guided tour of the castle.
Have you got a leaflet about the bus tours round York, please?
I hate it when I see people dropping litter.

market	[ˈmɑːkɪt]	a place where people buy and sell products
monument	[ˈmɒnjʊmənt]	something that you build to help people remember an important event or person; *ancient monuments*
mosque	[mɒsk]	a building where Muslims go to pray
museum	[mjuːˈziːəm]	a building where you can look at interesting and valuable objects; *visit a museum*
notice	[ˈnəʊtɪs]	a piece of writing in a place where everyone can read it
outskirts	[ˈaʊtskɜːts]	the parts of a town or a city that are furthest away from its centre; *live in the outskirts*
park	[pɑːk]	a public area of land in a town with grass and trees, where people go to relax and enjoy themselves; *a public park*
parking lot (*American English*)		*see* **car park**
parking meter	[ˈpɑːkɪŋ miːtə]	a machine in a street that you put money into to pay for leaving your car there
parking space	[ˈpɑːkɪŋ speɪs]	a space where a car can be parked
pavement	[ˈpeɪvmənt]	a path with a hard surface, usually by the side of a road (*In American English*, use **sidewalk**)
pedestrian	[pɪˈdestrɪən]	a person who is walking in a town or city
pedestrian crossing	[pɪˌdestrɪən ˈkrɒsɪŋ]	a place where drivers must stop to let people cross a street (*In American English*, use **crosswalk**)
places of interest	[ˌpleɪsɪz əv ˈɪntrəst]	buildings or parts of a city which are interesting to visit
population	[ˌpɒpjʊˈleɪʃən]	all the people who live in an area
post office	[ˈpəʊst ɒfɪs]	a building where you can buy stamps and post letters

---

EXAMPLES
The notice said 'Please close the door.'
I found a parking space right outside the block of flats.
He was hurrying along the pavement.
She visited museums and other places of interest.

restroom (*American English*)		*see* **toilet**
restaurant	['restərɒnt]	a place where you can buy and eat a meal
ring road	['rɪŋ rəʊd]	a road that goes around a large town to keep traffic away from the centre (*In American English, use* **beltway**)
road	[rəʊd]	a long piece of hard ground that vehicles travel on; *a main road*; *a road accident*
season ticket	['siːzən tɪkɪt]	a ticket for a number of journeys, that you usually buy at a reduced price; *a weekly/ monthly/annual season ticket*
shop	[ʃɒp]	a place where you buy things; *a local/ corner shop*; *a gift shop*; *a chip shop*; *a shop assistant*; *a shop window* (*In American English, use* **store**)
shopping centre	['ʃɒpɪŋ sentə]	an area in a town where a lot of shops have been built close together
sidewalk (*American English*)		*see* **pavement**
sign	[saɪn]	a piece of wood, metal, or plastic with words or pictures on it that warn you about something, or give you information; *a street sign*
square	[skweə]	an open place with buildings around it in a town or city; *the town square*; *the main/ central square*
store (*American English*)		*see* **shop**
street	[striːt]	a road in a city or a town; *the main street*; *a side street*; *city streets*
suburb	['sʌbɜːb]	one of the areas on the edge of a city where many people live; *the suburbs*; *a leafy/ wealthy suburb*
subway	['sʌbweɪ]	**1** a path that goes under a road so that people can cross safely **2** (*mainly American English*) *see* **the underground**

EXAMPLES
The sign said, 'Welcome to Glasgow.'
He lives at 66 Bingfield Street.

synagogue	['sɪnəgɒg]	a building where Jewish people go to pray
taxi	['tæksi]	a car that you can hire, with its driver, to take you somewhere; *take/catch a taxi*
taxi rank	['tæksi ræŋk]	a place where taxis wait for customers (*In American English*, *use* **taxi stand**)
taxi stand (*American English*)		*see* **taxi rank**
toilet	['tɔɪlət]	**1** a large bowl with a seat that you use when you get rid of waste from your body **2** a room that contains one or more toilets (*In American English*, *use* **restroom**)
tour	[tʊə]	a trip to an interesting place or around several interesting places; *a bus/coach tour*
tourist	['tʊərɪst]	a person who is visiting a place on holiday
tourist information office	[ˌtʊərɪst ɪnfə'meɪʃən ɒfɪs]	an office that gives information about the local area
tower	['taʊə]	a tall, narrow building, or a tall part of another building; *a church tower*
town	[taʊn]	a place with many streets, buildings and shops, where people live and work; *your home town*; *a seaside town*; *the town centre*
traffic	['træfɪk]	all the vehicles that are on a particular road at one time; *heavy traffic*; *road traffic*; *rush hour traffic*
train station	['treɪn steɪʃən]	a place where trains stop so that people can get on or off
trash can (*American English*)		*see* **bin**
the underground [ði: 'ʌndəgraʊnd]		in a city, the railway system in which electric trains travel below the ground in tunnels; *take the underground* (*In American English*, *use* **subway**)

EXAMPLES
Where are the nearest public toilets?
Michael took me on a tour of the nearby islands.
I'm going into town.
Where is the train station?

| zebra crossing | [ˌzebrə ˈkrɒsɪŋ] | a place on the road that is painted with black and white lines, where people can cross the road safely |
| zone | [zəʊn] | an area where something particular happens; *an industrial zone* |

VERBS

| go shopping | | to go to the shops to buy things |
| go sightseeing | | to travel around a town to visit famous and interesting places |

ADJECTIVES

busy	[ˈbɪzi]	full of people who are doing things; *a busy street/road*
clean	[kliːn]	not dirty
crowded	[ˈkraʊdɪd]	full of people; *crowded streets*; *a crowded bus/train*
dirty	[ˈdɜːti]	covered with unwanted substances such as litter
downtown	[ˌdaʊnˈtaʊn]	belonging to the part of a city where the large shops and businesses are; *a downtown hotel*
industrial	[ɪnˈdʌstriəl]	used for describing a city or a country in which industry is very important; *an industrial town/city*
lost	[lɒst]	not knowing where you are; unable to find your way; *I'm lost.*
suburban	[səˈbɜːbən]	in or relating to the suburbs; *a suburban street/district*
urban	[ˈɜːbən]	relating to a city or a town; *urban areas*

EXAMPLE

This is a crowded city of 2 million.

ADVERBS

left [left] opposite the side that most people write with; *turn left*

right [raɪt] to the side that is towards the east when you look north; *turn right*

straight ahead [ˌstreɪt əˈhed] in one direction only; without a curve or bend; *go straight ahead*

PHRASE

no entry if a sign says 'no entry', it means that people are not allowed to go into a particular street or area

trains

arrival	[ə'raɪvəl]	the occasion when a train arrives somewhere; *arrivals and departures*
barrier	['bærɪə]	a fence or a wall that prevents people or things from moving from one area to another
buffet	['bʌfeɪ]	the part of a train where food and drink is sold (*In American English, use* **dining car**)
carriage	['kærɪdʒ]	one of the sections of a train where people sit; *a railway/train carriage*
compartment	[kəm'pɑːtmənt]	**1** one of the separate spaces in a train carriage (= section of a train); *a first-class compartment* **2** a part of a train that is used for keeping luggage in; *a luggage compartment*
conductor	[kən'dʌktə]	a person on a train whose job is to check tickets
connection	[kə'nekʃən]	a train that leaves after another one arrives and allows you to continue your journey by changing from one to the other
departure	[dɪ'pɑːtʃə]	the occasion when a train leaves somewhere; *a train departure*
destination	[ˌdestɪ'neɪʃən]	the place a train is going to; *arrive at your destination*
dining car (*American English*)		*see* **buffet**
driver	['draɪvə]	the person who is driving a train; *a train driver*
engine	['endʒɪn]	the front part of a train that pulls the rest of it
fare	[feə]	the money that you pay for a trip in a train; *a train fare*
fast train	['fɑːst treɪn]	a train that travels very fast, and goes directly to a place, making few stops

---

EXAMPLES

The buffet car is now open.

I was afraid that I would miss my connection.

freight train (mainly American English)		*see* **goods train**
goods train	['gʊdz treɪn]	a train that carries goods and not people (*In American English, use* **freight train**)
intercity train	[ˌɪntəˈsɪti ˈtreɪn]	a fast train that travels long distances between cities, making few stops
journey	['dʒɜːni]	an occasion when you travel from one place to another; *a train journey*
left-luggage locker	[ˌleftˈlʌgɪdʒ lɒkə]	a small cupboard at a train station where you can leave luggage that you want to collect later
left-luggage office	[ˌleftˈlʌgɪdʒ ɒfɪs]	a place at a train station where you can pay to leave luggage for a short time
level crossing	[ˌlevəl ˈkrɒsɪŋ]	a place where a railway line crosses a road
line	[laɪn]	a route that trains move along; *the railway line*
lost property office	[ˌlɒst ˈprɒpəti ɒfɪs]	a place at a train station where you can go to look for things that you have lost and that someone else has found
luggage	['lʌgɪdʒ]	the bags that you take with you when you travel; *lost luggage*
luggage rack	['lʌgɪdʒ ræk]	a shelf on a train for putting luggage on
passenger	['pæsɪndʒə]	a person who is travelling in a train
platform	['plætfɔːm]	the area in a train station where you wait for a train; *a railway platform*
porter	['pɔːtə]	a person whose job is to carry people's luggage in a train station
railroad (American English)		*see* **railway**
railway	['reɪlweɪ]	a metal track between two places that trains travel along; *a railway track* (*In American English, use* **railroad**)

EXAMPLES

We stayed on the train to the end of the line.
We apologise to any rail passengers whose journey was delayed today.
The next train to London will depart from platform 3.
The road ran beside a railway.

reservation	[ˌrezə'veɪʃən]	a seat that a transport company keeps ready for you; *a seat reservation*
return	[rɪ'tɜːn]	a ticket for a journey to a place and back again
season ticket	['siːzən tɪkɪt]	a ticket for a number of train journeys, that you usually buy at a cheaper price
seat	[siːt]	something that you can sit on; *reserve a seat*
single	['sɪŋgəl]	a ticket for a journey from one place to another but not back again
sleeper	['sliːpə]	a train with beds for passengers on overnight journeys
slow train	['sləʊ treɪn]	a train that travels slowly, making many stops
station	['steɪʃən]	a place where trains stop so that people can get on or off; *a train station*
steam engine	['stiːm endʒɪn]	an engine that uses steam as a means of power
subway (mainly American English)		*see* **the underground**
suitcase	['suːtkeɪs]	a case for carrying your clothes when you are travelling; *pack/unpack a suitcase*
ticket	['tɪkɪt]	a small piece of paper or card that shows that you have paid to travel on a train; *buy a ticket*; *a train ticket*
ticket collector	['tɪkɪt kəlektə]	a person who collects the tickets of passengers when they get off a train
ticket office	['tɪkɪt ɒfɪs]	the place where you buy tickets at a train station

EXAMPLES
Is this seat free?
This seat is taken.
I'll take you to the station.
I'll come and pick you up at the station.
In 1941, the train would have been pulled by a steam engine.

timetable	['taɪmteɪbəl]	a list of the times when trains arrive and depart; *a train timetable*
track	[træk]	one of the metal lines that trains travel along; *a railway track*
train	[treɪn]	a long vehicle that is pulled by an engine along a railway; *catch a train*; *get on/off a train*; *take the train*; *train travel*
the tube	[ðə tju:b]	same as **the underground**
the underground [ði: 'ʌndəɡraʊnd]		in a city, the railway system in which trains travel below the ground; *the London underground*; *an underground train* (*In American English, use* **subway**)
waiting room	['weɪtɪŋ ru:m]	a room in a train station where people can sit down while they wait
whistle	['wɪsəl]	a small tube that you blow into in order to produce a loud sound; *blow a whistle*

VERBS

approach	[ə'prəʊtʃ]	to move closer to something
arrive	[ə'raɪv]	to come to a place from somewhere else
book	[bʊk]	to arrange to have or use something at a later time; *book a train ticket*
cancel	['kænsəl]	to say that a train that should travel will not be travelling
delay	[dɪ'leɪ]	to make someone or something late; *The train is delayed.*
depart	[dɪ'pɑ:t]	to leave
miss	[mɪs]	to arrive too late to get on a train; *miss your train*

EXAMPLES
He came to Glasgow by train.
I heard the train approaching.
Their train arrived on time.
Many trains have been cancelled.
Thousands of rail passengers were delayed yesterday.

ADJECTIVES

due	[djuː]	expected to happen or arrive at a particular time; *Find out when the next train is due.*
first-class	[ˌfɜːstˈklɑːs]	relating to the best and most expensive seats on a train; *a first-class carriage; a first-class ticket*
high-speed	[ˌhaɪˈspiːd]	that travels very fast; *a high-speed train*
late	[leɪt]	after the time that something should happen
non-smoking	[ˌnɒnˈsməʊkɪŋ]	a non-smoking area is a public place where people are not allowed to smoke
overcrowded	[ˌəʊvəˈkraʊdɪd]	with too many people
smoking	[ˈsməʊkɪŋ]	a smoking area is a public place where people are allowed to smoke; *the smoking section/area*

EXAMPLES

Your train is due to leave in three minutes.
The train is late.
The trains have separate non-smoking compartments.

weather

air [eə] the mixture of gases all around us that we breathe; *fresh air*; *warm/hot air*

atmosphere ['ætməsfɪə] the layer of air or other gases around a planet

climate ['klaɪmət] the normal weather in a place; *a warm/cold climate*; *climate change*

cloud [klaʊd] a white or grey thing in the sky that is made of drops of water

darkness ['dɑːknəs] the state of being dark, without any light

drought [draʊt] a long period of time with no rain

east [iːst] the direction that is in front of you when you look at the sun in the morning; *The sun rises in the east.*

flood [flʌd] an occasion when a lot of water covers land that is usually dry

fog [fɒg] thick cloud that is close to the ground

frost [frɒst] ice like white powder that forms outside when the weather is very cold

gale [geɪl] a very strong wind

hail [heɪl] small balls of ice that fall like rain from the sky

heat [hiːt] when something is hot

hurricane ['hʌrɪkən] a storm with very strong winds and rain

ice [aɪs] frozen water

lightning ['laɪtnɪŋ] the very bright flashes of light in the sky that happen during a storm; *thunder and lightning*; *a flash of lightning*

EXAMPLES

Keith opened the window and felt the cold air on his face.
There is an extra hour of darkness on winter mornings.
The drought has killed all their crops.
The car crash happened in thick fog.
A strong gale was blowing.
Our clothes dried quickly in the heat of the sun.
The ground was covered with ice.
One man died when he was struck by lightning.

mist	[mɪst]	a lot of tiny drops of water in the air, that make it difficult to see; *mist and fog*; *morning mist*
monsoon	[mɒnˈsuːn]	the season in Southern Asia when there is a lot of very heavy rain; *the monsoon rains*; *the monsoon season*
north	[nɔːθ]	the direction that is on your left when you are looking at the sun in the morning
puddle	[ˈpʌdəl]	a small pool of water on the ground
rain	[reɪn]	water that falls from the clouds in small drops; *heavy/pouring rain*; *go out in the rain*
rainbow	[ˈreɪnbəʊ]	a half circle of different colours that you can sometimes see in the sky when it rains
raindrop	[ˈreɪndrɒp]	a single drop of rain
sky	[skaɪ]	the space above the Earth that you can see when you stand outside and look upwards; *in the sky*
snow	[snəʊ]	soft white frozen water that falls from the sky
snowflake	[ˈsnəʊfleɪk]	one of the soft, white bits of frozen water that fall as snow
south	[saʊθ]	the direction that is on your right when you are looking at the sun in the morning
storm	[stɔːm]	very bad weather, with heavy rain and strong winds; *violent/severe storms*; *tropical storms*
sun	[sʌn]	**1** the ball of fire in the sky that gives us heat and light **2** the heat and light that comes from the sun

EXAMPLES

In the north, snow and ice cover the ground.
Young children love splashing in puddles.
Outside a light rain was falling.
Today we have clear blue skies.
Six inches of snow fell.
The sun is shining.
Suddenly, the sun came out.
They went outside to sit in the sun.

sunshine	['sʌnʃaɪn]	the light and heat that comes from the sun
temperature	['temprətʃə]	how hot or cold it is; *warm/cold temperatures*; *average temperature*
thermometer	[θə'mɒmɪtə]	an instrument for measuring how hot or cold something is
thunder	['θʌndə]	the loud noise that you sometimes hear from the sky during a storm
thunderstorm	['θʌndəstɔːm]	a very noisy storm
tornado	[tɔː'neɪdəʊ]	a storm with strong winds that spin around very fast and cause a lot of damage
tsunami	[tsʊ'nɑːmi]	a very large wave that flows onto the land and destroys things
umbrella	[ʌm'brelə]	a thing that you hold over your head to protect yourself from the rain; *put up your umbrella*
weather	['weðə]	the temperature and conditions outside, for example if it is raining, hot or windy; *cold/bad/wet weather*; *hot/warm weather*
weather forecast	['weðə fɔːkɑːst]	a statement saying what the weather will be like for the next few days; *watch/listen to the weather forecast*
west	[west]	the direction that is in front of you when you look at the sun in the evening
wind	[wɪnd]	air that moves

[VERBS]

blow	[bləʊ]	when a wind or breeze blows, the air moves
freeze	[friːz]	to become solid because the temperature is low

---

EXAMPLES

She was sitting outside a cafe in bright sunshine.
What's the weather like?
The sun sets in the west.
A strong wind was blowing from the north.
The wind is blowing.
Last winter the water froze in all our pipes.

melt	[melt]	to change from a solid substance to a liquid because of heat
rain	[reɪn]	when it rains, water falls from the clouds in small drops
shine	[ʃaɪn]	to give out bright light; *The sun is shining.*
snow	[snəʊ]	when it snows, soft white frozen water falls from the sky
thaw	[θɔː]	if snow or ice thaws, it becomes warmer and changes to liquid

ADJECTIVES

cloudy	['klaʊdi]	with a lot of clouds in the sky; *a cloudy day/ sky*
cold	[kəʊld]	without any warmth; *cold weather*; *cold air*
cool	[kuːl]	having a low temperature, but not cold; *cool air*
dry	[draɪ]	without any rain
freezing	['friːzɪŋ]	very cold
hot	[hɒt]	describing the weather when the temperature is high; *a hot day*
humid	['hjuːmɪd]	wet and warm; *humid air*; *humid weather/ conditions*
mild	[maɪld]	not too hot and not too cold; *a mild winter*; *mild weather*
rainy	['reɪni]	raining a lot; *a rainy day*
stormy	['stɔːmi]	with strong winds and heavy rain; *stormy weather*

EXAMPLES

The snow melted.
It's raining.
It snowed heavily all night.
The snow thawed.
The Sahara is one of the driest places in Africa.
It's freezing.
It's too hot to play tennis.

sunny	['sʌni]	with the sun shining brightly
tropical	['trɒpɪkəl]	belonging to or typical of the hot, wet areas of the world; *a tropical climate*; *tropical heat*
windy	['wɪndi]	with a lot of wind; *a windy day*

EXAMPLE
The weather was warm and sunny.

geographical place names

Here is a list of the names of well-known places in the world.

Afghanistan /æfˈgænɪˌstɑːn/
Africa /ˈæfrɪkə/
Albania /ælˈbeɪnɪə/
Algeria /ælˈdʒɪərɪə/
American Samoa
/əˌmerɪkən səˈməʊə/
Andorra /ænˈdɔːrə/
Angola /æŋˈgəʊlə/
Antarctica /ænˈtɑːktɪkə/
Antigua and Barbuda
/ænˈtiːgə ənd bɑːˈbuːdə/
the Arctic /ði ˈɑktɪk/
Argentina /ˌɑːdʒənˈtiːnə/
Armenia /ɑːˈmiːnɪə/
Asia /ˈeɪʒə/
the Atlantic /ði ətˈlæntɪk/
Australia /ɒˈstreɪlɪə/
Austria /ˈɒstrɪə/
Azerbaijan /ˌæzəbaɪˈdʒɑːn/
Bahamas /bəˈhɑːməz/
Bahrain /bɑːˈreɪn/
Bangladesh /ˌbæŋgləˈdeʃ/
Barbados /bɑːˈbeɪdɒs/
Belarus /ˌbeləˈrʊs/
Belgium /ˈbeldʒəm/
Belize /bəˈliːz/
Benin /beˈniːn/
Bhutan /buːˈtɑːn/
Bolivia /bəˈlɪvɪə/
Bosnia and Herzegovina
/ˈbɒznɪə ənd ˌhɜːsəgəʊˈviːnə/
Botswana /bɒtˈswɑːnə/
Brazil /brəˈzɪl/
Brunei /bruːˈnaɪ/
Bulgaria /bʌlˈgeərɪə/
Burkina-Faso /bɜːˌkiːnəˈfæsəʊ/
Burma /ˈbɜːmə/
Burundi /bəˈrʊndi/
Cambodia /kæmˈbəʊdɪə/

Cameroon /ˌkæməˈruːn/
Canada /ˈkænədə/
Cape Verde /ˌkeɪp ˈvɜːd/
the Caribbean /ðə ˌkærɪˈbiːən/
the Central African Republic
/ðə ˌsentrəl ˌæfrɪkən riˈpʌblɪk/
Chad /tʃæd/
Chile /ˈtʃɪli/
(the People's Republic of) China
/(ðə ˌpiːpəlz riˌpʌblɪk əv) ˈtʃaɪnə/
Colombia /kəˈlʌmbɪə/
Comoros /ˈkɒməˌrəʊz/
(the Republic of) Congo
/(ðə riˌpʌblɪk əv) ˈkɒŋgəʊ/
**(the Democratic Republic of)
Congo** /(ðə deməˌkrætɪk
riˌpʌblɪk əv) ˈkɒŋgəʊ/
Costa Rica /ˌkɒstə ˈriːkə/
Côte d'Ivoire /ˌkəʊt diːˈvwɑː/
Croatia /krəʊˈeɪʃə/
Cuba /ˈkjuːbə/
Cyprus /ˈsaɪprəs/
the Czech Republic
/ðə ˈtʃek riˌpʌblɪk/
Denmark /ˈdenmɑːk/
Djibouti /dʒɪˈbuːti/
Dominica
/ˌdɒmɪˈniːkə, dəˈmɪnɪkə/
the Dominican Republic
/ðə dəˈmɪnɪkən riˌpʌblɪk/
East Timor /ˌiːst ˈtiːmɔː/
Ecuador /ˈekwəˌdɔː/
Egypt /ˈiːdʒɪpt/
El Salvador /el ˈsælvəˌdɔː/
England /ˈɪŋglənd/
Equatorial Guinea
/ˌekwəˌtɔːrɪəl ˈgɪniː/
Eritrea /ˌerɪˈtreɪə/
Estonia /eˈstəʊnɪə/

Ethiopia /ˌiːθiˈəʊpiə/
Europe /ˈjʊərəp/
Fiji /ˈfiːdʒiː/
Finland /ˈfɪnlənd/
France /ˈfrɑːns/
Gabon /gəˈbɒn/
Gambia /ˈgæmbiə/
Georgia /ˈdʒɔːdʒjə/
Germany /ˈdʒɜːməni/
Ghana /ˈgɑːnə/
Great Britain /ˌgreɪt ˈbrɪtən/
Greece /griːs/
Greenland /ˈgriːnlənd/
Grenada /griˈneɪdə/
Guatemala /ˌgwætəˈmɑːlə/
Guinea /ˈgɪniː/
Guinea-Bissau /ˌgɪniːbiˈsaʊ/
Guyana /gaɪˈɑːnə/
Haiti /ˈheɪti/
Holland /ˈhɒlənd/
Honduras /hɒnˈdjʊərəs/
Hungary /ˈhʌŋgəri/
Iceland /ˈaɪslənd/
India /ˈɪndiə/
Indonesia /ˌɪndəˈniːziə/
Iran /ɪˈrɑːn. ɪˈræn/
Iraq /ɪˈrɑːk, ɪˈræk/
(the Republic of) Ireland
  /(ðə rɪˌpʌblɪk əv) ˈaɪələnd/
Israel /ˈɪzreɪəl/
Italy /ˈɪtəli/
Jamaica /dʒəˈmeɪkə/
Japan /dʒəˈpæn/
Jordan /ˈdʒɔːdən/
Kazakhstan
  /ˌkæzækˈstæn, ˌkɑːzɑːkˈstɑːn/
Kenya /ˈkenjə/
Kiribati /ˌkɪriˈbɑːti/
Kuwait /kuːˈweɪt/
Kyrgyzstan /ˌkɪəgiˈstɑːn/
Laos /laʊs/

Latvia /ˈlætviə/
Lebanon /ˈlebənən/
Lesotho /ləˈsəʊteʊ/
Liberia /laɪˈbɪəriə/
Libya /ˈlɪbiə/
Liechtenstein /ˈlɪktənˌstaɪn/ ·
Lithuania /ˌlɪθjuːˈeɪniə/
Luxembourg /ˈlʌksəmˌbɜːg/
Macedonia /ˌmæsiˈdəʊniə/
Madagascar /ˌmædəˈgæskə/
Malawi /məˈlɑːwi/
Malaysia /məˈleɪziə/
the Maldives /ðə ˈmɔːldiːvz/
Mali /ˈmɑːli/
Malta /ˈmɔːltə/
the Marshall Islands
  /ðə ˈmɑːʃəl ˌaɪləndz/
Mauritania /ˌmɒriˈteɪniə/
Mauritius /məˈrɪʃəs/
the Mediterranean
  /ðə ˌmedɪtəˈreɪniən/
Mexico /ˈmeksɪˌkəʊ/
Micronesia /ˌmaɪkrəʊˈniːziə/
Moldova /mɒlˈdəʊvə/
Monaco /ˈmɒnəˌkəʊ/
Mongolia /mɒnˈgəʊliə/
Montenegro /ˌmɒntiˈniːgrəʊ/
Morocco /məˈrɒkəʊ/
Mozambique /ˌməʊzæmˈbiːk/
Myanmar /ˈmjænmɑː/
Namibia /nəˈmɪbiə/
Nauru /nɑːˈuːruː, ˈnaʊruː/
Nepal /niˈpɔːl/
Netherlands /ˈneðələndz/
New Zealand /ˌnjuː ˈziːlənd/
Nicaragua /ˌnɪkəˈrægjʊə/
Niger /ˈnaɪdʒə, niːˈʒeə/
Nigeria /naɪˈdʒɪəriə/
Northern Ireland
  /ˌnɔːðən ˈaɪələnd/
North Korea /ˌnɔːθ kəˈriːə/

Norway /ˈnɔːweɪ/
Oman /əʊˈmɑːn/
the Pacific /ðə pəˈsɪfɪk/
Pakistan
    /ˌpɑːkiˈstɑːn, ˌpækiˈstɑːn/
Panama /ˈpænəˌmɑː, ˌpænəˈmɑː/
Papua New Guinea
    /ˌpæpjʊə njuːˈɡɪniː/
Paraguay /ˈpærəˌɡwaɪ/
Peru /pəˈruː/
the Philippines /ðə ˈfɪləˌpiːnz/
Poland /ˈpəʊlənd/
Portugal /ˈpɔːtjʊɡəl/
Puerto Rico
    /ˌpwɜːtəˈriːkəʊ, ˌpweətəˈriːkəʊ/
Qatar /kʌˈtɑː/
Romania /rəʊˈmeɪnɪə/
Russia /ˈrʌʃə/
Rwanda /rʊˈændə/
St Kitts and Nevis
    /sənt ˌkɪts ənd ˈniːvis/
St Lucia /sənt ˈluːʃə/
St Vincent and the Grenadines /sə
    nt ˈvɪnsənt ənd ðə ˌɡrenəˈdiːnz/
Samoa /səˈməʊə/
San Marino /ˌsæn məˈriːnəʊ/
São Tomé and Principe
    /ˌsaʊ təˈmeɪ ənd ˈprɪnsiˌpeɪ/
Saudi Arabia /ˌsaʊdi əˈreɪbɪə/
Scotland /ˈskɒtlənd/
Senegal /ˌseniˈɡɔːl/
Serbia /ˈsɜːbɪə/
the Seychelles /ðə ˌseɪˈʃelz/
Sierra Leone /siːˌeərə liːˌəʊn/
Singapore /ˌsɪŋəˈpɔː/
Slovakia /sləʊˈvækɪə/
Slovenia /sləʊˈviːnɪə/
the Solomon Islands
    /ðə ˈsɒləmən ˌaɪləndz/
Somalia /səˈmɑːlɪə/
South Africa /ˌsaʊθ ˈæfrɪkə/

South Korea /ˌsaʊθ kəˈriːə/
Spain /speɪn/
Sri Lanka /ˌsriː ˈlæŋkə/
Sudan /suːˈdɑːn, suːˈdæn/
Suriname /ˌsʊəriˈnæm/
Swaziland /ˈswɑːziˌlænd/
Sweden /ˈswiːdən/
Switzerland /ˈswɪtsələnd/
Syria /ˈsɪrɪə/
Taiwan /taɪˈwɑːn/
Tajikistan /tɑːˌdʒiːkiˈstɑːn/
Tanzania /ˌtænzəˈniːə/
Thailand /ˈtaɪˌlænd/
Togo /ˈtəʊɡəʊ/
Tonga /ˈtɒŋɡə/
Trinidad and Tobago
    /ˌtrɪnidæd ənd təˈbeɪɡəʊ/
Tunisia /tjuːˈnɪzɪə/
Turkey /ˈtɜːki/
Turkmenistan /tɜːkˌmeniˈstɑːn/
Tuvalu /ˌtuːvəˈluː/
Uganda /juːˈɡændə/
Ukraine /juːˈkreɪn/
the United Arab Emirates
    /ðiː juːˌnaɪtid ˌærəb ˈemirəts/
the United Kingdom
    /ðiː juːˌnaɪtid ˈkɪŋdəm/
the United States of America
    /ðiː juːˌnaɪtid ˌsteɪts əv
    əˈmerikə/
Uruguay /ˈʊərəˌɡwaɪ/
Uzbekistan /ʊzˌbekiˈstɑːn/
Vanuatu /ˌvænuːˈɑːtuː/
the Vatican City
    /ðə ˌvætikən ˈsɪti/
Venezuela /ˌveniˈzweɪlə/
Vietnam /ˌvjetˈnæm/
Wales /weɪlz/
Yemen /ˈjemən/
Zambia /ˈzæmbɪə/
Zimbabwe /zɪmˈbɑːbweɪ/

irregular verbs

INFINITIVE	PAST TENSE	PAST PARTICIPLE
arise	arose	arisen
be	was, were	been
beat	beat	beaten
become	became	become
begin	began	begun
bend	bent	bent
bet	bet	bet
bind	bound	bound
bite	bit	bitten
bleed	bled	bled
blow	blew	blown
break	broke	broken
bring	brought	brought
build	built	built
burn	burned *or* burnt	burned *or* burnt
burst	burst	burst
buy	bought	bought
catch	caught	caught
choose	chose	chosen
cling	clung	clung
come	came	come
cost	cost *or* costed	cost *or* costed
creep	crept	crept
cut	cut	cut
deal	dealt	dealt
dig	dug	dug
dive	dived *or* dove	dived
do	did	done
draw	drew	drawn
dream	dreamed *or* dreamt	dreamed *or* dreamt
drink	drank	drunk
drive	drove	driven
eat	ate	eaten
fall	fell	fallen
feed	fed	fed
feel	felt	felt
fight	fought	fought
find	found	found
fly	flew	flown
forbid	forbade	forbidden
forget	forgot	forgotten
freeze	froze	frozen
get	got	gotten, got

INFINITIVE	PAST TENSE	PAST PARTICIPLE
give	gave	given
go	went	gone
grind	ground	ground
grow	grew	grown
hang	hung *or* hanged	hung *or* hanged
have	had	had
hear	heard	heard
hide	hid	hidden
hit	hit	hit
hold	held	held
hurt	hurt	hurt
keep	kept	kept
kneel	kneeled *or* knelt	kneeled *or* knelt
know	knew	known
lay	laid	laid
lead	led	led
lean	leaned	leaned
leap	leaped *or* leapt	leaped *or* leapt
learn	learned	learned
leave	left	left
lend	lent	lent
let	let	let
lie	lay	lain
light	lit *or* lighted	lit *or* lighted
lose	lost	lost
make	made	made
mean	meant	meant
meet	met	met
pay	paid	paid
put	put	put
quit	quit	quit
read	read	read
ride	rode	ridden
ring	rang	rung
rise	rose	risen
run	ran	run
say	said	said
see	saw	seen
seek	sought	sought
sell	sold	sold
send	sent	sent
set	set	set
shake	shook	shaken

INFINITIVE	PAST TENSE	PAST PARTICIPLE
shine	shined or shone	shined or shone
shoot	shot	shot
show	showed	shown
shrink	shrank	shrunk
shut	shut	shut
sing	sang	sung
sink	sank	sunk
sit	sat	sat
sleep	slept	slept
slide	slid	slid
smell	smelled	smelled
speak	spoke	spoken
speed	sped or speeded	sped or speeded
spell	spelled or spelt	spelled or spelt
spend	spent	spent
spill	spilled or spilt	spilled or spilt
spit	spit or spat	spit, or spat
spoil	spoiled or spoilt	spoiled or spoilt
spread	spread	spread
spring	sprang	sprung
stand	stood	stood
steal	stole	stolen
stick	stuck	stuck
sting	stung	stung
stink	stank	stunk
strike	struck	struck or stricken
swear	swore	sworn
sweep	swept	swept
swell	swelled	swollen
swim	swam	swum
swing	swung	swung
take	took	taken
teach	taught	taught
tear	tore	torn
tell	told	told
think	thought	thought
throw	threw	thrown
wake	woke or waked	woken or waked
wear	wore	worn
weep	wept	wept
win	won	won
wind	wound	wound
write	wrote	written

measurements

LENGTH

millimetre (mm)
centimetre (cm)
metre (m)
kilometre (km)
mile (= 1.61 kilometres)

WEIGHT

milligram (mg)
gram (g)
kilogram (kg)
tonne
ounce (1oz = 28g)
pound (1 lb = 454g)
stone (= 6.4kg)

CAPACITY

millilitre (ml)
litre (l)
pint (= 0.57 litres)
gallon (= 4.55 litres)

EXAMPLES

This tiny plant is only a few centimetres high.
They drove 600 miles across the desert.
The box weighs 4.5 kilograms.
The boat was carrying 30,000 tonnes of oil.
Each carton contains a pint of milk.
Adults should drink about two litres of water each day.

1	one
2	two
3	three
4	four
5	five
6	six
7	seven
8	eight
9	nine
10	ten
11	eleven
12	twelve
13	thirteen
14	fourteen
15	fifteen
16	sixteen
17	seventeen
18	eighteen
19	nineteen
20	twenty
21	twenty-one
22	twenty-two
30	thirty
40	forty
50	fifty
60	sixty
70	seventy
80	eighty
90	ninety
100	a/one hundred
101	a/one hundred and one
1,000	a/one thousand
10,000	ten thousand
100,000	a/one hundred thousand
1,000,000	a/one million

NUMBERS OVER 20

We write numbers over 20 (except 30, 40, 50, etc) with a hyphen.

25	twenty-five	45	forty-five
82	eighty-two	59	fifty-nine

A OR ONE?

100	a/one hundred	1,000,000	a/one million
1,000	a/one thousand		

One is more formal, and is often used in order to be very clear and precise.

LARGE NUMBERS

We often use a comma to divide large numbers into groups of three figures.

1,235,578	one million, two hundred and thirty-five thousand, five hundred and seventy-eight

EXAMPLES
The total amount was one hundred and forty-nine pounds and thirty pence.
These shoes cost over a hundred pounds.

ORDINAL NUMBERS

1st	first	19th	nineteenth
2nd	second	20th	twentieth
3rd	third	21st	twenty-first
4th	fourth	22nd	twenty-second
5th	fifth	30th	thirtieth
6th	sixth	40th	fortieth
7th	seventh	50th	fiftieth
8th	eighth	60th	sixtieth
9th	ninth	70th	seventieth
10th	tenth	80th	eightieth
11th	eleventh	90th	ninetieth
12th	twelfth	100th	hundredth
13th	thirteenth	101st	hundred and first
14th	fourteenth	200th	two hundredth
15th	fifteenth	1,000th	thousandth
16th	sixteenth	10,000th	ten thousandth
17th	seventeenth	100,000th	hundred thousandth
18th	eighteenth	1,000,000th	millionth

EXAMPLES

Kate won first prize in the writing competition.

It's Michael's seventh birthday tomorrow.

My office is on the twelfth floor.

I'm doing a project about fashion in the eighteenth century.

We're celebrating the 200th anniversary of independence next year.

The company announced that it has just served its millionth customer.

people of the world

There are different ways that the noun for a place changes to become the noun for a person from that place, or to become the adjective for that place. For places ending in '-a', the person noun and the adjective usually end in '-an', for example Australia→Australian.

> I live in Australia.
> I am an Australian.
> I am Australian.
> ...the Australian flag.

Here are some other examples of words that work this way:

Place nouns that end in –a → person nouns and adjectives that end in –an
Africa→African, America→American, Asia→Asian, Austria→Austrian, Bulgaria→Bulgarian, Cuba→Cuban, India→Indian, Kenya→Kenyan, Malaysia→Malaysian, Russia→Russian, Slovakia→Slovakian, Slovenia→Slovenian

There is no plural form for 'person' words that end in '-s' or '-ese', for example 'a Swiss' and 'a Chinese'. The singular form of these words are also not used very often, and it is more common to say 'a Swiss man' or 'a Chinese woman'.

Other place names change in different ways. Here is a list of some of the well-known ones:

If there is a language related to a particular country, the name of the language is usually the same as the adjective describing the country, for example *Polish, Japanese, Italian*.

EXAMPLES
Have you ever been to Peru?
She was born in China.
Five Germans and twelve Spaniards were on board the flight.
Can you speak Welsh?
He is fluent in Vietnamese.
He is English.
...a Mexican restaurant.
...the French president.

Place (noun)	Adjective	Person (noun)
Afghanistan	Afghan	an Afghan
Argentina	Argentinean	an Argentine
Bangladesh	Bangladeshi	a Bangladeshi
Belgium	Belgian	a Belgian
Brazil	Brazilian	a Brazilian
Britain	British	a Briton
Canada	Canadian	a Canadian
Chile	Chilean	a Chilean
China	Chinese	a Chinese
the Czech Republic	Czech	a Czech
Denmark	Danish	a Dane
Egypt	Egyptian	an Egyptian
England	English	an Englishman or an Englishwoman
Europe	European	a European
Finland	Finnish	a Finn
France	French	a Frenchman or a Frenchwoman
Germany	German	a German
Greece	Greek	a Greek
Hungary	Hungarian	a Hungarian
Iceland	Icelandic	an Icelander
Iran	Iranian	an Iranian
Iraq	Iraqi	an Iraqi
Ireland	Irish	an Irishman or an Irishwoman
Italy	Italian	an Italian
Japan	Japanese	a Japanese
Mexico	Mexican	a Mexican
Morocco	Moroccan	a Moroccan
The Netherlands	Dutch	a Dutchman or a Dutchwoman
New Zealand	New Zealand	a New Zealander
Norway	Norwegian	a Norwegian
Pakistan	Pakistani	a Pakistani
Peru	Peruvian	a Peruvian
Poland	Polish	a Pole
Portugal	Portuguese	a Portuguese
Scotland	Scottish	a Scot or a Scotsman or a Scotswoman
Spain	Spanish	a Spaniard
Sweden	Swedish	a Swede
Switzerland	Swiss	a Swiss
Taiwan	Taiwanese	a Taiwanese
Turkey	Turkish	a Turk
Vietnam	Vietnamese	a Vietnamese
Wales	Welsh	a Welshman or a Welshwoman

times and dates

TELLING THE TIME

Here are the most common ways of saying and writing the time.

four o'clock	nine o'clock	twelve o'clock
four	nine	twelve
4.00	9.00	12.00

four in the morning	nine in the morning	twelve in the morning
4 a.m.	9 a.m.	12 a.m.
midday		
noon		

four in the afternoon	nine in the evening	twelve at night
4 p.m.	9 p.m.	12 p.m.
midnight		

half past eleven
half-eleven
eleven-thirty
11.30

quarter past twelve (*British*)	quarter to one (*British*)
twelve-fifteen	twelve forty-five
12.15	12.45
quarter after twelve (*American*)	quarter of one (*American*)

twenty-five past two (*British*)	ten to eight (*British*)
two twenty-five	seven-fifty
2.25	7.50
twenty-five after two (*American*)	ten of eight (*American*)

EXAMPLES

What time is it? – It's five o'clock.
Excuse me, do you have the time? – Yes, it's half past eleven.
The class starts at 11 a.m. and finishes at 1.30 p.m.
We arrived at the airport just after nine.
I'll met you at quarter to eight.

WRITING DATES

There are several different ways of writing a date.

20 April   April 20
20th April   April 20th

(say 'the twentieth of April' or 'April the twentieth')

If you want to give the year, you put it last.

December 14th 2015

(say 'December the fourteenth, twenty fifteen')

You can write a date in figures. In British English, you put the day first, then the month, then the year. In American English, you put the month first, then the day, then the year.

In British English, December 14th 2015 is:

14/12/15   *or*   14.12.15

In American English, December 14th 2015 is:

12/14/15   *or*   12.14.15

EXAMPLES
The new shop opens on 5th February.
I was born on June 15th, 1970.
Date of birth: 15/6/1970

index

index